Palgrave Studies in the Enlightenment, Romanticism and the Cultures of Print

General Editors: **Professor Anne K.** Mellor and **Professor Clifford Siskin** Editorial Board: **Isobel Armstrong**, Birkbeck & IES; **John Bender**, Stanford; **Alan Bewell**, Toronto; **Peter de Bolla**, Cambridge; **Robert Miles**, Victoria; **Claudia L. Johnson**, Princeton; **Saree Makdisi**, UCLA; **Felicity Nussbaum**, UCLA; **Mary Poovey**, NYU; **Janet Todd**, Cambridge

Palgrave Studies in the Enlightenment, Romanticism and the Cultures of Print will feature work that does not fit comfortably within established boundaries—whether between periods or between disciplines. Uniquely, it will combine efforts to engage the power and materiality of print with explorations of gender, race, and class. By attending as well to intersections of literature with the visual arts, medicine, law, and science, the series will enable a large-scale rethinking of the origins of modernity.

Titles include:

Melanie Bigold
WOMEN OF LETTERS, MANUSCRIPT CIRCULATION, AND PRINT AFTERLIVES IN THE EIGHTEENTH CENTURY
Elizabeth Rowe, Catharine Cockburn, and Elizabeth Carter

Katey Castellano
THE ECOLOGY OF BRITISH ROMANTIC CONSERVATISM, 1790–1837

Noah Comet
ROMANTIC HELLENISM AND WOMEN WRITERS

Ildiko Csengei
SYMPATHY, SENSIBILITY AND THE LITERATURE OF FEELING IN THE EIGHTEENTH CENTURY

Alexander Dick
ROMANTICISM AND THE GOLD STANDARD
Money, Literature, and Economic Debate in Britain 1790–1830

Elizabeth Eger
BLUESTOCKINGS
Women of Reason from Enlightenment to Romanticism

Ina Ferris and Paul Keen (*editors*)
BOOKISH HISTORIES
Books, Literature, and Commercial Modernity, 1700–1900

John Gardner
POETRY AND POPULAR PROTEST
Peterloo, Cato Street and the Queen Caroline Controversy

George C. Grinnell
THE AGE OF HYPOCHONDRIA
Interpreting Romantic Health and Illness

Anthony S. Jarrells
BRITAIN'S BLOODLESS REVOLUTIONS
1688 and the Romantic Reform of Literature

Emrys Jones
FRIENDSHIP AND ALLEGIANCE IN EIGHTEENTH-CENTURY LITERATURE
The Politics of Private Virtue in the Age of Walpole

Jacqueline M. Labbe
WRITING ROMANTICISM
Charlotte Smith and William Wordsworth, 1784–1807

April London
LITERARY HISTORY WRITING, 1770–1820

Robert Morrison and Daniel Sanjiv Roberts (*editors*)
ROMANTICISM AND *BLACKWOOD'S MAGAZINE*
'An Unprecedented Phenomenon'

Catherine Packham
EIGHTEENTH-CENTURY VITALISM
Bodies, Culture, Politics

Nicola Parsons
READING GOSSIP IN EARLY EIGHTEENTH-CENTURY ENGLAND

Murray G.H. Pittock
MATERIAL CULTURE AND SEDITION, 1688–1760
Treacherous Objects, Secret Places

Jessica Richard
THE ROMANCE OF GAMBLING IN THE EIGHTEENTH-CENTURY BRITISH NOVEL

Andrew Rudd
SYMPATHY AND INDIA IN BRITISH LITERATURE, 1770–1830

Sharon Ruston
CREATING ROMANTICISM
Case Studies in the Literature, Science and Medicine of the 1790s

Yasmin Solomonescu
JOHN THELWALL AND THE MATERIALIST IMAGINATION

Richard Squibbs
URBAN ENLIGHTENMENT AND THE EIGHTEENTH-CENTURY PERIODICAL ESSAY
Transatlantic Retrospects

David Stewart
ROMANTIC MAGAZINES AND METROPOLITAN LITERARY CULTURE

Rebecca Tierney-Hynes
NOVEL MINDS
Philosophers and Romance Readers, 1680–1740

P. Westover
NECROMANTICISM
Travelling to Meet the Dead, 1750–1860

Esther Wohlgemut
ROMANTIC COSMOPOLITANISM

Palgrave Studies in the Enlightenment, Romanticism and the Cultures of Print
Series Standing Order ISBN 978–1–403–93408–6 hardback
978–1–403–93409–3 paperback
(*outside North America only*)

You can receive future titles in this series as they are published by placing a stand-ing order. Please contact your bookseller or, in case of difficulty, write to us at the address below with your name and address, the title of the series and the ISBN quoted above.

Customer Services Department, Macmillan Distribution Ltd, Houndmills, Basingstoke, Hampshire RG21 6XS, England

John Thelwall and the Materialist Imagination

Yasmin Solomonescu
Assistant Professor, University of Notre Dame, USA

First published 2014 by
PALGRAVE MACMILLAN

Palgrave Macmillan in the UK is an imprint of Macmillan Publishers Limited, registered in England, company number 785998, of Houndmills, Basingstoke, Hampshire RG21 6XS.

Palgrave Macmillan in the US is a division of St Martin's Press LLC, 175 Fifth Avenue, New York, NY 10010.

Palgrave Macmillan is the global academic imprint of the above companies and has companies and representatives throughout the world.

Palgrave® and Macmillan® are registered trademarks in the United States, the United Kingdom, Europe and other countries.

ISBN 978–1–137–42613–0

This book is printed on paper suitable for recycling and made from fully managed and sustained forest sources. Logging, pulping and manufacturing processes are expected to conform to the environmental regulations of the country of origin.

A catalogue record for this book is available from the British Library.

A catalog record for this book is available from the Library of Congress.

Typeset by MPS Limited, Chennai, India.

For Joseph

Contents

List of Illustrations

Acknowledgements

Many people and organizations have helped make the writing of this book at once possible and pleasurable. For their generous support of my research, I wish to thank the Social Sciences and Humanities Research Council of Canada (SSHRC), Doctoral and Postdoctoral Fellowship Programs; Trinity Hall, Cambridge; the Cambridge Commonwealth Trust; the Canadian Centennial Scholarship Fund; the Gordon Sinclair Foundation; and the Institute for Scholarship in the Liberal Arts, University of Notre Dame.

The publishers and I are grateful to the following for permission to reproduce archival or copyright material: the Derby Local Studies Library for permission to quote from Thelwall's three faircopy volumes entitled *Poems, Chiefly Suggested by the Scenery of Nature* and for permission to reproduce part of a page from that collection; the National Library of Scotland for permission to quote from Thelwall's letters to Robert Anderson of 9 Feb. and 12 March 1804; John F. Delaney Letters, Department of Special Collections, Hesburgh Libraries of Notre Dame, for permission to quote from Thelwall's letters to Thomas Hardy of 24 Aug. 1796, 19 May 1797 and 12 Dec. 1805; the HCL Widener Library for permission to reproduce Thelwall's 'Ode from the Land of Mountains' from *The Vestibule of Eloquence*; the British Museum for permission to reproduce James Gillray's *Copenhagen House*; and the Fitzwilliam Museum for permission to reproduce on the cover William Blake's 'I want! I want!' Plate 9 in *For the Sexes: The Gates of Paradise*. This book benefitted from the expert assistance of librarians, curators and managers at all of those institutions, as well as at the British Library; the Cambridge University Library; the King's College London Library; the Jerwood Centre, Grasmere; the National Art Library, Victoria and Albert Museum; and the Morgan Library and Museum.

Earlier versions of material in Chapters 2 and 3 appeared as 'Articulations of Community in *The Peripatetic*', in *John Thelwall: Radical Romantic and Acquitted Felon*, ed. Steve Poole, The Enlightenment World 11 (London: Pickering and Chatto, 2009), pp. 83–93, and 'Mute Records and Blank Legends: John Thelwall's "Paternal Tears"', *Romanticism* 16, no. 2 (2010), 152–63, respectively. The publishers and I are grateful to Pickering and Chatto and Edinburgh University Press for permission to reproduce that material here.

Every effort has been made to trace rights holders, but if any have been inadvertently overlooked the publishers would be pleased to make the necessary arrangements at the first opportunity.

ଔ

This book first took shape as a dissertation at the University of Cambridge under the exceptionally skilled and generous guidance of Mary Jacobus. I am deeply grateful to her for supporting and challenging me as needed, then and now. For their keen insight and unflagging encouragement at key stages of the project's development, I also wish to thank my dissertation examiners Peter de Bolla and Jon Mee, and my postdoctoral fellowship advisor Ian Balfour. I owe an equally great debt to the following colleagues and mentors: Judith Thompson and Michael Scrivener, for years of inspiring interchange (of ideas and documents) and thoughtful responses to drafts of this book; Richard Sha and Nicholas Roe, whose scholarship and conversation significantly influenced the book's framing; and not least Alan Richardson, my mentor through the Keats-Shelley Association of America, who provided invaluable commentary and guidance at critical moments. Warm thanks to him and the K-SAA for their commitment to supporting early-career scholars.

Many wonderful colleagues at the University of Notre Dame have also helped shape this book by their advice and example. I would particularly like to thank Terry Eagleton, Steve Fallon, Chris Fox, Peter Holland, Romana Huk, Greg Kucich, Jesse Lander, Kate Marshall, Sara Maurer, Sarah McKibben, Valerie Sayers, John Sitter, David Thomas, Chris Vanden Bossche, Laura Dassow Walls and Henry Weinfield, as well as the members of the Contemporary Transformations in Modern Europe writing group: Tobias Boes, John Deak, Julia Douthwaite, Lauren Faulkner, Robert Fishman, Tom Kselman, Alexander Martin, Ian Newman, Pierpaolo Polzonetti and Lesley Walker.

The wider community of mentors, colleagues and friends who offered a listening ear, sound counsel and many nameless acts of kindness along the way includes Zygmunt and Maggie Baranski, Alan Bewell, Julia Carlson, Philip Connell, Ildiko Csengei, Damian Walford Davies, Molly Desjardins, David Fairer, Tim Fulford, Michael Gamer, Daisy Hay, Hanna Janiszewska, Julie Joosten, Ludmilla Jordanova, Louise Joy, Paul Keen, Steve Poole and William St. Clair.

For their professionalism and expertise, I am particularly grateful to my editors at Palgrave Macmillan, Ben Doyle and Sophie Ainscough, my editorial consultant, Linda Auld, and my copyeditor, Mervyn Thomas. Profound thanks also to the book's anonymous reader and the series editors, Anne Mellor and Clifford Siskin, for their enthusiasm for the project. Needless to say, any missteps remain entirely my own.

My parents, Armand Solomonescu and Zoe Khoee Ward, and my sister, Hana Solomonescu, provided steady encouragement and welcome diversion, as did Victoria and Eddie Rosenberg. My grandmother, Elvira Grigorian Khoee, has been a model of good-natured perseverance. But my greatest and most cherished debt is to Joseph Rosenberg, for support and inspiration material, ideal, and in all ways vital. This book is dedicated to him with love.

List of Abbreviations

Derby manuscript	John Thelwall, *Poems, Chiefly Suggested by the Scenery of Nature; to Which are Added Odes &c. Amatory and Congratulatory, Translations, and Attempts at Humour*, 3 vols, manuscript, Derby Local Studies Library, England.
PEJ	John Thelwall, *The Politics of English Jacobinism: Writings of John Thelwall*, ed. Gregory Claeys, University Park: Pennsylvania State University Press, 1995.
Rhythmus	John Thelwall, *Selections for the Illustration of a Course of Instructions on the Rhythmus and Utterance of the English Language*, London, 1812.
SPW	John Thelwall, *Selected Political Writings of John Thelwall*, ed. Robert Lamb and Corinna Wagner, 4 vols, London: Pickering and Chatto, 2009.

Introduction

'Mister Surgeon Thelwall'

On 27 October 1795, the day after John Thelwall had addressed a mass meeting of the 'Friends of Parliamentary Reform' at Copenhagen Fields, Islington, the anti-Jacobin periodical the *Tomahawk* published the following squib 'On Mister Surgeon Thelwall':

> Poor *Mister* Thelwall has exhausted
>   All his little stock of wit,
> The fellow *merits* – to be hoisted;
>   So high he soars – *to pick a bit*.
>
> He dealt with *resurrection-men*,
>   To make the *Quick rise* now he's at;
> But sure we cannot wonder, when
>   The fellow is a *Democrat*!
>
> If he would eat in peace his bread,
>   Why let him follow ancient thriving;
> Go pick the BONES then of the dead
>   And not the POCKETS of the *living*![1]

Alluding to Thelwall's acquittal at the Treason Trials of 1794, when the ministry of William Pitt attempted to suppress the reform movement by charging its leaders with high treason for allegedly conspiring to overthrow the constitution and depose the king, the lampoonist 'Jack Bull' implies that Thelwall merits a new trial for boldly resuming his political lectures and speeches shortly after his release from prison. If he does not wish to be 'hoisted' by his own petard, Thelwall should desist from picking bones (with those in power) and pockets (presumably those of his audiences), and limit himself to 'pick[ing] the bones' of the dead, that is, dabbling in medicine, a profession that relied on 'resurrection men' to supply corpses for dissection. Yet even such dabbling is not safe from censure for, as 'Bull' suggests, Thelwall's medical interests are inextricable from his radical politics: one cannot wonder at his efforts to 'make the *Quick rise*' for 'The fellow is a *Democrat!*'. A third major field of interest, literature, may be implied by the puns on picking bones and pockets: both were central to Thelwall's satirical 'Sheep-Shearing Song', cited as evidence at his trial, which proclaims the British people's resistance to being 'fleeced' by those in power: 'For well we know if tamely thus / We yield our wool like drones, / Ye will not only fleece our backs, / But, gad! you'll pick our bones'.[2]

The relationship between Thelwall's scientific interests and his political and literary pursuits was apparent not only to 'Jack Bull'.[3] The critic Francis Jeffery would denounce him squarely as 'The Champion of Materialism, the Orator of Chalk Farm, and the Committee Man of the London Corresponding Society'.[4] Taking a more sympathetic view, the antiquary and topographer John Britton noted of Thelwall's acquittal in 1794 that he was then only 'commencing his career of usefulness', which 'continued through two other equal cycles, or periods of time, with increased energy, zeal, and devotion to the united causes of literature, science, and political reform'.[5] After some 150 years' obscurity, attributable partly to his radical stigma and partly to the rarity of his works, Thelwall regained attention as an early hero of the British Left in E. P. Thompson's *The Making of the English Working Class* (1963).[6] Thanks to Thompson, Gregory Claeys, John Barrell and others, Thelwall is now known once more as a leading English 'Jacobin' of the 1790s and the movement's foremost theorist after Thomas Paine.[7] In the past decade his equally innovative literary oeuvre has also attracted renewed interest, notably in Michael Scrivener's *Seditious Allegories: John Thelwall and Jacobin Writing* (2001), which presents him as a window onto the protean radical culture of the 1790s, and Judith Thompson's *John Thelwall in the Wordsworth Circle: The Silenced Partner* (2012), which recovers his 'silenced' role in William Wordsworth and Samuel Taylor Coleridge's poetic partnership.[8] With the collections *John Thelwall: Radical Romantic and Acquitted Felon* (Poole, 2009) and *John Thelwall: Critical Reassessments* (Solomonescu, 2011), the field of Thelwall studies takes steps beyond the 'Revolutionary Decade', particularly into the elocutionary phase of his career.

While this scholarship has effectively launched Thelwall's recovery, it only begins to account for a body of work that spanned decades, disciplines, networks and modes of communication, perhaps more extensively than that of any contemporary. More to the point, the prevalent critical emphasis on Thelwall's 'Jacobin' or high-Romantic contexts has largely eclipsed the fact that he was not only a noteworthy political and literary figure, but also an amateur natural philosopher who made among the earliest and most controversial forays into the period's 'vitality debates', debates about the principles of life and cognition that preoccupied two generations of thinkers and writers, finding their most famous expression in Mary Shelley's *Frankenstein* (1818). As 'Frankenstein's science' and the associated science of the mind undergo scholarly re-evaluation, the nature and ramifications of 'Mister Surgeon Thelwall's' contributions remain vastly underappreciated.[9] Yet they stand radically to revise our understanding of his oeuvre and of the Romantic era's creative triangulation of avant-garde science, radical politics and literary imagination to which it was central.

Drawing on new archival materials and spanning the four decades of Thelwall's career, this book examines the aesthetic and ideological ramifications of his heterodox 'materialist' view that the properties and processes of living nature, from vitality and cognition to agency and imagination, could be explained with reference to certain immutable laws of organic matter. In so doing, it brings a new perspective to bear on the rehabilitation of a long-neglected figure, while simultaneously showing through the prism of Thelwall's works that materialism was not merely a relic of Enlightenment empiricism and the utopian optimism of the 1790s, but a vital element of British thought and culture well into the nineteenth century. Thelwall first articulated his unconventional views in 1793, in two papers delivered before the Guy's Hospital Physical Society, composed of the leading surgeons and anatomists of the day. In the first he sought to account for 'animal vitality', or the principle of life, 'upon the simple principles of materialism', provoking a discussion that lasted for six successive meetings. Rejecting the two dominant theories of the day, which regarded vitality as the result of a particular organization of matter or the action of an immaterial external principle, Thelwall argued instead that it arose from the conjunction of suitably organized matter and a material stimulus, and he tentatively identified the latter with the 'electrical fluid' that had been popularized by the experiments of Joseph Priestley and Benjamin Franklin.[10] Thelwall's 'excellent and very valuable paper' on vitality earned him a letter of thanks from the Physical Society that may have emboldened him to deliver a new paper 'On the Origin of Sensation' later that year. But this time his attempt to explain 'the phenomena of mind [...] upon principles *purely Physical*' was rejected after heated debate, at least in part for its atheistic implications.[11] Thelwall quit the Society in protest, but he did not abandon the 'habit of thinking and of reasoning physiologically' that he acquired there.[12] Rather, this book's primary argument is that his scientific materialism merged with his radical politics and literary imagination in previously unexplored ways to anchor his career for the next four decades, as he attempted in speech and writing to spark democratic change in the body politic. The resulting experiments with literary form and oral performance appeal not just to individual reason – a pre-eminent agent of change for many contemporary radicals – but above all to an embodied conception of the sympathetic imagination, the ability to project oneself imaginatively into the experiences of another. In so doing they engage some of the era's most urgent questions and preoccupations: What is the body's relationship to the mind and imagination? What forms of language can 'speak' most effectively to and from them? Under what circumstances does the imagination become 'diseased', breeding solipsistic self-interest, zealotry or mob violence, or entrenching prejudices of class, race or gender? How can the imagination avoid such intemperance or effect its own 'cures'? Underpinning all of these questions is a concern with how the imagination can be made an agent of individual and social change – an 'unacknowledged legislator of the World', in Percy Shelley's famous phrase – especially in times of crisis and repression.[13] For Thelwall these were matters not only of intellectual speculation, but also of day-to-day practice as a reformer, writer, orator, teacher and therapist. His works stand out for their sustained attention and adaptation to challenges to the sympathetic imagination posed by factors including self-interest, political repression, personal loss and the 'tyranny' of habit and custom.

In charting Thelwall's evolving responses to these challenges, this book highlights at various points his complex treatment of two central problems of scientific and philosophical materialism: its deterministic tendency to reduce individuals to the status of passive subjects of external influence, and its apparent failure to account for the creative imagination. For those who consider Thelwall's works interesting only insofar as they 'indicate the direction of the breeze that was soon to fill the sails of a fleet of British poets, some of whom would successfully navigate the strange seas of thought that Thelwall but dimly perceived',[14] it may come as a surprise to find that, like Coleridge, he contested a mechanical view of cognition such as he found in the philosopher David Hartley and, in dialogue with Coleridge and Edmund Burke, among others, ultimately articulated a theory of the imagination as a faculty rooted in visual sense perception that is nonetheless capable of visionary transcendence. With that theory, Thelwall provides a wedge with which to prise open the rigid scholarly opposition between a radical ideology taken up with 'things as they are' and a 'Romantic ideology' of inward vision devoted to the imaginative transcendence of the material present.[15]

As the first detailed examination of Thelwall's body of work from the vantage of his materialism, this book aims not only to help rehabilitate that corpus, but also to challenge the longstanding critical view that Romanticism marked the triumph of various forms of anti-materialism, notably idealism and its scientific corollary, vitalism – a belief in the 'irreducibility of the living to the mechanical or chemical'.[16] That perspective, with deep roots in the writings of Coleridge and Immanuel Kant, finds new life in studies such as Neil Vickers's *Coleridge and the Doctors* (2004), which emphasizes the prevalence of orthodox mind-body dualism in the period, and Denise Gigante's *Life: Organic Form and Romanticism* (2009), which identifies a Romantic-era Zeitgeist preoccupied with the self-generating, self-sustaining powers of organic form.[17] While one alternative has been to denounce the 'Romantic ideology' of organic form and creative imagination as an evasion of historical realities, another, emergent strand, represented notably by the work of Alan Richardson, Richard Sha, Marjorie Levinson and Sharon Ruston, seeks to redirect attention to what Richardson calls 'an antidualistic, materialist register' in Romantic writing that has been 'badly ignored'.[18] Richardson has more recently described the critical re-evaluation of Romantic-era conceptions of the imagination along materialist, physiological and neurocognitive lines as 'one of the most exciting research areas in the field'.[19] As Geoffrey Hartman observes, '[t]he impact of matter on the imagination begins to matter'.[20]

So far, however, that impact has been assessed with reference primarily to the canonical Romantic poets. This is notably the case in Ruston's illuminating *Shelley and Vitality* (2005) and Levinson's provocative 2007 essay on Wordsworth and the Dutch materialist philosopher Benedict de Spinoza, as well as in Noel Jackson's and Paul Gilmore's studies of how material sensory experience grounded aesthetic theory and practice in late eighteenth- and early nineteenth-century Britain and America – studies wherein Coleridge and Keats are also prominent.[21] Nicholas Roe's *The Politics of Nature: William Wordsworth and Some Contemporaries* (2nd edn, 2002) stands out for its suggestion that the materialist principles expressed in Thelwall's 'animal vitality' paper of 1793 laid a foundation for the Romantic poetry of transcendence, but does not extend that insight to the range of his oeuvre.[22] For others, by contrast, Thelwall's materialist credentials are no longer self-evident. George S. Rousseau notes that many of his works 'are permeated with vitalistic metaphors and reflect a culture of vitalism in which he was immersed', adding that '[t]here was no philosophy of uniformity underlying his activities'.[23] Similarly, Catherine Packham examines Thelwall's political writings of the 1790s from the perspective of an eighteenth-century tradition of vitalism that she defines comprehensively as a rejection of earlier mechanical models of living nature.[24] These assessments are to some extent justified by the discursive overlap between vitalism and materialism at the time, notably as a result of the ambiguous ontological status of electricity: materialists and anti-materialists alike identified that mysterious fluid as the vital principle, as Chapter 1 will show.[25] At the same time, however, such assessments also attest to the long-prevalent understanding of Romanticism as essentially vitalistic. Restoring attention to the materialist underpinnings of Thelwall's entire career, this book ultimately argues that materialism and idealism (including vitalism) were neither interchangeable nor mutually exclusive traditions, but equally integral strands in the double-helix DNA of Romanticism. If this relationship can be described as dialectical, it is not so in the Hegelian sense of teleologically transforming oppositions into unities. As Pierre Macherey has observed,

[i]f there is a 'struggle' between materialism and idealism, [...] [i]t is not some external dialogue between two independent and divergent protagonists, the debate between whom might finally be settled in favour of one rather than the other. If materialism there is, then it is in the very development of idealism that it must be sought[.][26]

Insofar as Thelwall's writing gestures towards this dialogical or double-helix formation, it presents a timely reminder, amid the 'new materialist' turn of recent critical theory, of that tradition's long history and complex relation to idealist alternatives.[27]

To be clear, this book does not use the term 'materialism' to designate Thelwall's natural philosophy exclusively. Raymond Williams reminds us that in the eighteenth and early nineteenth centuries the word and its cognates referred not only to a 'varying set of arguments which propose[d] matter as the primary substance of all living and non-living things, including human beings', but also to a 'related or consequent but again highly various set of explanations and judgments of mental, moral and social activities'.[28] For this reason, as Paul Gilmore notes, a meaningful use of the term today should seek to address various interrelated kinds of materiality: of the body; of the aesthetic object; of language and the signifier; and of the limitations imposed on all of these by social, economic and political life.[29] In the title of this book the phrase 'materialist imagination' indicates its dual focus on the imaginative works in which Thelwall sought to produce material effects on the minds and bodies of audiences in the service of sociopolitical reform, and on his materialist understanding of the imagination as a faculty rooted in embodied sense perception. The extension of scientific materialism to politics, literature, elocution and aesthetics represents one of Thelwall's most important, and least appreciated, contributions to Romantic culture. In his works we see how theories of organic matter intersect with contemporaneous ideas about language, cognition, necessity and change, laying a foundation for the historical materialism of the later nineteenth century.

This book's revisionary approach to Thelwall and the materialist imagination is based on an extensive body of new archival materials. Chief among these are three manuscript volumes of his poetry held by the Derby Local Studies Library, England, which contain several previously unknown compositions, notably an unfinished satire on contemporary poets including Wordsworth, Robert Southey and Letitia Elizabeth Landon.[30] Also central to my argument are a hitherto unattributed essay of 1803 in which Thelwall refutes Burke's influential theory of language and aesthetic response; the original dedication of his *Poems, Chiefly Written in Retirement* to the democrat-physician Peter Crompton; an unpublished letter from Crompton to Thelwall during his three-year retreat from public life; Thelwall's candid marginalia on Coleridge's *Biographia Literaria* and on a volume of poems by William Lisle Bowles that was a gift from Coleridge; and his contributions to periodicals including the *Biographical and Imperial Magazine*, the *Champion* and the *Panoramic Miscellany*. The ensuing chapters place these new materials – selections from which appear in the book's appendices – in dialogue with Thelwall's better-known works, notably his verse-prose hybrid *The Peripatetic* (1793), his collections *Poems Written in Close Confinement* (1795) and *Poems, Chiefly Written in Retirement* (1801), his novel *The Daughter of Adoption* (1801), and his prolific elocutionary and political writing. In all of these works Thelwall emerges as, in Francis Jeffrey's phrase, 'The Champion of Materialism', one who sustained a highly nuanced engagement with the tradition's key premises well into the nineteenth century, and whose literary and historical fate was intimately bound up with its repudiation.[31]

While Jeffrey stands out for his understanding (however scornful) of Thelwall's centrality to materialist thought and practice in the Romantic period, it was Coleridge who offered the most fitting description of the resulting body of work with the phrase 'vigorous song', a compliment paid in a sonnet 'To John Thelwall' in 1796 when Coleridge still tenuously believed in the 'corporeality of *thought* – namely that it is motion'.[32] Deriving from the Latin for liveliness, activity or force, 'vigorous' denotes the physical strength of bodies and the figurative energy of minds and language.[33] Another version of Coleridge's sonnet describes Thelwall's song instead as 'nervous', a term derived from the Latin *nervosus*, meaning sinewy, which conveys even more explicitly the physiological sources of the song's energy.[34] In use as a stylistic term since the sixteenth century, 'nervous' had by the eighteenth century become a widespread term of praise for expression that was brisk and forceful, and a hallmark of those qualities in the writer or speaker, whose style was thought to be connected with his nervous responsiveness to the world.[35] Coleridge's sense of the embodied, material quality of Thelwall's 'vigorous song' is also evident in his remark a year later, in response to Thelwall's criticism of his early poetry, 'your nerves are exquisite *electrometers* of Taste'.[36] As Coleridge was no doubt aware, the lexicon of nervous, vigorous song also had a strong ideological valence. A commonplace of late eighteenth-century radical analyses of language is the contrast between the weak, effeminate expression of the upper classes, often associated with decadent aristocracy, and the robust, masculine expression of the common people, typically aligned with virtuous republicanism.[37] Thelwall would later lament the decline of Wordsworth's 'nervous line' together with his political apostasy, as we will see.[38] 'Vigorous song', then, evokes precisely the conjunction of materialist aesthetic, scientific and ideological qualities in Thelwall's oeuvre that Coleridge first admired and then strenuously rejected, and that this book undertakes to recover.[39]

That recovery proceeds in the spirit of Thelwall's materialism by tracing the vitality of his works to particular conjunctions of matter and stimulus, writer and moment. Accordingly, the book's method combines close literary analysis with a 'positive' form of reading Romantic literature in its historical and personal contexts.[40] The ensuing chapters share Paul Magnuson's sense that all Romantic texts are public utterances that arise from particular locations, communities and debates.[41] Their aim, however, is not simply to re-inscribe Thelwall within the familiar networks and narratives of Romanticism, but in some sense to defamiliarize him by shifting attention to the wider intellectual and social spheres in dialogue and dispute with which his ideas found expression. If, as E. P. Thompson asserted and recent criticism confirms, Thelwall 'straddled the world of Wordsworth and Coleridge, and the world of the Spitalfields weavers', he also had a firm footing in the scientific circles of London, Edinburgh and the provinces to which this book restores attention.[42] Moreover, since the avant-garde science of the period provided Thelwall with a lexicon as well as a model of change in complex bodies, my method also involves a form of 'literal archaeology' that attempts to recover the materialist inflections of keywords in his oeuvre that might otherwise be treated as purely metaphorical.[43] At the heart of that lexicon is electricity, an 'exquisitely subtile' (or exceedingly fine) fluid that Thelwall regarded as the principle 'by which all heat and action are originally generated and maintained' in the animal body as in the natural world.[44] Thelwall's instructor at Guy's Hospital, the eminent surgeon John Hunter, and later his fellow pupil Astley Cooper would attribute sympathetic communication within the body to the circulation of an electrical nervous fluid.[45] For Thelwall, electricity also offers a powerful model and metaphor for the communication between bodies and embodied minds that he seeks to achieve with language. Its lexical field includes terms related to its apparatus and manifestations, such as 'electric jar', 'hermetic hand', conductor, wand, charge, lightening and fire. These mingle in Thelwall's materialist lexicon with terms derived from physiology (nerves, fibres, brain, pulse, throb, vibration, sensation, stimulus), chemistry (limbec, vapour), and mechanism or the science of motion (machine, automaton).[46] Like the medical language that permeates John Keats's poetry, Thelwall's materialist lexicon is not limited to scientific meanings, but nonetheless 'anchored' by them.[47] This mobility made it especially useful for addressing issues of liberty, equality and reform under repression.

The organization of the book's six chapters, roughly following the dates and genres of Thelwall's major works, highlights the development of his materialist thought and practice across the span of his career, his relentless experimentation with communicative forms, and his changing response to personal and political circumstance. This organization also highlights his enduring commitment to democratic reform, a commitment that challenges the master narratives of Romantic introspection and apostasy whereby young radicals become old reactionaries.[48] In an influential essay on the 'fragmented ideology' of reform in the period, Mark Philp calls for more nuanced attention to its varied responses to rapidly shifting historical and discursive parameters.[49] Thelwall put the point succinctly when, speaking in 1795 before a mass audience against proposed laws to curtail free speech and assembly, he observed that '[u]niformity of principle and versatility of means are perfectly reconcilable; and he who wishes to promote the public cause must vary his mode of action with the change of time and circumstances: as the same line of conduct may be at one time beneficial, and at another injurious'.[50] Thus, while this book is interested in the displacement of history and politics in Thelwall's works, it sees this displacement, when it happens, as evidence not of 'Romantic ideology' but of radical strategy: a means of preserving vitality under stifling conditions of repression. From that perspective, Thelwall's imaginative and elocutionary works appear not merely as quietist alternatives to his frustrated political ambitions, but as the very means by which, in changing circumstances, he sought to promote his democratic, egalitarian and humanitarian principles.

Chapter 1 lays a foundation for following Thelwall through his varied 'mode[s] of action' by examining the concurrent development in the early 1790s of his materialist notions of vitality and cognition and his reformist ambitions to 'quicken' a new consciousness in the body politic by appeals to the sympathetic imagination. The chapter begins by situating Thelwall's bold speculations about 'animal vitality' in relation to those of his contemporaries – including John Hunter, Joseph Priestley, Erasmus Darwin and William Lawrence – and then considers how those speculations informed and inflected his project of democratic reform. The little-examined link between Thelwall's medical and political theories is shown to be his materialist understanding of cognition, which sought to reconcile David Hartley's doctrine of mental associations with a radical faith in individual agency shared notably with William Godwin. Responding to critics who fault Thelwall for failing to develop an equivalent to Paine's radical style, the chapter ends with a look ahead to a late essay in which he elevates suggestive literary language over 'plain' speech and writing for its ability to address the imagination as well as the understanding.

Chapters 2 to 4 explore the literary expressions of Thelwall's radical materialism as he confronted the challenges of self-interest, repression, mourning and disillusionment in the mid- to late 1790s. Chapter 2 focuses on *The Peripatetic; or, Sketches of the Heart, of Nature and Society* (1793), a highly digressive work in verse and prose that takes the reader on a tour of the English countryside at a period of profound socio-economic transformation. Often read as an attempt to reform literary convention or as a source of inspiration for Wordsworth, *The Peripatetic* is interpreted here as embodying, thematically and formally, the fusion of science, politics and the imagination in Thelwall's writing at this time. His controversial papers on 'Animal Vitality' and 'The Origin of Sensation', both contemporaneous with *The Peripatetic*, are shown to inform its unifying interest in the connections among perception, cognition and benevolent action, as well as its strategies for appealing to those faculties in readers. The chapter thus launches the book's discussion of Thelwall's career-long fascination with the reformatory potential of an embodied imagination, while also demonstrating his awareness of its limits, especially when measured against the force of direct sensory experience and the claims of self-interest.

Concerns about the individual's capacity to overcome solipsistic self-interest come to the fore in the two volumes that are the focus of Chapter 3: *Poems Written in Close Confinement* (1795), composed during Thelwall's seven-month imprisonment pending trial for high treason, and *Poems, Chiefly Written in Retirement* (1801), composed during his three-year retreat to Wales. Whereas some critics regard these collections as precursors to, or interlocutors of, the introspective individualism of the 'Greater Romantic Lyric', this chapter considers how they employ a richly metaphorical lexicon of health, pathology and healing to address questions of sociopolitical change even under repression. In so doing, it argues, the collections define an alternative aesthetic characterized by what one poem describes as a 'turn / From *Self* to *Sentient Nature*' – the imaginative ability to perceive oneself as part of an animate whole that Thelwall thought indispensible to reform.[51] In both collections this outward turn is dependent on the poet's sense of connection with a wider community of reformers. Drawing on new archival evidence, the chapter suggests that the *Retirement* poems in particular should be read with reference not only to the Wordsworth-Coleridge circle that failed to sustain Thelwall in crisis, but also to the wider medico-political community that succeeded.

In the aftermath of the anti-Jacobin backlash of the mid- to late 1790s Thelwall became increasingly preoccupied with the deterministic implications of materialism, and particularly with the prospect of embodied cognition giving way to a mechanical automaticity of response – the 'automatonism' that Coleridge also feared. Chapter 4 looks at how in three works composed at the turn of the century – the Arthurian drama *The Fairy of the Lake*, the unfinished epic poem *The Hope of Albion*, and the late 'Jacobin' novel *The Daughter of Adoption* – Thelwall adapts the genre of romance, specifically the politically charged version theorized by Godwin that Jon Klancher calls 'republican romance', to re-imagine how would-be reformers reduced to the status of mere automatons might become heroes once more.[52] Whereas a host of supernaturally empowered antagonists counteract the radical agency of Arthur in *The Fairy* and the exiled prince Edwin in *The Hope*, the heroine of *The Daughter* manages against the odds to live out her 'new philosophy' of equality and universal benevolence, but only by tempering her radical idealism with a pragmatic understanding of the power of material circumstance, habit and feeling over individual thought and action. All three 'republican romances' thus testify to a heightened concern with the potential limitations and dangers of mind-body reciprocity, while holding fast to a belief in the possibility of reform.

Chapters 5 and 6 carry the book's argument beyond the 'Revolutionary Decade' to take stock of the newly discovered manuscript poetry and prolific but uncollected elocutionary writings that span the period 1800 to 1830. Chapter 5 considers how in the early nineteenth century Thelwall adapted to the narrow range of legally permitted public utterance by turning his attention to the material basis of elicitation and response as a self-made professor of elocution and speech therapist. While the scattered state of his elocutionary corpus has long precluded a comprehensive assessment of his system, this chapter shows it to have been rooted in the principle of 'rhythmus', the careful coordination of volition with the organic necessity of action and reaction in the speaking body. That principle also underpins Thelwall's poetry of this period, notably the unpublished collection *Poems, Chiefly Suggested by the Scenery of Nature*, recently recovered as part of the three manuscript volumes in Derby. The chapter presents both facets of Thelwall's career after 1800, the poetic and the elocutionary, as continuations by different means of his reformist project, and it attributes their shared emphasis on 'restrained vehemence' – the virtuous self-regulation of one's passion – to the revolutionary excesses of the previous decade and widespread anti-radical, anti-materialist sentiment that ensued, which threatened to obstruct Thelwall's newly recovered powers of expression.

Thelwall's physiological insights into the dynamics of expression and cognition in the early nineteenth century underpinned not only his elocutionary career, but also his development of a materialist aesthetics and theory of the imagination. By way of conclusion, Chapter 6 examines a cluster of critically neglected late poems, criticism and marginalia from which it becomes clear to what extent Coleridge's sense of his and Thelwall's 'irreconcilably different opinions in Politics, Religion, & Metaphysics, (& probably in Taste too)' was overstated.[53] In dialogue with Coleridge and Burke, Thelwall's late works challenge the dichotomy between materialism and idealism, and by extension between passive subjectivity and voluntaristic creativity, propounded by Coleridge and still prominent in criticism today. In restoring attention to those works, the chapter testifies to an enduring sense of the transformative potential of the imagination that makes Thelwall not just an exemplary radical, but also a quintessential Romantic, even while his materialist convictions led him to dissent from Romanticism's transcendental, idealizing impulses. Like the book as a whole, it aims to breathe new life into Thelwall's oeuvre and the tradition of British materialism to which it was central.

1
Vital Principles
From the Animal Body to the Body Politic

But what is this something – this vivifying principle?[1]

John Thelwall wanted to give his heart to medical science. He and the surgeon Astley Cooper had an agreement whereby, if Thelwall died first, Cooper would receive his heart for medical study. It was apparently remarkable for its pathology, as well as for its radical sensibility. According to his second wife and biographer, Henrietta Cecil, Thelwall suffered from a strange condition that sometimes caused his heart to beat so loudly that it was audible from several yards away. On one occasion it startled a passer-by in the street; on another it awoke Cecil in the middle of the night, when she mistook its beating for someone knocking at the door. Cooper joked that his friend had 'an exceedingly good head – but an excessively bad heart!'.[2] Although that defective organ eventually caused Thelwall's death in 1834 when he suffered 'some affection' of it, probably a heart attack, while on an elocutionary lecture-stop in Bath, it seems doubtful that Cooper ever sought fulfilment of their agreement.[3] He knew, in any case, that Thelwall had already given his heart to medical science four decades earlier, when he attended lectures at Guy's and St. Thomas's hospitals in London and immersed himself in the debates about vitality and cognition that were to pulse through his life's work. Thelwall's early engagement with medical science was a vital context for his pursuits across disciplines and decades, yet it has long lain buried beneath his profile as a radical agitator and one-time friend of Wordsworth and Coleridge. If we are adequately to reassess his body of work, we must first recover the ideas about the human mind and body that were at its very heart.

Since Michel Foucault's pioneering study of the eighteenth-century transformation of medicine into 'a science of the individual' and Roy Porter's and George Rousseau's investigations of contemporaneous understandings of the relationship between the body and the self, the intersections of Romantic-era literary and scientific cultures have become prominent areas of analysis.[4] With few exceptions, however, scholars have tended to give only cursory attention to Thelwall's place in what Alan Richardson describes as 'one of the most daring intellectual ventures of [... the] era – the reinvention, along naturalistic, physiological, and ecological lines, of the study of human nature'.[5] This chapter demonstrates how, in the crucible of early 1790s' political debate, Thelwall's medical training became compounded with his radical politics and developing theories of language and the imagination to provide a model and a lexicon for his vision of reform. The first section examines the idiosyncrasies of his belief that the properties and processes of living nature could be explained with reference to certain immutable laws of matter, situating his theory in relation to those of his better-known contemporaries, including Joseph Priestley, Erasmus Darwin, John Hunter and William Lawrence. The second section shows how Thelwall's heterodox speculations about animal life provided a model for 'quickening' a reformist consciousness in the body politic through the medium of language, while the third explores the bridge between his scientific and political theories: his materialist conception of the mind. Although the paper in which Thelwall set forth his ideas about cognition was lost amid the controversy surrounding its presentation in 1793 before the leading surgeons and anatomists of the day, we can infer its contents from a range of other documents, in which he endorses a doctrine of mental association as propounded by the philosopher David Hartley, while following his mentor William Godwin in attempting to keep open a place for individual agency. Responding to critics who fault Thelwall for failing to develop an equivalent to Thomas Paine's 'intellectual vernacular', the chapter ends with a look ahead to an essay of 1826 in which he articulates his faith in the 'ambiguous magic' of literary language – the capacity to spark associative trains of thought that made it a powerful instrument of reform.[6] By recovering these theoretical underpinnings of Thelwall's career, the chapter lays a foundation for the ensuing readings of his literary and elocutionary works not merely as alternatives to his political activism, but as the principal means by which he sought to elicit the sympathetic imagination in the cause of reform. A brief excursus into Thelwall's early years will help contextualize his interest in medical science.

Living, in a material world

Born 27 July 1764 in Covent Garden to a downwardly mobile family of Saxon descent, Thelwall showed polymathic interests from a young age. Following the death of his father, he was pulled from school at age nine to work behind the counter of the family silk shop and suffered routine beatings by his mother and epileptic older brother. He found comfort in voracious reading – 'plays, poetry, and history, moral philosophy, metaphysics, and even divinity'[7] – and made unsuccessful attempts to become a historical painter and actor-dramatist, before leaving home at 16 to become apprenticed first to a west-end tailor, and then to an attorney. He kept up his self-education, even carrying a candle in his pocket so that he could read as he walked home at night.[8] But he soon came to detest the career of 'venal pleading' as much as the 'disgusting trade' of the tailor shop.[9] In 1786, just a year before his qualification for the bar, Thelwall abruptly cancelled his articles of indenture and 'launch[ed] into the world as a literary adventurer'.[10] The following year he published the two-volume sentimental collection *Poems on Various Subjects* as well as *Orlando and Almeyda: A Legendary Tale, in the Manner of Dr. Goldsmith*, and around the same time he became editor of the *Biographical and Imperial Magazine*, composing much of its miscellaneous content himself.[11] Financial self-sufficiency enabled him in July 1791 to marry Susan Vellum, whom he had met on a visit to Rutland two years earlier, when she was only 'a simple, innocent, unsophisticated little maiden' of 15.[12]

Soon after his marriage Thelwall settled in Southwark, near Guy's and St. Thomas's hospitals. This location facilitated his immersion in the world of medical research that was attracting widespread public interest. Possibly inspired by his grandfather, a naval surgeon who was found guilty of high treason for treating his enemies' wounds during the Spanish War of 1718,[13] Thelwall began attending lectures on anatomy given by his friend Henry Cline, as well as on chemistry and physiology, and also sat in on operations and dissections. His medical circle soon included Edward Coleman, expert in cases of asphyxia, John Walker, future specialist in vaccination, and James Parkinson, who later identified the disease that bears his name.[14] The latter two would, like Thelwall, become equally well known for their radical politics.[15] Thelwall now also befriended Cline's pupil Astley Cooper, future surgeon to the king, instructor of John Keats, and prospective recipient of Thelwall's noisy heart.[16] Along with Cooper, Thelwall became active in the management of the Physical Society, a sort of 'informal university' and continuing education programme for the pre-eminent members of the Borough hospitals, who met weekly to discuss medical issues.[17] It was before this society that Thelwall caused a sensation when, on 26 January 1793, he delivered a bold paper on 'animal vitality' that was debated for six successive meetings.[18]

Vitality was a hot topic at the end of the eighteenth century, when discoveries in chemistry, physiology and other areas of natural philosophy were offering up new grounds of speculation about the principle of life. Thelwall had kept abreast of these developments as editor of the *Biographical and Imperial Magazine*, publishing reports on Joseph Priestley's experiments with 'dephlogisticated air' (or oxygen), George Fordyce's Royal Society lecture on muscular motion, Erasmus Darwin's study of the expansion of air, and Johann Kaspar Lavater's *Essays on Physiognomy*, among other scientific items.[19] The magazine also shows Thelwall to have been a keen follower of the Humane Society, founded in 1776 by his friend William Hawes to resuscitate drowning victims and promote research into life-saving techniques.[20] In June 1790 two items from the Society's reports received particular attention in the magazine: the discovery by the Baron de Hupsch that 'a human body, apparently dead, may be resuscitated by being electrified', and the invention by a Mr. Roulaud, of the University of Paris, of a machine consisting of a double-bellows for 'restoring Respiration to Persons drowned, or otherwise suffocated'.[21]

Air, electricity, muscular motion – virtually all subjects of scientific inquiry at the time converged on a single question:

> Whether life itself is to be considered as a distinct and positive essence, or, simply, as the result of a particular harmony and correspondence of the whole, or aggregate combination, preserved and acted upon by a particular stimulus?[22]

In his 1793 paper before the Physical Society, published later that year as *An Essay, Towards a Definition of Animal Vitality*, Thelwall undertakes to answer this question 'upon the simple principles of materialism'.[23] The essay's epigraph – *'Felix, qui potuit rerum cognoscere causas'* ('Happy is he who can understand the causes of things') – comes from a line in Vigil's *Georgics* that echoes Lucretius's *De Rerum Natura* (*On the Nature of Things*), a foundational text of materialist natural philosophy.[24] Thelwall's attempt to understand the cause of life proceeds by submitting the prevailing theories of the day to a version of the heuristic now known as Occam's razor: he prefers whichever theory 'involves the fewest absurdities, or is best supported by analogy, and the correspondence of the general laws of Nature'.[25] On this basis Thelwall dismisses the two prevailing theories of the day, starting with the theory that 'life is to be considered as a distinct and positive essence' which is 'superadded' to organized matter.[26] This was a version of vitalism, the 'belief in the existence of a mysterious force running through *all matter* in the universe'.[27] Sometimes referred to as 'transcendentalism' for its distinction between a perishable, material body and an immortal, immaterial soul, the theory was consistent with the Church-sanctioned Newtonian theory of matter as an inert, impenetrable substance consisting of 'corpuscules' that were endlessly recombined by divine principles or powers.[28] Thelwall traces the transmission of this theory among ancient writers – Aristotle, Plato, Plutarch, Moses and St. Paul – before calling attention to its resurgence in 'modern philosophy', notably the works of the country's foremost surgeon John Hunter (uncle of Matthew and Joanna Baillie).[29] Thelwall had regularly attended Hunter's lectures and was well acquainted with his argument that the principle of life was located in the blood.[30] While he agrees that the blood has a role in sustaining the animal organism, he rejects Hunter's 'doctrine of the Vitality of the blood' because it implies that the blood itself is alive, a claim that 'seems to contradict the known laws and phenomena of nature', and also contradicts the opinion of 'some later philosophers' that the blood is less indispensable to life than the brain.[31] The latter remark suggests Thelwall's familiarity with the avant-garde brain science of the 1780s and 1790s, advanced notably by F. J. Gall in Austria and Erasmus Darwin in England.[32] By contrast, he compares Hunter's doctrine with that of

> an ancient sect of Atheists, who, to get rid of the necessity of a Deity, insisted upon the original and eternal Vitality of matter, and accounted for the growth and nourishment of living things, by arguing, that the particles that nourished them were themselves possessed of a living principle.[33]

A strict empiricist, Thelwall rejects this pantheistic – or more accurately 'hylozoistic' – creed as inconsistent with the evidence of the senses.[34] The universe, he reasons, must consist in either matter or vacuum, 'and how vacuum, or nothing, can be so modified as to produce Life, I leave to the consideration of the Metaphysicians'.[35] By insisting on the epistemological rather than ontological nature of his speculations, Thelwall may be seeking to deflect charges of atheism such as had been levelled against the French materialist *philosophes* Denis Diderot, Paul-Henri Dietrich, Baron d'Holbach, Claude-Adrien Helvétius and Julien Offroy de La Mettrie, as well as their English counterparts, including Darwin and Joseph Priestley.

Thelwall's refusal to engage ontological questions notwithstanding, his refutation of Hunter has strong affinities with Priestley's attack on 'modern philosophical dualism' in *Disquisitions Relating to Matter and Spirit* (1777), where Priestley argued controversially that matter itself had the capacity for thought.[36] Priestley was rare among late eighteenth-century natural philosophers in asserting the ontological unity of creation without denying the role of divine agency in directing the forces of attraction and repulsion that, in his view, defined matter.[37] Such views led Priestley to argue that life arises from a particular organization of matter without the superaddition of an external substance. His reasoning is encapsulated by his observation that 'the powers of sensation or perception, and thought, as belonging to man, have never been found but in conjunction with a certain *organized system of matter*; and therefore, [...] those powers necessarily exist in, and depend upon, such a system'.[38] While sharing Priestley's metaphysical monism, Thelwall rejects the 'immanentist' theory of vitality that he helped make famous. Although Priestley is not named in the *Animal Vitality* essay (and the immanentist arguments of the French physiologist Marie-François-Xavier Bichat and the English surgeon William Lawrence post-dated it[39]), his position is implicit in Thelwall's insistence that a particular organization of matter is a necessary but not sufficient condition for life. An egg consists of highly organized matter, Thelwall reasons, but prior to incubation it is not alive. On similar grounds, he dismisses the theory that life consists in action – 'the performance of the Animal functions' – observing that a creature might be incapacitated in various ways but still remain alive.[40]

Having dismantled the two dominant theories of the day, Thelwall states his case for a plausible third: that life is the result of a particular organization of matter (the 'pre-disposing' cause) acted upon by a particular stimulus (the 'remote cause'). When the two combine, the result is 'that meliorated or altered state of the organized frame' which enables the vital functions to be performed (the 'proximate cause' of life). The 'ultimate effect' of this conjunction is life itself.[41] Thelwall defines organization as an 'arrangement of dissimilar parts' that produces 'a harmony and communication of the whole' and makes it 'susceptible' to the vital stimulus.[42] What, then, was 'this something – this vivifying principle'? It was apparently imbibed by the blood on its passage through the lungs, but recent experiments had ruled out the possibility that it was 'atmospheric air', which apparently could not traverse the membranes of the arteries or lungs. Thelwall speculates that the stimulus is rather 'something of a powerful and exquisitely subtle nature' contained in the atmosphere – something like the 'electrical fluid, [...] whose agency, in so many phenomena of Nature, we are daily detecting'. He concludes the essay by surmising that this quasi-electrical fluid will one day be identified as the vital principle itself – 'the real principle by which all heat and action are originally generated and maintained!'.[43]

The concept of an 'electrical fluid' had wide credence at the time thanks to Priestley's *History and Present State of Electricity* (1767) and Benjamin Franklin's experiments to prove the electrical nature of lightening,[44] and thanks also to the popularity of spectacular public demonstrations. Thelwall may have attended one in which a Leyden jar – a glass jar filled with water and electrified by a wire attached to a conductor – was used to pass a current through one or even hundreds of people.[45] He probably also knew about the 'magnetic' frog experiments of Luigi Galvani, whose conclusion that an electrical vital fluid proceeded from the animal was disproved by Alessandro Volta in 1792.[46] Certainly, Thelwall was familiar with the medical applications of electricity. As editor of the *Biographical and Imperial Magazine* he had taken notice of the Humane Society's reports of dead bodies reanimated by electricity, and as a pupil at Guy's and St. Thomas's hospitals he would have witnessed its therapeutic application as practiced by Hunter and others for the relief of conditions ranging from smallpox and paralysis to hysteria.[47] In positing that the 'electrical fluid' is the vital principle itself, however, Thelwall aligns himself with a medical avant-garde that exhibited a 'cautious fascination' with its role in vitality.[48] Darwin, for instance, speculated in *The Botanic Garden* (1789–91) – one of the books seized from Thelwall's home on his arrest in 1794 – about the existence of 'a material received from the air by respiration; which is so necessary to life, that the embryon must learn to breath [*sic*] almost within a minute after its birth, or it dies'. Darwin tentatively identified this material with the vital principle, adding that '[p]erhaps the spirit of animation itself is thus acquired from the atmosphere, which if it be supposed to be finer or more subtle than the electric matter, could not long be retained in our bodies, and must therefore require perpetual renovation' through respiration.[49]

The heterodoxy of Thelwall's theory of life comes into sharper relief when we compare it with those of the surgeon William Lawrence and his mentor John Abernethy, whose debates in the 1810s are a now-familiar context for Percy and Mary Shelley's interest in vitality.[50] The debates centred on Abernethy's argument, derived from Hunter, that life was dependent not on the body's material organization, but on the existence of a 'subtile, mobile, invisible substance, superadded to the evident structure of muscles, or other forms of vegetable and animal matter, as magnetism is to iron, and as electricity is to various substances with which it may be connected'.[51] Drawing on the chemical experiments of Humphry Davy, Abernethy speculated that this 'subtile' substance was analogous if not identical to electricity.[52] Unlike Thelwall, however, he did not regard electricity as material; rather, as Sharon Ruston notes, he considered it to occupy some 'middle ground' between the material body and immaterial soul.[53] Lawrence, by contrast, argued against his teacher that vitality was not superadded to matter but a quality of organized matter itself. His theory has been described as no less 'vitalistic' than Abernethy's insofar as it rejected earlier mechanistic accounts of living bodies.[54] Nonetheless, his insistence on the strictly material causes of vitality, combined with his desire to separate medical and theological inquiry, led to his suspension from employment and eventual recantation. This fate was primarily a consequence of the association between his views and the atheistic materialism of the French physiologists, but might also be traced to the avant-garde science of 1790s' English radicals, among the most vocal of whom was the 'Champion of Materialism', Thelwall.[55]

Quickening the body politic

The convergence of materialist science and radical politics in Thelwall's thought itself had a precedent in the mid-seventeenth century's 'Vitalist Moment'. As John Rogers has shown, this period coinciding with the English Revolution (1649–52) was marked by an 'explosion of alternative materialist philosophies' that posited the self-moving quality of matter in the natural and political worlds alike, setting themselves against the premise of arbitrary authority common to Puritan and mechanistic discourses.[56] Among the disparate group of poets, reformers and natural philosophers who endorsed such views, one of the most famous was John Milton, from the perspective of whose 'animist materialism' matter and spirit differed in degree rather than quality, both being manifestations of one 'animate, self-active, and free' corporeal substance.[57] Stephen M. Fallon has established that for Milton, 'a revolutionary who distrusted the masses', animist materialism offered ontological support not only for the concept of free will (which Thomas Hobbes had famously denied), but also for 'a political vision of republican rule of and for all the people by the chosen few'.[58] For others, the theory of self-moving matter could also justify a more populist, egalitarian politics of self-rule. Rogers considers that this radical implication helps explain the brevity of the 'Vitalist Moment', which gave way to a mechanistic conception of atomistic individuals whose behaviour was determined by their subjection to a higher authority, rather than by their innate virtue and reason.[59]

The period's 'alternative materialist philosophies' nonetheless resurfaced at various moments in the long eighteenth century.[60] This was notably the case in England in the aftermath of the Revolution of 1688, when Isaac Newton's two theories of matter – one postulating inert particles or 'corpuscules' subject to forces of attraction and repulsion, the other suggesting the existence of a 'subtle', elastic fluid called 'aether' permeating all matter – were appropriated into the rhetoric of opposing political philosophies. According to the 'court ideology' developed by Newton and his disciplines, guidance by active and benevolent external powers was equally necessary in the natural and political worlds. Conversely, according to the republican natural philosophers who co-opted Newton's ideas, the corpuscules that composed matter were in fact active and autonomous, themselves productive of the forces that regulated them, and a harmonious political order was likewise a matter of internal self-regulation by an active citizenry.[61] In the writings of the eighteenth-century French *philosophes* and subsequently those of English radicals like Priestley and William Godwin, materialism became virtually synonymous with atheism and republicanism – an association whose perils were demonstrated in 1791 when a church-and-king mob destroyed Priestley's Birmingham home and laboratory, spurring his emigration to America three years later.

Notwithstanding the dangers of unorthodox scientific opinion, the 'early habit of thinking and of reasoning physiologically' that Thelwall acquired at the London hospitals came to inform his theory and practice for the next 40 years, converging with the radical principles that he likewise adopted in the early 1790s.[62] At 19 he had begun speaking at the debating societies then popular in London, giving his first address at Coachmakers' Hall, the meeting place of the Society for Free Debate, where he became known as the 'Lisping Orator' for the speech impediment that he would not overcome for several decades. He later credited that society with challenging his youthful church-and-king 'dogmatism' and teaching him to think for himself.[63] (One especially potent topic of debate was the slave trade, which he opposed with 'an almost diseased enthusiasm', as Chapter 5 of this book attests.[64]) Thelwall's conversion from 'zealous ministerialist' to zealous reformer accelerated with the onset of the French Revolution.[65] A believer in the 'principles of ancient freedom' – the inheritance of Anglo-Saxon rights and liberties that many Whigs and radicals thought to have been lost with the Norman Conquest – he welcomed the revolution as an 'unprecedented attempt to form a philosophical system of government, not upon military violence and temporary expedients, but upon digested principles of reason and humanity'.[66] Those principles, combined with Thelwall's 'abhorrence' of the widespread corruption that characterized British parliamentary elections at the time, spurred him to become a poll-clerk in the Westminster election of 1790, a position he then gave up to campaign on behalf of the veteran reformer John Horne Tooke, a staunch supporter of British legal and constitutional liberties and of the American Revolution. Tooke lost the election but won a disciple in Thelwall, who came to regard the older man as his 'intellectual and political father'.[67] This radical mentorship was supplemented by Thelwall's reading of Paine's *Rights of Man* and Godwin's *Enquiry concerning Political Justice* around this time.[68] He would soon set to popularizing their principles in his writings and lectures, asserting that 'one Thomas Paine is worth a dozen Aristotles'. He would note, however, that 'it was not *Tom Paine* but *Edmund Burke* that made me so zealous a reformer, and convinced me of the necessity of annual Parliaments and universal suffrage'.[69] Burke's defence of the country's inherited institutions and attacks on English 'Jacobinism' would galvanize Thelwall's writing for many years to come.

But perhaps the most effective catalyst of Thelwall's radical politics was his involvement with various reform societies in London as the government began to crack down on the freedoms of speech and the press amid mounting concern over the spread of revolutionary sentiment. After trying unsuccessfully to prevent suppression of his cherished Society for Free Debate, Thelwall in October 1793 joined Division 25 of the London Corresponding Society or 'LCS', a working-class organization founded by the shoemaker Thomas Hardy to represent the disenfranchised and campaign for annual parliaments and universal manhood suffrage.[70] Thelwall quickly distinguished himself as one of the LCS's most gifted speakers and organizers, and in April 1794 he was named as its delegate to the more genteel Society for Constitutional Information and began hosting meetings of their joint committees.[71] During these years he also began lecturing on politics, first from an assembly room in Southwark, then from rooms in Soho, and finally from a lecture hall in Beaufort Buildings, the Strand, where he also took up residence.[72]

As articulated in his lectures and writings of this period, Thelwall's vision of reform turns on a materialist interpretation of the age-old analogy between the animal body and the body politic: both, in his view, are animated by a conjunction of internal and external factors. A republican who deemed constitutional monarchy an acceptable interim system, Thelwall believed the health of the polis to depend on 'that sort of combination and among the people, that sort of intelligence, communication, and organised harmony among them, by which the whole will of the nation can be immediately collected and communicated'.[73] Therefore, until parliamentary reform instituted a 'full and fair' representation in the Commons, it was incumbent on the people to make their collective body seen and their collective voice heard. As he put it in a striking passage in *The Natural and Constitutional Right of Britons to Annual Parliaments, Universal Suffrage, and the Freedom of Popular Association* (1795),

> as the Royal Power is concentrated in a single person, girt and surrounded by Ministers of his own appointment; and as the aristocratic body is also intimately encorporated; if the people are not permitted to associate and knit themselves together for the vindication of their rights, how shall they frustrate attempts which will inevitably be made against their liberties? The scattered million, however unanimous in feeling, is but chaff in the whirlwind. It must be pressed together to have any weight.[74]

Thelwall alludes to Burke's contention in *Reflections on the Revolution in France* (1790) that members of a civil society must be held together by '*a power out of themselves*'.[75] Burke considered that one of the lost advantages of the French *ancien régime* was its 'pressing down the whole by the weight of a real monarchy'.[76] For Thelwall, by contrast, a healthy body politic needs not only an external source of vitality, but also an appropriate internal organization: the people must be 'pressed together' to have any weight or substance. In his lectures he insists that popular discontent will be only a 'wandering ghost' unless the people collectively present their governors with the 'living body' of their complaints.[77]

The 'wandering ghost' becomes a 'living body' through a process that directly echoes Thelwall's essay on animal vitality. In a 1794 lecture 'On the Moral Tendency of a System of Spies and Informers', he cites the recent surge in prosecutions for libel as evidence that

> now the great mass of the people is quickened into mental existence. The sparks, successively struck off in the different struggles and contests for the emoluments of this corruption, have flown throughout the whole circle of society; and though the degrees of warmth are dissimilar, there is scarcely an individual, especially in towns and cities, where men are pressed together, and minds come into immediate contact, that is not in some degree animated with the desire of political enquiry.[78]

Here as in the previously quoted passage, the image of men and minds 'pressed together' evokes what Thelwall regards as two key instruments for a collective quickening. One is the printing press, which gave literal and figurative substance to popular opinion. Like Godwin, Thelwall saw literature in a broad sense – works of information and imagination – as the engines of a 'universal moral revolution' that would alter the 'whole substrata' of political institutions.[79] He credited the spread of literature during the sixteenth century with first awakening the British people to a sense of their rights, and he argued that the Revolution of 1649 had failed only because the great mass of the people had not partaken of this enlightenment and therefore allowed themselves to be guided by fanatics. In revolutionary France, by contrast, the press had helped spread the principles of 'Sans Culottism' through the whole body of the people, and '[t]he whole mass being quickened, the whole mass acted'. 'Sans Culottism' was the Revolution's 'vital principle' and literature was its lifeblood.[80] A second key instrument for quickening public opinion was the extra-parliamentary public sphere of associations and assemblies, where the people could 'press together' to discuss their interests and grievances, fostering what Godwin called the 'collision of mind with mind'.[81] Referring to his role as public orator and lecturer, Thelwall described himself as 'a part – a little, little member of the great animal of human society – a palpilliary [*sic*] nerve upon one of the extremities!' adding, 'I must do that duty to the whole, for which by my structure and organization I am adapted'.[82] He was making the point that just as the health of the animal body depended on a proper 'harmony and communication' of the various organs, so the health of the 'great animal of human society' depended on individuals like him, the nerves of the system, or what he later called 'the organ[s] of all communication between the enlightened and the uninformed'.[83] As Nicholas Roe observes, Thelwall shared and no doubt helped inspire the ambition of 1790s' radical societies to re-animate the body politic by diffusing political information through networks of correspondence and cooperation, just as vitality was diffused through the nervous and vascular networks of the animal body.[84]

For those who opposed reform, however, assemblies and mass meetings of its supporters raised the spectre of uncontainable mob violence. Justifying the government's charge of high treason against Thelwall and other leading members of the reform movement in 1794, Sir James Eyre, Lord Chief Justice of the Common Pleas, noted 'how easily an impetuous Man may precipitate such Assemblies into Crimes of unforeseen Magnitude, and Danger to the State'.[85] Demonstrating that anxieties about the regulation of mob enthusiasm cut across ideological lines, Godwin likewise attacked Thelwall for helping to provoke the notorious 'Gagging Acts' of 1795 – laws that expanded the definition of treason and restricted public meetings for political discussion – by delivering lectures that sought to animate the brute matter of the common people, 'persons not much in the habits of regular thinking'.[86] On similar grounds, Burke in *Letters on a Regicide Peace* (1796) proposed the exclusion from public debate of the eighty thousand people he considered to be 'pure Jacobins; utterly incapable of amendment; objects of eternal vigilance'.[87] Thelwall shot back with his most eloquent defence of the plebeian public sphere, insisting in *Rights of Nature, against the Usurpations of Establishments* (1796) that '[m]an is, by his very nature, social and communicative – proud to display the little knowledge he possesses, and eager, as opportunity presents, to encrease [*sic*] his store'. Therefore, '[w]hatever presses men together, [...] though it may generate some vices, is favourable to the diffusion of knowledge, and ultimately promotive of human liberty. [... A] sort of Socratic spirit will necessarily grow up, wherever large bodies of men assemble'.[88]

Confident – for now, at least – in such bodies' capacity for virtuous self-regulation, Thelwall offered his very words as a stimulus of their political vitality. In June 1790 he had published in the *Biographical and Imperial Magazine* an excerpt from the Humane Society's reports that announced the invention in Paris of a machine for 'restoring Respiration to Persons drowned, or otherwise suffocated', as we have seen. The machine consisted of a 'double bellows' whereby 'bad air' could be drawn out of the lungs and 'atmospheric air' forced in, 'oblig[ing] the lungs to perform the act of inspiration and expiration, and gradually induc[ing] the organ to resume its function, if the subject be not absolutely dead'.[89] Thelwall regarded his lectures and writing as equivalents to that life-restoring machine. He advised his audiences that if reading the 'aristocratic works' of Burke, Arthur Young and others failed to make them 'thorough democrats', they should not hesitate to 'take [his] lungs for a pair of bellows to blow an alchymist's fire withal'.[90] Just as alchemy, the medieval forerunner of chemistry, sought to transmute base metal into gold, so Thelwall hoped that his words would transmute the opinions of his audiences to the radical gold standard of egalitarianism and universal benevolence. In a letter of September 1795 to his wife, he noted with pride that his most recent lectures in the Strand had

> shaken the pillars of corruption, till every stone of the rotten edifice trembled. Every sentence darted from breast to breast with electric contagion, and the very *aristocrats* themselves, numbers of whom throng to hear me, were frequently compelled by irresistible impulse to join in the acclamations, however they disliked the doctrine.[91]

With Thelwall this is not merely a rhetorical play on the biblical concept of *logos*, the creative word. He believes that language can materially affect the bodies and minds of an audience, darting to their hearts with 'electric contagion'. The phrase conjures images of Franklin's experiments with lightening and also evokes the electrical fluid that surgeons including Hunter (and later Cooper) thought responsible for rapid neural communication within the body.[92] Far from sharing Burke's alarm at the 'electrick communication' of the press, Thelwall presents the 'electric contagion' of language as salutary means of toppling the pillars corruption – a first step toward social renovation.[93] It remains to be seen how exactly he thought language might accomplish this.

The material mind

Emboldened, perhaps, by a letter of thanks from the Physical Society for his 'excellent and very valuable' paper on animal vitality, Thelwall delivered a second paper in December 1793 'On the Origin of Sensation' that sought to explain 'the phenomena of mind [...] upon principles *purely Physical*'.[94] Although only a logical extension of his earlier argument about life, this account of the mind verged too closely on atheistic materialism – particularly that of La Mettrie, author of *L'Homme machine* (1747; trans. *Man a Machine*, 1749) – even for the progressive Physical Society. After heated debate, the society rejected the paper as having 'no application to the science of medicine or surgery', and Thelwall and several others withdrew in protest.[95]

Although Thelwall's controversial second paper has been lost, we can infer its argument from several other sources, starting with his remarks to the Physical Society on another occasion as recorded by Astley Cooper's nephew. Thelwall had apparently argued against the execution of a convicted murderer on grounds that 'there was not a particle of the being who had committed the crime, still existing in the man who was to be executed for it'.[96] He assumes here that the human mind and body are alike material and subject to 'principles *purely Physical*'. On this model, one can literally and figuratively become a 'new man', transformed over time in mental as in bodily 'particles'. In the late eighteenth-century the foremost British exponent of the view that mental processes could be explained in terms of the modifications of matter was Joseph Priestley, who rejected traditional dualism to argue that matter itself had the capacity for thought, as noted earlier. Yet despite the resemblance between their positions, Thelwall never cites Priestley in his writings on the mind. A surer influence is Godwin, whom he may have heard speak on that subject at the Philomathian Society, a London debating club to which they both belonged, even before he read Godwin's *Political Justice* in 1793.[97] Godwin was one of the period's most famous exponents of the doctrine of necessity, which held that human opinion and action are determined by inexorable laws of cause and effect. Following John Locke in rejecting the doctrine of innate ideas, Godwin describes consciousness as a 'vast chain of perceptions and notions' that are 'regularly generated in the mind by a series of impressions, and digested and arranged by association and reflexion'.[98] In the second edition of *Political Justice*, published in 1796, he explains further that

> All our knowledge, all our ideas, everything we possess as intelligent beings, comes from impression. All the minds that exist set out from absolute ignorance. They received first one impression, and then a second. As the impressions became more numerous, and were stored by the help of memory, and combined by the faculty of association, so the experience increased, and with the experience the knowledge, the wisdom, everything that distinguishes man from what we understand by a 'clod of the valley'.[99]

Godwin's main source for these remarks is the materialist psychology of David Hartley, who in *Observations on Man* (1749) had described processes whereby sense impressions from the outside world caused 'vibrations' in the body that, passing along the 'medullary substance' of the nerves, set off corresponding vibrations (or 'vibratiuncles') in the brain. The brain then combined the resulting 'simple ideas' into 'complex ideas' according to laws of 'association'.[100] While Godwin endorses the doctrine of association, he parts ways with Hartley over the 'scheme of material automatism' that it implies, which was anathema to his faith in the capacity of the individual to make rational choices that would be consistent with truth and the general good.[101] To reconcile individual agency with the deterministic implications of necessity and association, he distinguishes sensation from judgement – our ability to prefer courses of action most consistent with truth and reason – and makes the latter 'an essential link in the chain' that connects sensory impression with opinion and action.[102]

Adapted thus, Hartley's doctrine of association provided a psychological foundation for Godwin's faith in human perfectibility.[103] For if 'the voluntary actions of men originate[d] in their opinions', and those opinions in turn originated in 'external circumstances', then by changing people's circumstances one could in turn change their opinions and actions.[104] From this perspective, as Isaac Kramnick explains, 'active intervention through scientific manipulation of circumstances – in other words, education – could produce "improvements" by necessarily altering the causal chain of associations in the machine that was man's mind'.[105] On this basis Godwin looks ahead to a day when education and the exercise of individual judgement will make redundant the rule of law and other unjust institutions of society. Yet even while endorsing the 'collision of mind with mind' in unrestricted conversation, he insists that a durable change of opinions must ultimately come from within, from a rational weighing of ideas and options for action.[106] He therefore criticizes Thelwall's lectures and speeches in the belief that a reformer should supply information without proselytizing.[107]

Notwithstanding this difference, that Thelwall, too, endorsed the doctrine of association and sought to reconcile it with individual agency is apparent from his little-known essay 'On the Influence of the Scenery of Nature on the Intellectual and Moral Character, as well as on the Taste and Imagination', first published in his newspaper the *Champion* in 1820. There he asserts that to deny the doctrine of association is

> to regard a human being as a sort of abstract entity, whose ideas are all innate and independent of perception; and whose senses are mere superfluous appendages, not ministers to his intellectual *perfectibility:* a sort of fillagree on the outside of a tea caddee [*sic*], that neither contributes to the flavour nor the preservation of the aromatic luxury within.[108]

Rejecting the 'fillagree' metaphor, Thelwall contends instead for the permeability of the boundary between the mind and its surroundings, insisting that 'it is from without that we have imbibed whatever is within us; and present scenery and present associations have always a certain influence on the current of our thoughts and feelings'.[109] He denies, therefore, that the individual is merely a 'bundle of abstractions'. His description of the senses as 'ministers' to the intellect implies that they are not sovereigns; they have 'a certain influence' on the mind's progress toward 'intellectual perfectibility', but not an exclusive one. Thelwall thus follows Godwin in rejecting the assumption of passivity or 'material automatonism' implicit in Hartley's scheme. Tellingly, in a series of character sketches that he published in the *Biographical and Imperial Magazine* in 1789–90, the question of whether man might be 'a mere machine' is attributed to the sceptical narrator Apathus.[110]

The place of individual agency, including of the imagination, in Thelwall's theory of the mind emerges more clearly in an anecdote that he recounted at the Capel Court debating society in November 1793. The night's debate centred on the question of whether love of liberty, love of life or love of 'the fair sex' had the greatest influence on human action. The first speaker had argued for love of life, citing the example of a tortured black slave who, after having his hands and feet chopped off on the order of his masters, was placed in a frying pan over the fire. When a fellow slave rushed forward to end his suffering, the victim demonstrated his love of life by raising his 'poor bleeding stumps' to ward off the death-blow. Thelwall responded with a materialist re-interpretation of the story, insisting that the slave's action was

> merely involuntary, [...] it being natural to all animals, after they had been long used to perform certain actions in consequence of any particular stimulus, applied either to the sight or any other of the senses, to continue those actions, by mere mechanical impulse, whenever the usual objects are presented, without reflecting what it is they are doing.[111]

The assertion raises the question of whether, in Thelwall's opinion, one always acts by 'mere mechanical impulse', or only when self-preservation is at stake. He implicitly takes the latter view when he draws a bold analogy between the slave's response and that of a gamecock he once owned, a 'haughty old tyrant would never let my farmyard be quiet'. Lording it over the other birds with his 'ermine spotted breast, [...] the flowing robe of plumage tucked up at his rump, and, above all, that fine ornamented

thing upon his head there – (his crown, or *coxcomb*, I believe you call it
[...])', the gamecock would 'tax' the other birds' seed and deny them the
remains. These gestures so strongly provoked Thelwall's hatred of 'barefaced despotism' that he one day grabbed a nearby scythe and chopped
off King Chaunticlere's head. Yet even headless, the petty tyrant continued to flap and kick about, while his barnyard subjects continued
to bow and scrape before him.[112] Ostensibly, the anecdote corroborates
Thelwall's point that gamecocks, chickens and humans are all slaves to
their mechanical impulses. But with Thelwall himself the case is different: his action is not purely automatic, but arises from a complex mental
process of association (between the gamecock and a tyrant, between the
chickens and an oppressed people), sympathetic identification (with the
victims), and future projection (of a more egalitarian society). Reason –
'the operations of the mind, employed in the research, comparison,
and digestion, of knowledge' – may enter into the process insofar as
the young Thelwall of the anecdote, hitherto an admirer of aristocracy,
now acts on 'some lurking principles of aversion to barefaced despotism'.[113] Yet it is notable to what extent his sympathetic imagination is
shown to have the upper hand. That same year Thelwall would assert
in *The Peripatetic* that '*Reason is not the sole Arbiter in the human mind.
Imagination has also a considerable share in the enjoyment and perturbations of the soul: nor will her vivid impressions always submit to the
cool and regular deductions of Philosophy*'.[114]

The imagination's importance to reform is explained in greater detail
in Thelwall's lecture 'On the Moral Tendency of a System of Spies and
Informers', where he notes that one of the most pernicious features
of the government's widespread system of surveillance is its inhibi-
tion of man's freedom to enquire into his rights and duties within the
body politic, and the pleasures of imaginative self-transcendence such
enquiry entails:

> He looks in the face of his fellow creature; and he sees indeed a
> brother – or a part rather of his own existence; another self – He
> contemplates in every individual the faculties of sufferance and
> enjoyment, and feels one nerve of sympathy connecting him with
> the whole intellectual universe. [...] [T]he native of Gallia and the
> professor of Mahometanism are regarded with the same benevolence
> as the man of his own sect and country; and the sooty African need
> lift his fettered hands no more to *remind* him that he is a MAN AND A
> BROTHER! – He enfolds the universe in one large embrace, and finds
> an eternal source of rational gratification in contemplating the felic-
> ity, or labouring to mitigate the calamities of his fellow creatures.[115]

Although prompted to these reflections by the culture of surveillance, Thelwall is not primarily concerned here with the imagination as an 'allusive and elusive' means of expression.[116] More important is its ability to dissolve the limits of the self and the distinctions of race, religion and nationality, fostering a sense of mutual rights and duties rooted in humanity's physiological commonality: the would-be reformer 'contemplates in every individual the faculties of sufferance and enjoyment, and feels one nerve of sympathy connecting him with the whole intellectual universe'. The language of medical science merges with that of 'radical sensibility' – the ideological appropriation of earlier eighteenth-century ideas about natural affections and universal benevolence[117] – to anchor a vision of reform that is at once radical and materialist. This convergence of science, politics and the imagination is likewise apparent in the anecdote of 'King Chaunticlere', specifically in its seditious suggestion that just as Thelwall is capable of responding to the gamecock's aggressions with deliberate action, so the British people may act against their oppressors with similar resolve.[118] Catherine Packham notes that this vision of political liberation harnesses both the rational and the instinctual modes of the animal body.[119] It bears emphasis, however, that according to the logic of the anecdote, 'mental action' can prevail over 'muscular action' and the tyranny of habit only under conditions of acute oppression. As Thelwall remarks on another occasion,

> Hume's Commonwealth slept for sixty years, and the Eutopia for whole centuries, on the shelves of the learned; and even the popular language of Thomas Paine would not have provoked any very alarming discussion, if the general *condition* of mankind had not predisposed them to exclaim – *We are wretched! – Let us enquire the cause!*[120]

This sense of contingency would become prominent in Thelwall's writing after the anti-Jacobin backlash of the late decade; in the early 1790s, however, the circumstances of war, food shortages, excessive taxation, parliamentary corruption, the consolidation of land and the examples of America and France all seemed to have created a suitable predisposition in the British body politic. It was a propitious moment to apply the stimulus of language to help restore vitality to a decaying state.

But what kind of language was best suited to this intervention? Several critics have called Thelwall to account for failing to put into practice the radical language theory of his mentor John Horne Tooke and thus achieve an equivalent to Paine's 'intellectual vernacular'.[121] In *Epea Pteroenta: or, The Diversions of Purley* (1786–1805), Tooke claimed that all words had a material origin: they were the 'signs of things' (i.e., nouns and verbs), or else abbreviations of those signs introduced for the sake of expediency (the 'winged words' of Tooke's Greek title, including adverbs, conjunctions and pronouns). Regarding the operations of the mind as 'merely the operations of Language', he defended the linguistic competencies of every 'man of common plain sense' against the elitist assertions of the linguists James Harris and James Burnett, Lord Monboddo.[122] While these egalitarian, materialist premises surely appealed to Thelwall, unlike his mentor he believed that figurative language addressed to the imagination might be as conducive to reform as clear language addressed to 'common plain sense', as the works discussed in the ensuing chapters attest. As a segue to those chapters – including fuller discussion of Thelwall's theory of language in Chapter 6 – it is worth briefly looking ahead to his 1826 essay on 'euphony' in his journal the *Panoramic Miscellany*, which opens with a contrast between the language appropriate to science and that befitting conversation, literature and appeals to the imagination more generally. Thelwall rehearses the longstanding view that scientific language should 'speak plainly and unequivocally to the understanding alone', without 'pretence of synonymes [sic]': every idea should have its 'specific name', and 'the signification of these must be fixed, not by arbitrary, but by strict and logical definition'. By contrast, in conversation as in 'literary disquisition' – that is, 'in whatever appeals to the imagination, or has reference only to general ideas' – a speaker or writer should make use of the language's array of 'apparent synonymes' to achieve 'grace', 'harmony' and 'vividness', his object being not to 'analyse and contradistinguish' but to 'call up ideas, or present images to the mind, in their generalities and their aggregates'. Thelwall writes of appeals to the imagination that,

> In such cases, 'more is meant than meets the ear;' much is left to the fancy, or the memory, – to the imagination, or the feeling of the hearer, or reader; and he, who most powerfully excites these to activity in the minds of those he addresses, by the fewest particulars, and with the least aproximation [sic] to detail, is, in fact, most eloquent. For this purpose, a *part* is perpetually used for the whole – an integral fraction, for a complex aggregate – an individual trait, for a complicated association of attributes.

Used in such suggestively figurative ways, language is a source of 'ambiguous magic': 'not the mathematician's compass, but the wizzard's spell'.[123] It was precisely this capacity of literary or imaginative language to spark associative trains of thought that made it appealing to Thelwall as an instrument of reform, one that was potentially more effective than the faculty of reason. We can begin to appreciate the aesthetic and ideological consequences of these views by turning to his 1793 work *The Peripatetic*. This highly experimental verse-prose hybrid bases its digressive, dialogical form on a materialist theory of cognition in an attempt to elicit the reader's sympathy in the cause of reform. At the same time, however, it also launches Thelwall's career-long interrogation of the efficacy of such appeals against the claims of self-interest and the force of direct sense perception.

2
Errant Sympathies
The Peripatetic

> *Reason is not the sole Arbiter in the human mind.*
> Imagination has also a considerable share in the enjoy-
> ment and perturbations of the soul: nor will her vivid
> impressions always submit to the cool and regular
> deductions of Philosophy.[1]

Thelwall's earliest literary attempt at sparking a new consciousness in
the body politic was his 1793 work *The Peripatetic; or, Sketches of the
Heart, of Nature and Society; in a Series of Politico-Sentimental Journals,
in Verse and Prose of the Eccentric Excursions of Sylvanus Theophrastus,
Supposed to be Written by Himself.* Following the pedestrian excursions
of the poet-philosopher Sylvanus Theophrastus and various companions, the work gives us a running (or walking) commentary on the
sociopolitical and cultural state of England in the early 1790s. A striking
feature of this condition-of-England fiction *avant la lettre* is its 'politico-
sentimental' mingling of genres, styles and voices in a series of more
than 100 brief sections. In the preface Thelwall describes it as 'uniting
the different advantages of the novel, the sentimental journal, and the
miscellaneous collection of essays and poetical effusions'.[2] He might
also have mentioned the travelogue, epic poem, gothic tale, political
lecture, autobiography and character-sketch. These disparate elements
are held together by the sentimental subplot of Belmour and Sophia,
young lovers kept apart by the dictates of paternal tyranny. Thelwall
claimed to have introduced this narrative thread and the character of
the narrator to boost *The Peripatetic*'s circulation at the suggestion of
a 'literary friend' – probably Thomas Holcroft, a strong proponent of
'[u]nity of design' in the novel.[3] Not merely opportunistic add-ons,
however, both elements are also central to the work's preoccupation

34

with the causes and cures of self-interest in the British body politic. The solipsistic Belmour raises the question of how such states of mind can be redirected to 'the interests, or the miseries of mankind', while the free-roaming narrator offers a counter-model of healthy mental associations and sympathetic responsiveness, albeit with a tendency to ineffectual abstraction.[4]

Thelwall's engagement with the pathological and therapeutic tendencies of the mind in *The Peripatetic* offers an early instantiation of the formal and discursive alliance among materialist science, radical politics and literary imagination that formed in his writings at this time.[5] Published the same year as the *Essay, Towards a Definition of Animal Vitality*, *The Peripatetic* draws on that work for an ideal of harmonious organization in the body politic, just as it draws on the theory of embodied cognition advanced in Thelwall's equally controversial paper 'On the Origin of Sensation' of the same year for a model of the mind's responsiveness to external stimuli.[6] The materialist theories of vitality and cognition set forth chiefly in these papers also illuminate the hybrid, dialogical 'physiology' of *The Peripatetic* itself. Typically read as a radical re-formation of conventional literary categories and source of inspiration for Wordsworth, the work is also noteworthy for its attempt to function as a 'proper provocative' to sociopolitical reform: a print-cultural equivalent to the resuscitative techniques that rescue Belmour after his attempted suicide.[7] Notwithstanding its happy ending, however, *The Peripatetic* also launches Thelwall's career-long exploration of the tension between materialist theory and action by acknowledging the contingency of the sympathetic imagination on one's past and present experience – or, to put it in the terms of the medical analogies that permeate *The Peripatetic*, on a proper conjunction of the stimulus of language with suitably 'pre-disposed' mental and bodily matter.

The 'feeling observer': from perception to action

From his opening remarks on the power of outdoor rambles to counter 'valetudinarian languor', *The Peripatetic*'s narrator Sylvanus Theophrastus establishes the health and disorders of body and mind as central themes of his 'Sketches of the Heart, of Nature and Society'.[8] In this respect, as in many others, Sylvanus is a stand-in for the author himself, a fellow valetudinarian who would visit the family cottage at Lambeth for the relief of his chronic asthma and pleurisy, and who studied anatomy and physiology at Guy's and St Thomas's hospitals from 1791 to 1793.[9] As in Thelwall's political writings, the vitality of

the animal body provides a model in *The Peripatetic* for the proper func-
tioning of the political organism. This is notably the case in the section
entitled 'A Digression for the Anatomists', when on a visit to Deptford
the sight of some anatomically correct sculptures of human skulls on an
ancient church tower prompts Sylvanus to effuse about 'the form and
organization of man; the sublimest of all the world of creation'. Echoing
Thelwall's definition in the *Animal Vitality* essay of corporeal organization as an 'arrangement of dissimilar parts' that produces 'a harmony
and communication of the whole' and makes it 'susceptible' to the vital
stimulus,[10] Sylvanus describes in verse a system of 'human oeconomy'
dependent on a 'wond'rous train of sudden Sympathy' among the
heart, lungs and brain. The heart is 'life's awful reservoir! / That pours
to every part the vital store'; the lungs draw the 'pure electric fire' from
the air and transmit it to the 'passing streams' of blood; and the brain
'all the frame commands' through the 'subtile dictates' of neural transmission.[11] The materialist psychology of David Hartley, whereby sense
impressions are conducted to the brain by means of vibrations chan-
nelled along the nerves, informs Sylvanus's description of the brain as
the locus of cognition:

> Where vibrates sound, where splendid vision lives,
> Where Taste – where Smell her essence all receives,
> And Touch, fine-thrilling, each impression gives!

Moreover, just as Thelwall in *Animal Vitality* had refuted the surgeon
John Hunter's theory of the vitality of the blood by invoking recent
experiments on the vital function of the brain, so Sylvanus notes of the
latter organ,

> From this, when injur'd, all tumultuous fly
> The wond'rous train of sudden Sympathy:
> The Lungs, the Heart, their functions each disclaim:
> Dies thro' each Nerve the paralytic frame![12]

By contrast with this model of healthy organic interdependence,
Sylvanus's meandering examination of the British body politic finds
it suffering from a morbid constitutional imbalance. A hilltop view of
the Thames near London prompts him to exclaim against the growing
monopoly that prevents the 'channels' of the country's wealth from
'divid[ing] themselves into little streamlets, and communicat[ing] a
portion of their blessings to the lower orders of the state' – an implicit

critique of Adam Smith's *laissez-faire* economics.[13] Such critique had roots in Thelwall's own rambles in the countryside in the late 1780s and early 1790s, 'a tragic period for English labour' when widespread unemployment was exacerbated by harvest failures, a rapidly increasing population and the outbreak of war with France.[14] Thelwall credited these excursions with exploding his 'romantic' notions of 'rural felicity':

> I beheld there poor women, doubled with age, toiling from morning to night, over their wheels, spinning their flax and hemp; and I found that their condition was so miserable, that many of them were positively obliged to take their work once or twice a day home to the persons who employed them, in order to get the scanty pittance that was to purchase the meal by which they were to sustain their emaciated frames.[15]

Dissatisfied with theories that linked poverty with the precariousness of wages or the natural indolence and profligacy of the poor,[16] Thelwall used his political lectures and pamphlets of the mid-1790s to define a vision of economic justice based on the belief, adapted from Lockean natural rights theory, that for labourers and employers to enjoy equal rights in practice, they had to be on an equal contractual footing. This meant that 'the labourer ha[d] a right to a share of the produce, not merely equal to his support, but, proportionate to the profits of the employer'.[17] The system of proportionate advantage was a necessary condition for Thelwall's acceptance of the emergent industrial capitalism, which otherwise threatened to bloat one part of the nation and starve another.[18]

In *The Peripatetic*, the unequal circulation of wealth is only one symptom of the nation's disease; Sylvanus's experiences on the road reveal that the channels of human sympathy are also blocked before they can reach the extremities of the nation. The monopolizing landlord tears down cottages to protect his '*tender feelings*', the aristocratic rake resists the emasculating influence of 'Tormenting SENSIBILITY' and the 'Daughters of Albion's gay enlighten'd hour' '[p]retend to softness, delicacy, love', but blithely disregard the suffering of others, from their caged birds to the African slaves whose labour sweetens their tea.[19] The narrator's friend Belmour presents an especially instructive case of morbid sensibility. Lovesickness breeds a 'canker of the mind' that commits 'ravages' on his body, renders him apathetic to the outside world and triggers thoughts of suicide.[20] The case is much the same with a female 'maniac' encountered on the road who obsessively haunts the grave of her mother.[21] Such behaviour coincides with Thelwall's later definition of 'mania' as

> distempered imagination intensely coherent to the fantom of its crea-
> tion; so that present realities cannot divert it from its imaginative object,
> & things the most dissimilar are converted to its likeness – windmills
> become giants & flocks of sheep are armies – because the distempered
> sees with the eyes of his imagination instead of the eyes of sense.[22]

True to this definition, Belmour is later found projecting his sorrows onto a thrush that he finds lying in a doorway and assumes to have died of heartache for its lost mate.[23] His 'disordered imagination' confirms the medical opinion of one of Sylvanus's (and Thelwall's) favourite poets, the physician John Armstrong.[24] In a passage of *The Art of Preserving Health* (1744) that Thelwall later excerpted in an elocutionary handbook, Armstrong notes the deleterious effects of 'painful thinking', or dwelling at length on any one subject:

> anxious study, discontent and care,
> Love without hope, and hate without revenge,
> And fear and jealousy, fatigue the soul.
> Engross the subtile ministers of life,
> And spoil the labouring functions of their share.

By contrast with these models of pathological self-regard, *The Peripatetic* celebrates the mind's ability to wander freely outside the limits of the self, an ability that is closely associated with the excursions of the body. Bearing out Armstrong's belief that 'the mind, with various thoughts amus'd / Nor akes [*sic*] itself nor gives the body pain',[25] Sylvanus embarks on his excursions in pursuit of 'health and recreation', and soon turns his attention to political '[i]nformation and improvement'.[26] Pedestrianism is ideally suited to his goal of seeking out 'Real Misfortune' in its 'modest retirements': 'in the murky chambers of the artisan, and the cottage of the industrious peasant', along the byways and footpaths where coaches cannot venture.[27] In two main excursions to Rochester and Saint Albans, which take him along 'the central axis of England's economic, historical, and literary landscape',[28] Sylvanus practices what Robin Jarvis calls 'radical walking', 'a kind of extra-parliamentary direct action' motivated by a desire to 'break down the barriers of mutual ignorance and suspicion between classes by enquiring into the lives of the lower orders in a more careful and intimate way than would be possible by using "respectable" means of transport'.[29] Sylvanus's goal is 'enfranchisement of vision from the dull captivity of brick walls and square panes of glass'.[30] Borrowing a phrase from Wordsworth, we might say that he attempts to see into the *material* 'life of things', particularly the lives of the labouring poor.[31]

If pedestrianism in *The Peripatetic* evokes 'the restlessness [... and] *mobility* of the radical mind', as Jeffrey C. Robinson observes, yet its potential to provoke 'uprootedness and political divisiveness' is mitigated by the work's narrator.[32] Described in the preface as a 'feeling observer', Sylvanus fits the profile in two senses: he is a 'keen observer of the passions of mankind', as in his interactions with Belmour, and he is emotionally responsive to what he observes.[33] His frequent bursts of poetry capture his 'radical sensibility', the unconditional fellow-feeling that many at the time considered indispensable to social progress.[34] In one of more than 40 poetical effusions he hails the stork and pelican as emblems of 'the glorious maxims of relative and social duty' and the lark as emblem of 'soul-expanding love' and sympathetic response.[35] When he is not reciting his own verse Sylvanus quotes a sentimental eighteenth-century canon that includes Edward Young, James Thomson, Thomas Gray, William Collins, Oliver Goldsmith, James Beattie and Charlotte Smith. *The Peripatetic* makes it clear, however, that virtuous participation in the 'many-peopled sphere' demands more than just the 'extemporaneous effusions of a moral muse': the morals must be acted upon as well, in accordance with Thelwall's view – shared with contemporaries including William Godwin and Mary Wollstonecraft – that 'if virtue, in reality, means neither more nor less than intentionally doing that which is best for general happiness and welfare, it results [...] that all virtue must be of an *active*, not of a *passive* nature'.[36]

The process by which fellow-feeling leads to active virtue is the subject of several episodes that go beyond 'radical sensibility' to affirm the material roots of sympathy. In one, Sylvanus responds to his friend Ambulator's criticism of the 'visionary schemes' of philosophers, so readily forgotten in 'the theatre of public action', by declaring his allegiance to the Peripatetic School of Aristotle, whose fidelity to 'terrestrial substance' he contrasts with 'the visionary ravings of Plato'.[37] Sylvanus illustrates the contrast with the story of 'The Platonic Fair', a young devotee of sentimental novels whose naive belief in their doctrine of '*the chaste SYMPATHY OF SOULS: the virgin intercourse of ENAMOURED MINDS*' is the cause of her being deserted by a more materially minded lover. Sylvanus cannot believe that 'beings who have blood that circulates, and nerves that feel, should ever aspire to forget their materiality, and regulate their passions and conduct by *the pure dictates of immaterial essence*'.[38] In an episode entitled 'Hints for the Stoics', the memory of his original response to Belmour's tale of thwarted love causes him to feel a new pang of sympathy. He takes the sensation as confirmation that

> memory and reflection are something more than impassive vacancy – or immaterial suggestion: – that they dwell in the vital essence of the blood, and are modifications of that susceptible organization, without which the breath that gives us life were nothing.[39]

This version of 'emotion recollected in tranquillity' may well have inspired Wordsworth's notion of 'sensations sweet, / Felt in the blood, and felt along the heart, / And passing even into my purer mind / With tranquil restoration', as Nicholas Roe suggests.[40] But whereas Wordsworth emphasizes those moments when 'we are laid asleep / In body, and become a living soul',[41] Thelwall insists via Sylvanus on the material basis of all experience, even mental. He develops this point in the episode 'The Maniac', when the peripatetic company overhear the mournful song of a female maniac in a village churchyard, prompting the narrator's attack on the doctrine of self-love:

> Tell me, ye exquisite powers of nature, who attune the finer nerves to mournful sympathy! – why did my heart vibrate, and my pulse beat in solemn unison to the melting cadence? – Why was my breath suspended, and my foot rivetted [*sic*] to the consecrated turf? – And by what mysterious mechanism did the unconscious tear steal down my cheek responsive to the tremulous note? – Here was no selfish retrospect: no anticipation of correspondent suffering. – Ye Sceptics! there was none. – I had not seen the mourner – I knew not the complexion of her woes – Desire and Apprehension stood equally aloof. – And yet I pitied – and I wept![42]

The 'Sceptics' disputed here include Adam Smith, who argued that we are all naturally more sensitive to our own distresses than to those of others, and that the role of our 'internal spectators' is to protect us from the consequences of this self-concern.[43] Sylvanus not only denies that sympathetic response is contingent on self-love, but also insists that it is capable of provoking benevolent action even when the object of sympathy is unknown. Anticipating by more than a decade Johann Wolfgang von Goethe's comparison between human attraction and the laws of chemical affinity, Sylvanus elsewhere defends the existence of 'a kind of mental attraction, by which dispositions that assimilate, like the correspondent particles of matter, have a tendency to adhere whenever they are brought within the sphere of mutual attraction'.[44]

Perhaps the most revealing case study of the relationship between embodied sympathy and benevolent action occurs in Sylvanus's story of a prior encounter with an indigent haymaker. Owing to a still earlier run-in with a professional beggar who, when Sylvanus denied his plea, struck him violently with a crutch, he is at first suspicious of the haymaker's 'decent appearance' and 'pathetic voice'.[45] He is therefore about to ignore the haymaker's petition when he catches sight of the man's pitchfork and considers how easily he might wield it to 'relieve the oppressions of distress, which the hard conditions of society [...] have laid upon him'. The thought of revolutionary violence passes 'instantaneously' across Sylvanus's mind, and his body responds accordingly: 'I turned instantly around, and my hand, sympathizing with the feelings of my heart, waited not for the cold approbation of Reason, but went immediately and instinctively to my pocket'. The ensuing conversation confirms the judiciousness of the action: the haymaker has taken to the road in search of employment to support his family, and he now begs only because the rainy weather prevents him from working.[46] In dramatizing the process by which sympathy leads to judicious action, Thelwall appears to be rewriting an opening scene from one of the acknowledged models for *The Peripatetic*, Laurence Sterne's *A Sentimental Journey* (1768), in which Yorick refuses alms to a Franciscan monk despite being in a mood of expansive fellow-feeling at the moment he encounters the petitioner.[47] As James Chandler observes, in that scene and throughout the work's opening sequence, the ambiguous relationship between Yorick's bodily and mental responses invites readers to question the authority of his claim to have 'confounded the most *physical precieuse* in France: with all her materialism' such that 'she could scarce have called me a machine'.[48] Sylvanus's encounter with the haymaker may be read, by contrast, as an attempt to reassert the embodied nature of sympathetic response. His 'instantaneous' reaction evokes the theory of electrical neural transmission advanced by the surgeon John Hunter based on his experiments with an electric fish, the 'Gymnotus Electricus'.[49] It should be noted, however, that although Sylvanus describes his reaction as pre-rational, it is not in fact purely automatic or instinctive.[50] Rather, as in the contemporaneous anecdote of 'King Chaunticlere' discussed in Chapter 1, it depends on a rapid sequence of sense perception, sympathetic identification and imaginative future projection that mingles considerations of general welfare and self-preservation.

While it is certainly the case that in his encounters with the downtrod-
den and dispossessed Sylvanus embodies the sympathetic responsiveness that Thelwall believed should be felt by the whole nation, as James
Robert Allard points out,[51] his responses are not infallible. He is often
more concerned with establishing 'maxims' about how one ought to act
or effusing about the psychic rewards of benevolence than with actually
acting. On one occasion he gets so caught up in a long digression about
his childhood that Belmour gives him the slip.[52] On another he engages
in a protracted conversation about generosity and benevolence, leaving Ambulator to make enquiries about their now suicidally despond-
ent friend. Ironically, it is Ambulator's generous activity rather than
Sylvanus's ineffectual 'panegyric' about generosity that sets in motion
the train of events leading to Belmour's happy ending.[53] Although
apparently out of step with Thelwall's ideal of active virtue, Sylvanus's
fallibility can be explained in terms of his Peripatetic lineage. He is, after
all, a namesake and 'descendant of the philosopher Theophrastus', who
took over the Peripatetic school after Aristotle's death.[54] Theophrastus
is chiefly remembered for his *Characters*, a collection of 30 short prose
sketches describing the vices and follies of Athenians in the late fourth
century BCE. The work was translated into English several times from the
seventeenth century and gave rise to many native imitations, notably
in the *Tatler* and *Spectator*.[55] As a schematic representation of human
thought and character, the Theophrastan character is ideally suited to
The Peripatetic, which does not vest ultimate authority or exemplarity
in any one character, but leaves its key issues open to debate among
characters who embody various 'pervading principle[s]' and 'extrava-
gances of human nature'.[56] Sylvanus, who shares his first name with
an ancient Roman woodland god, unites the nature-lover and the
poet-philosopher; Arisor has all the wry humour of the cynic (his name
echoes the Latin *risibilis*, or 'risible'); Wentworth is the worthy if naive
'sentimentalist enthusiast' ('Wentworth Chatterton' was a penname of
Thelwall's); the philosophically inclined 'Julian' is so nicknamed after
the Roman emperor Flavius Claudius Julianus (a.k.a. 'the Apostate'),
famous for his renunciation of Christianity and literary and philosophical interests; and the fragile Belmour is a quintessential eighteenth-century man of feeling.[57] Ambulator, whose name evokes a contemporary
guide to London and the surrounding regions, embodies instructive
companionship.[58] His attitude towards the needy coincides perfectly
with Aristotle's definition of the generous person as one who 'avoid[s]
giving to just anyone, so that he will have something to give to the right
people, at the right time'.[59] But even Ambulator is not a reliable moral

centre. When he and Sylvanus encounter a 'robust and ruddy' gypsy youth 'with nothing evident of distress about him', he is at first taken in by the boy's 'plaintive cant' and is about to give him money 'almost mechanically' when he notices the boy's red cheeks, a possible sign of inebriation. Sylvanus seizes the opportunity to draw his friend away, reminding him that 'if *Labour*, as must be admitted constitutes the real wealth of the community, it can never be the part of a good member of society to contribute to the *useless* and the *idle*'.[60]

While such encounters demonstrate the fallibility of individual perception and judgement, they also confirm the corrective power of conversation. Godwin might as well have been referring to *The Peripatetic* when he described an ideal of free 'social communication' involving

> a number of individuals, who, having first stored their minds with reading and reflection, proceed afterwards, in candid and unreserved conversation to compare their ideas, to suggest their doubts, to remove their difficulties, and to cultivate a collected and striking manner of delivering their sentiments.

If these individuals were motivated by benevolence to extend their conversation to a wider circle, Godwin reasoned, the spread of knowledge would eventually be universal. He doubted, however, whether such conversation could be transferred to print without losing its powers of 'stimulus and surprise'. Books, he noted, have 'a sort of constitutional coldness' that rarely inspire us with the courage of 'striking into untrodden paths, and questioning tenets that have been generally received'.[61] Thelwall, by contrast, had a qualified optimism about the vitalizing powers of his 'work of digressions and conversations'.[62]

Transient influences

Reprinting the poetry of *The Peripatetic* in his newspaper the *Champion* in 1819–21, Thelwall appended to one instalment an essay in which he defended walking as more conducive than riding or driving to 'the deliberate wanderings which fancy may suggest, or surrounding objects may induce'. Thanks to these 'deliberate wanderings' – a phrase that captures the joint influence of material circumstance and individual judgement on human action – the 'imagination is plumed, and moral determination nerved'. The wanderer thus acquires 'sedateness of appreciation' and 'rectitude of determination', both essential complements to 'the ardours of patriotism and philanthropy'.[63] The desire to recreate this experience for the reader is what drives *The Peripatetic*'s seemingly haphazard, 'whimsical jarring' of topics, genres, styles and voices.[64] In the preface Thelwall acknowledges a debt to Sterne and Henry Fielding for the division of his work into more than 100 brief sections that shuttle rapidly from present to past, theme to theme and genre to genre, a structure that he finds better suited to 'rousing the attention of the reader to every change of subject' than 'the arbitrary and usual distinctions of book and chapter'.[65] A still more decisive influence on *The Peripatetic*'s episodic form is the narrator's pedestrianism, which provides a constant stimulus to his associative mind. The results, and their therapeutic potential for the characters and the reader, are vividly demonstrated by the cluster of encounters with gypsies narrated at the work's centre. The inaugural meeting with a 'robust and ruddy' gypsy youth who pleads for charity despite having 'nothing of evident distress about him' prompts Sylvanus to inveigh against gypsies as 'miserable tribes of wandering robbers', proto-Burkean defenders of 'ancient precedent and ancestral usage' and types of ignorance and idleness undeserving of charity.[66] Further encounters, actual and recollected, and the conversations they inspire gradually yield a series of more favourable representations, as gypsies become picturesque 'embellishments' of rural scenery, emblems of 'social familiarity', possible progenitors of modern civilization, figments of Gothic fantasy, champions of ancient English freedoms and models of 'departed Ostentation'.[67] As Jonathan Lamb notes of Sterne's *Sentimental Journey*, so we might say of *The Peripatetic*'s gypsies cluster that it shows how 'association, besides its tendency to confuse cause and effect, makes ideas cluster in truthful forms'.[68] It also suggests the importance of conversation to achieving that effect for the reader as well as the characters.

Although not strictly speaking a 'Jacobin' novel – 'the imaginative enactment of a philosophical argument' that links plot and character according to Godwin's principle of necessity – *The Peripatetic* nonetheless shares the subgenre's attempt to create a 'dialogic relationship' with readers by inviting them to participate in the debates it stages about the health of the body politic.[69] This approach is reflected in the titles of *The Peripatetic*'s various sections: '*Indications* of Commerce', '*Symptoms* of Loquacity', '*Hints* for the Stoics', '*Scraps* of Criticism', and '*Traits* of Singularity' (emphases added). It is up to the reader to make a meaningful picture out of these numerous 'Sketches of the Heart, of Nature and Society'.[70] Sylvanus suggests as much when he urges the reader to pursue the questions raised by *The Peripatetic* beyond the limits of the text, remarking that 'the condition of the labouring poor in this country [... is a] subject so copious, and the abuses and oppressions so numerous, that our journey was completed before our enquiry'.[71] We might say that *The Peripatetic* offers a version of the technique of the 'non finito', which Eric Rothstein defines as 'the art of making the reader or viewer supply what is unstated'.[72] Whereas in art criticism the 'non finito' describes paintings and sculptures deliberately left unfinished to encourage the viewer's cooperation in the creation of meaning, Rothstein applies the term to formally complete works of eighteenth-century literature that likewise urge the reader to 'an imaginative expansion of the text' by 'controlling the flow of stimuli from which readers will develop images'.[73] The goal is not to tax the imagination with exhaustive details or restrict it with analogies and examples, but to furnish it selectively with what theorists like Henry Home, Lord Kames, and Hugh Blair described as 'clear' and 'complete' images capable of producing strong impressions on the mind as a stimulus to 'imaginative expansion'.[74] The goal, in other words, is to produce what Kames described in *Elements of Criticism* (1762) as the illusion of 'ideal presence', a sort of 'waking dream' produced by literary representation that is vivid enough to create an illusion of reality. According to Kames,

> The reader's passions are never sensibly moved, till he be thrown into a kind of reverie; in which state, losing the consciousness of self, and of reading, his present occupation, he conceives every incident as passing in his presence, precisely as if he were an eye-witness.[75]

A similar idea is expressed by Sylvanus's companion Julian when he remarks that '*Reason is not the sole Arbiter in the human mind*. Imagination has also a considerable share in the enjoyment and perturbations of the soul: nor will her vivid impressions always submit to the cool and regular deductions of Philosophy'.[76] But if *The Peripatetic* employs various imaginative techniques – notably demystifying encounters with the disenfranchised and displays of sympathetic response – to make readers feel as if they were eye-witnesses to, and interlocutors of, the characters' experiences on the road, it also calls into question its efficacy as a stimulus of 'ideal presence' among those who, like Belmour, are consumed by self-interest.[77]

The imagination's variable sway over human conduct is displayed in hortatory stories of benevolence embedded throughout the narrative. We learn, for instance, of 'Philanthopa', who is moved to charity by the story of another woman's destitution, and thereby enables her to set up a small shop and regain self-sufficiency.[78] Ideally, every reader of *The Peripatetic* will respond to its stories of hardship with active virtue. Thelwall recognized, however, that this kind of moral re-education was not simply a matter of storytelling or exhortation. In 'A Digression for Parents and Preceptors', the narrator recalls having once told a 'pretty story' about a giant who traps humans to teach a young girl why she was wrong to trap a ladybird. The girl promptly frees her captive, and Sylvanus flatters himself that his 'harmless fiction' has helped make her 'a better member of society'. But almost in the same breath he acknowledges that 'the unfeeling mass of mankind' will be deaf to such stories.[79] As the metaphor suggests, just as vitality was (in Thelwall's view) contingent on an appropriate 'pre-disposition' of matter to the vital stimulus, so the attempt to spark a radical consciousness in audiences was contingent on the susceptibility of even the 'unfeeling mass of mankind' to the application of a 'proper provocative'.[80]

The narrator expands on this point in a section entitled 'Effervescences of Political Enthusiasm', in which he attempts a poetic *reductio ad absurdum* of the lovesick Belmour's social apathy, concluding that it is

> better far, forgetting and forgot,
>   Sequester'd, to the peaceful grave to glide,
> From Fortune's wheel withdraw our anxious lot,
>   And crimes we can't *prevent*, at least *avoid*.

This 'rhapsody' has an immediate effect: Belmour's 'mien assumed its wonted dignity, his eyes began to sparkle with indignation'.[81] But these 'effervescences' subside before Sylvanus can bring them to a boil:

> the fervour was of short duration; as is generally the case with that enthusiasm, which is the effect only of appeals to the imagination, rather than of principles resulting from actual feeling and present experience.[82]

Thelwall's 'effervescences of political enthusiasm' recall Joseph Priestley's experiments with volatile gases, as well as Edmund Burke's alarm about the 'first effervescence' of the 'wild *gas*' of liberty in revolutionary France, which created a 'troubled and frothy surface' that obscured the real damages inflicted by the experiment.[83] But whereas Burke hoped to see those effervescences subside, for *The Peripatetic* their transience is precisely the problem. In a sort of post-script to the episode, Sylvanus remarks that 'modern sophists' are mistaken when they

> pretend that reason is to be deluded by declamations on *fancied grievances*, or even that the most animated remonstrances against *real*

oppression can excite a serious discontent in the popular mind, till the enormity of the evil has *brought home the consequent suffering to every man's business and bosom*.[84]

The passage echoes Adam Smith's claim that to enter sympathetically into the feelings of another, a spectator must 'bring home to himself every little circumstance of distress which can possibly occur to the sufferer'.[85] Sylvanus is careful to distinguish between the rational, benevolent enthusiasm he wishes to elicit and the 'deluded' enthusiasm that 'modern sophists' like Burke attributed to radical agitators. Elsewhere he explains that although his friend Ambulator advocates the principles of liberty and equality, 'he is no enthusiast – [...]. He abhors the sanguinary crew'.[86] A few pages before this he presents us with a contrary definition of enthusiasm in a description of himself as a boy standing near the edge of a precipice and listening to the ebbing tide 'in sweet enthusiasm'.[87]

In the increasingly paranoid political climate of the 1790s, and especially after the Treason Trials of 1794, the distinction between firing the people with enthusiasm for social change and inciting them to violence would become a central preoccupation for Thelwall, as for many of his contemporaries. Yet *The Peripatetic*'s concern is not that the reader or listener might be carried too far, but that he might not be carried far enough, especially if he has no direct experience of suffering and injustice. As Jon Mee points out, the work 'disregards the kind of regulation that separated polite sensibility [...] from a more expansive movement out of the self and towards the multitude associated with enthusiasm'.[88] We see this notably at the conclusion of the 'Effervescences' episode when Sylvanus observes,

> Remove but the *real causes of complaint*; nay, keep them but at such a distance, that they may not *goad the bosoms* of those who have the capacity to act, and whatever may be the transient influence of poets and orators on the heated fancies of a few, every one will quickly find, like Belmour, some *personal feeling*, some *individual interest* to overpower the *sympathies of imagination*, and restore the momentary wanderer to *himself!*[89]

This key moment in Thelwall's oeuvre might be read as an acknowledgement of the limitations of sentimental appeals in eliciting a shared oppositional consciousness. According to Andrew McCann, *The Peripatetic* shows that such appeals can have only a fleeting and gratifying effect on the reader when they are articulated through literature, in which form they inevitably consolidate the structures that they are meant to undermine, private culture-consumption and the reproduction of capital. McCann concludes that Thelwall's awareness of the 'potential neutralization of his own political aims by the circulation of his text through the marketplace' led him to renounce literature as a means of reform and re-focus his efforts on the medium of political oratory.[90] Thelwall lends credence to such a reading by making sharp distinctions between his literary and political pursuits, as in the 'Epithalamium' that concludes *The Peripatetic*.[91] The narrator celebrates the weddings of Belmour and Ambulator as an apotheosis of 'Social Affection' but declares that this 'youthful strain' on his '*Sportive* lyre' will be his last, as he intends to swap it for the 'loud enthusiast shell' to sing of 'TRUTH and godlike LIBERTY!'.[92] Certainly, the fraught potential of 'politico-sentimental' appeals to the imagination would become a defining preoccupation of Thelwall's career in the wake of *The Peripatetic*, as he developed his theory of aesthetic response and experimented widely with the stimuli of literary form and oral performance. However, as the ensuing chapters demonstrate, his recognition of the potential transience of such appeals never invalidated his belief in their potential to spark new forms of consciousness in the body politic. Even in *The Peripatetic*, the obstacle highlighted in the 'Effervescences' episode is not 'politico-sentimental' literature – Sylvanus's remarks apply just as much to orators as to poets – but mediation of any kind that deadens the sensory impressions which, from the perspective of materialist psychology, are responsible for setting off the associative trains of thought that can lead to benevolent action. If only 'actual feeling and present experience' can provide an effective stimulus to benevolent action, then the representation of such experience is only a simulacrum: at best it can produce an 'effervescence' of enthusiasm, but that will inevitably subside when the voice fades or the page is turned. Literary mediation, like physical distance, compromises the effectiveness of the stimulus of 'active feeling and present experience'.

This is confirmed towards the end of the narrative when Ambulator, enquiring at an inn for news of Belmour, meets an old man who is poring over a book, sighing pitifully and brushing away the occasional tear. Ambulator is surprised to see anyone so moved by 'a tale of fiction' and wonders what 'agony of sensation' would agitate the man if 'the picture of the miseries of the great mass of his countrymen [were] brought, in living colours, to his sight!'.[93] He suspects that what moves the old man is not 'mere invention' but some personal experience recalled by his reading. Conversation proves Ambulator right: the man is reading *Tom Jones* and has reached the scene where the young protagonist falls into a pond trying to recover Sophia's bird, a scene that reminds him of a similar incident involving his niece (none other than Belmour's beloved) and her childhood companion (none other than Belmour). The revelation thus confirms Ambulator's sense that for fiction to elicit the sympathetic imagination of its readers, they must have some 'cognitive contact' with the experiences recounted.[94]

The happy ending of *The Peripatetic*, in which Belmour is resuscitated after an attempted suicide by drowning, holds out the hope that readers might be similarly 'cured' of their solipsistic self-interest thanks to the 'cognitive contact' stimulated by the work's hybrid, dialogical, associative form.[95] This optimism is qualified, however, by the characters' awareness of a malignant form of 'association': John Reeves's Association for the Preservation of Liberty and Property against Republicans and Levellers, formed in 1792 and devoted to circulating anti-radical propaganda, harassing reformers and bringing legal charges against them. Sylvanus alludes to the organization's stifling effects when he warns Ambulator to 'suppress [his] freedom of speech, and remember THE ASSOCIATION!'.[96] Reeves may in fact have been behind the attempted suppression of *The Peripatetic*, whose original publisher – probably Thomas Rickaby, who had published the *Animal Vitality* essay earlier that year – urged Thelwall to omit his political opinions or '[turn] them to the other side of the question'. When Thelwall refused, Rickaby broke their contract and attempted to confiscate the manuscript, acting under pressure from a 'municipal inquisitor'.[97] Thelwall justifies his tenacity in publishing the work by remarking in the preface that

> the subject of our political abuses is so interwoven with the scenes of distress so perpetually recurring to the feeling observer, that it were impossible to be silent in this respect, without suppressing almost every reflection that ought to awaken the tender sympathies of the soul.[98]

Less than a year later, however, a much more serious threat to the values and vitality of the reform movement would make such silence unavoidable. Under these circumstances, poetry would offer a new experimental means of countering the debilitating effects of repression and disillusionment in Thelwall's readers and, before long, in himself.

3

From Self to Sentient Nature

Poems Written in Close Confinement and
Poems, Chiefly Written in Retirement

The channels of vital sustenance have been dried up[.][1]

In the *Animal Vitality* essay Thelwall observes that to heal a wound it is necessary 'to keep the living parts in contact, and exclude the air, and other injurious, extraneous particles, till Nature has sufficient opportunity of exerting her restoring powers'. The blood will 'enter intimately into the different portions of the severed parts' and, 'driving towards its usual course, [...] at last find its way again [... to] the injured parts, and complete their restoration'.[2] A figurative version of this course of treatment proved vital to Thelwall in the mid-1790s, when the government attempted to kill off the radical reform movement by charging its leaders with high treason and, when that failed, by enacting 'gagging' laws that effectively asphyxiated it. Political disillusionment turned to despair with the sudden death in 1799 of Thelwall's six-year-old daughter, 'she [...] in whom I liv'd— / In whom all hope was center'd'.[3] At these moments of personal and political crisis, Thelwall turned to poetry as a means of healing psychic wounds and restoring vitality in himself and his readers. The results were *Poems Written in Close Confinement* (1795), composed during his seven-month imprisonment pending trial for high treason, and *Poems, Chiefly Written in Retirement* (1801), a product of his three-year retreat to Wales.

The past decades' resurgence of interest in Thelwall has brought new attention to bear on his *Confinement* and *Retirement* verse. Challenging E. P. Thompson's claim that Thelwall 'had the misfortune to be a mediocre poet', scholars have tended to read his collections as precursors to, or interlocutors of, the 'Greater Romantic Lyrics' of his more famous contemporaries, or as specimens of the introspective, individualist tendency of the Romantic lyric more generally.[4] While such approaches are borne out by Thelwall's complex relationship with Wordsworth and Coleridge during these years, yet, as Judith Thompson acknowledges in her recent recovery of that 'silenced' poetic partnership, they should not obscure the distinctiveness of his corpus, including its activist and therapeutic dimensions.[5] This chapter explores the materialist under-pinnings of Thelwall's alternative aesthetics, specifically his attempt in the *Confinement* and *Retirement* collections to resist or work through forms of introversion that, as Chapter 2 has shown, he regarded as inimical to reform, insofar as they signalled a break-down of the mind's free-ranging associative responses to the world. By contrast with the 'out-in-out' movement of the 'Greater Romantic Lyric' as defined by M. H. Abrams, which remains fundamentally introspective even when its gaze turns outward, the characteristic movement of Thelwall's *Confinement* and *Retirement* poems is a resolute 'in-out': an imaginative attempt to resettle the mind's eye on the world beyond the self.[6] In one poem Thelwall figures this as a 'turn / From *Self* to *Sentient Nature*', the ability to regard oneself as part of an animate whole that he thought essential to virtuous action.[7] The poems' fusion of radical politics and materialist science is also apparent in their shared lexicon of nerves and blood, which serves at once to address issues of liberty and reform under repression and to overcome that condition. Whereas the experimental sonnets, odes and songs of the *Confinement* collection attempt to 'rouse the patriotic feeling' from inside the prison walls, the supple blank verse of the *Retirement* collection charts a path from a state of mind resembling suspended animation to renewed radical agency.[8] Vitality in both collections is dependent on the poet's sense of belonging to a community of fellow reformers, even after contact among those 'living parts' had been 'severed' by the repressive measures of the late 1790s. Based on new archival evidence, this chapter shows that the *Retirement* collection in particular should be read with reference not only to the Wordsworth-Coleridge circle that failed to sustain Thelwall in crisis, but also to the reformist community centred around the democrat-surgeon Peter Crompton that succeeded.

'Transcripts of the heart'

Thelwall's concluding wish in *The Peripatetic* to trade his 'Sportive lyre' for the 'loud enthusiast shell' was soon granted.[9] In the spring of 1794, thanks to its network of spies and informers, the government of William Pitt received word that the London Corresponding Society (or LCS) was planning to hold a convention in London as a show of strength in the wake of the previous autumn's disastrous meeting of reform societies in Edinburgh, when several delegates were arrested, charged and transported to Botany Bay. Suspending the Habeas Corpus Act, the government launched a decisive crackdown, starting with the arrest on 12 May of the LCS founder and secretary Thomas Hardy. The next night Thelwall hosted an emergency meeting of the LCS and was arrested as it dispersed.[10] Along with Thomas Holcroft, John Horne Tooke and other leading radicals, Thelwall spent the next seven months in prison, first in a large, airy room in the Tower of London, and then in the notoriously overcrowded and disease-ridden Newgate jail.[11] Only after five months did he and his fellow prisoners learn that they were being charged with nothing less than high treason, an offence punishable by hanging.[12] According to the English statue of treasons of 1351 (25 Edward III), it was treason to 'compass or imagine the death of our lord the king' or to 'levy war' against him.[13] Under this statute one could not be charged with actually killing the king, but only with 'compassing' or 'imagining' his death, and it was incumbent on the prosecution to show that each defendant had committed some 'overt act' that demonstrated such an intention. Although by the 1790s it was agreed that conspiracies to depose the king constituted 'overt acts' of treason, the trials of 1794 raised the question of whether the category of 'overt acts' might include actions that had the indirect or unintended consequence of endangering the king's life.[14] In Thelwall's case, evidence of an alleged intention to overthrow the constitution and depose the king included his membership in various radical societies; his political lectures and speeches; his composition of three satirical songs; his participation in radical toasts; his use of the word 'Citizen'; his ownership of unlawful knives; his applause of seditious passages at a performance of Thomas Otway's *Venice Preserved*; and a half-finished letter – one of many papers confiscated on his arrest – in which he expressed support for the radical French Montagnard party.[15]

The possibility of being sentenced to death on the strength of such evidence made it imperative for Thelwall to show his intentions in a different light. Accordingly, one of his first concerns on being jailed was to petition for the use of paper, pens, ink and books. Thus armed, he set to work on his defence and the collection *Poems Written in Close Confinement*, both published the following year. 'Of the poems', Coleridge would remark in a letter of February 1797, 'the two Odes are the best—Of the two Odes the last, I think——it is in the best style of Akenside's best Odes.—Several of the sonnets are pleasing—& whenever I was pleased, I paused, & imaged you in my mind in your captivity'.[16] This admiration lay behind his 1796 sonnet 'To John Thelwall' in praise of his 'vigorous song', one version of which described the song instead as 'nervous', as noted in the introduction.[17] Both adjectives capture the conjunction of materialist science, radical politics and literary imagination in Thelwall's body of work, but the latter is an especially apt descriptor of the *Confinement* poems: these 12 sonnets, two Pindaric odes, four ballads, and one Anacreontic ode are at once an expression of benevolent nervous sensibility, a display of political nerve and an attempt to reinvigorate an enervated British populace.

A lexicon of nervous illness permeates the collection, particularly its metaphors for the condition of the British people under an unreformed government. Tyranny 'Ensnares the dazed senses, till our hearts / Sink, palsied, in degenerate lethargy', while the 'fell opiate' Luxury deludes with 'gaudy visions' of opulence. Slavery 'unnerve[s] the soul' and 'vain Magnificence' plunges it into a 'trance'. Britain's 'burning cheek, and kindling eye' are no longer signs of 'free-born energies', but symptoms of decay.[18] The only ones immune to the disease are the brave few who uphold the

> sacred creed,
> That not for self alone—not for the few
> Whom kindred ties endear, we live. The soul
> By Justice warm'd pants for the kindred whole.[19]

Such men are 'patriots' in the earlier eighteenth-century sense of vindicating the liberties of 'freeborn' Britons from political corruption,[20] but they are also defined in the *Confinement* collection by their ability to imagine the future rewards of their labours. In 'Meditation's glass' they foresee the 'scenes of woe' that their children will know 'Beneath the Despot's rod'; their 'generous breast can feel / An offspring's future woe or future weal'.[21]

The materialist subtext of these assertions becomes apparent when we turn to lectures on the 'prospective principle of virtue' that Thelwall delivered shortly after his acquittal, in which he distinguishes that principle from the 'the retrospective system [...] of brooding over the past'. Whereas the latter can produce at best only 'despondency and lethargy', and at worst the excesses of the French Terror, the former is essential to 'political amelioration'.[22] It depends on the realization that the individual is merely a small element of the 'continuous system of animated being' that makes up the universe. Responding to those who invoked the slow pace of reform as an excuse for inaction, Thelwall reasons,

> Those storms which compose the individuals that surround me, some few years hence may perhaps be winnowed in the gale; in the eternal revolutions of matter they may be transmuted into various forms, flow in the wave, mount with the element of fire, or mingle with their parent dust: but have we therefore no interests in the enjoyments of posterity?—Yes, we have. In contemplation we enjoy them [...]. And though you may not live to see the whole of those benefits you are toiling to produce, if you cannot anticipate them and enjoy them, in prospect, while you are toiling, I pity the cold-ness and sordidness of your imagination.[23]

While Thelwall's main point is that prospective imagination enables reformers to transcend the mortal limits of the self, he also implies that the 'eternal revolutions of matter' ensure the survival of the very atoms that comprise them, establishing a material continuity among the gen-erations. He thus puts a radical and materialist spin on Burke's notion of society as a partnership 'between those who are living, those who are dead, and those who are to be born',[24] making that continuity the very grounds for reform: 'year after year, generation after generation, ages after ages, and myriads of ages after myriads, may pass away, and still society exist to reap the benefits of our exertions; then our energy becomes as it were immortal'.[25]

This premise of material continuity is manifest in Sonnet XI, 'The Phœnix', inspired by a letter in the *Morning Chronicle* that excoriated Pitt for his self-aggrandizing pursuit of war with France.[26] Identifying 'Phocion' as an heir of the 'phœnix' 'Junius' – the author of a series of mid-eighteenth-century attacks on the ministries of the Duke of Grafton and Lord North – Thelwall credits him with reviving the defendants' spirits:

> with eager joy we view
> Thy daring flight, and thy bold course pursue
> With new-reviving ardour, from thy wings
> Shook thro' the bright'ning æther.[27]

The motif of the persecuted rebel whose inspiring spirit rises from the ashes of his destruction has a corollary in Milton's *Samson Agonistes*, where Samson is compared with 'that self-begotten bird' which 'Revives, reflourishes, then vigorous most / When most unactive deemed, / And though her body die, her fame survives'.[28] Inflected by this allusion, the phoenix metaphor in Sonnet XI suggests that the defendants of 1794 are only the latest incarnations of an inextinguishable spirit of patriotism. As Thelwall exclaims in 'Stanzas on Happiness', 'he can glory so to bleed / As Russell *and as* Sidney *bled!'*.[29] The invocation recurs throughout the collection like a refrain, linking the poems internally, like so many pages in the 'breviary' of Thelwall's 'sentiments and principles', and externally, with a tradition of 'patriot' tributes to the republican martyrs.[30] All are parts of the larger 'Jacobin' body of some 80,000 that Burke regarded as a cancer on society, and that Thelwall celebrates as willing, like Samson, to pull down the pillars of corruption even at pain of death.[31]

Thelwall's object in the *Confinement* collection is to transfer such patriot enthusiasm to others – to effect a sort of blood transfusion through the instrument of the pen. He describes the poems in a preface as 'transcripts of the heart', adding, 'I have spoken what I felt; not considered what I should speak; a method, at least, the most honest, and sometimes the most successful, in appealing to the hearts of others'.[32] As this *cri de coeur* suggests, one strategy is to enact virtuous patriotism in verse much as he did at reformist meetings and lectures before his arrest. The result is a kind of physiognomical poetry – one approximating the pseudo-science of inferring a person's character from a study of his or her physical features[33] – in which the words on the page stand as indices of the moral qualities of the poet. In Sonnet XII, 'The Crisis', composed a few days before his trial, he explicitly invites readers to anatomize his motives and responses:

> Now search my breast with scrutiny severe:
> > That breast which frequent in the swelling pride
> > Of youthful ardour, the stern threats defied
> Of distant danger: mark, if now base fear
> > Palsy its boasted virtue—or if now
> (Forgetful of the truths so oft upheld)
> > Abject beneath the imperious foot I bow
> Of terror-vested Power—suppliant!—depress'd!—
> Or one emotion feel, but what the breast
> Of Hampden or of Sidney might have swell'd.[34]

Attending to the 'oratorical ethos and aesthetics of voice' that permeates the *Confinement* poems, Judith Thompson calls attention to Sonnet

XII's imagery of resuscitation and 'mouth-to-mouth inspiration'.[35] Yet what Thelwall particularly wishes to demonstrate here are the qualities of his heart: before a jury of his readers, he lays bare the qualities of unflinching virtue and self-possessed ardour that he associates with the seventeenth-century republican heroes John Hampden and Algernon Sidney, after whom he would name two of his sons. As he notes in the preface, 'They who look for the sighs of personal regret, and the elegiac tenderness of complaint, will certainly be disappointed'.[36] His ambition to 'rouse the patriotic feeling' in himself and his readers helps explain his refusal to dwell on personal hardship: the poems are not about his plight, but about the universal status of any would-be British 'patriot' under conditions of repression.[37]

Such stoicism is dramatized in 'The Cell', a sonnet in ringing iambic tetrameter that Thelwall composed on first entering the 'den of horrors' that was Newgate. The description was not histrionic: Thelwall was confined in 'the dead hole, or charnel-house—the common receptacle for the putrid carcases of felons who die of diseases in the jail'.[38] Echoing the prison collection's epigraph from Milton's *Comus* –

> Fool, do not boast:
> Thou can'st not touch the freedom of my mind,
> ———Altho' this corporal rind
> Thou hast immanacled[39]

– Thelwall's sonnet celebrates the freedom of his mind 'Within the Dungeon's noxious gloom':

> he, unaw'd by guilty fears,
>   (To Freedom and his Country true)
> Who o'er a race of well-spent years
>   Can cast the retrospective view,
> Looks inward to his heart, and sees
> The objects that must ever please.[40]

In marked contrast with Coleridge's 'The Dungeon' and 'This Lime-Tree Bower My Prison' and Wordsworth's 'The Convict' – poems that in various ways celebrate the healing influence of nature on the metaphorically imprisoned soul – the speaker of the 'The Cell' transcends the material conditions of his confinement by looking 'inward to his heart'. This inward gaze is not to be confused with the more individualistic introspection of the 'Greater Romantic Lyric'.[41] What Thelwall sees on

looking inward is the memory of his past exertions in the public cause
of reform, a memory that sustains his commitment under persecution.

A comparable outward movement of the speaker's mind occurs
in 'Ode II', a loosely Pindaric ode whose three parts comprise two
Shakespearean sonnets and a variably constructed third stanza in iambic pentameter. This intricate form serves to develop a one-sided debate
with a parent wondering whether to educate his sons in the radical
tradition. Thelwall again evokes *Samson Agonistes*, in which the hero's
father, seeing his son doubly 'darkened' by blindness and imprisonment, asks aloud, 'Who would be now a father in my stead?'.[42] The
anguish that afflicts both father and son among the Philistines becomes
in Thelwall's ode the grounds for at first discouraging the transmission
of patriot values, only to conclude the more emphatically in its favour:

> What then, to those who breathe the heart-felt vow
> At Freedom's shrine, and the pure flame avow
>   Of Virtue—what are dungeons?—what the gloom
> Of Solitude, to him who thus can turn
>   From *Self* to *Sentient Nature*—to the doom
> Of myriads yet in embrio, who shall learn
>   To bless his virtues, and enjoy secure
> The Liberty he toil'd for?[43]

With this epode or stand, the poem at the heart of the collection celebrates the concept at the heart of Thelwall's radical and materialist
vision of reform, a 'turn / From *Self* to *Sentient Nature*' wherein sentience
denotes the capacity for sensation in living matter. Turning to 'Sentient
Nature' means seeing the world as sentient: one 'continuous system of
animated being', as Thelwall put it in his lecture on 'prospective virtue'. The passage also recalls the 'Spies and Informers' lecture in which
he celebrates the effects of unrestricted information and enquiry on
the mind: 'Employed in the pursuit of these, man feels and enjoys the
noble superiority of his nature [...]. He contemplates in every individual the faculties of suffrance and enjoyment, and feels one nerve of
sympathy connecting him with the whole intellectual universe'.[44] In
'Ode II', this ideal of a 'turn / From *Self* to *Sentient Nature*' is enacted not
only by the enjambed line that redirects attention from 'dungeons' to
the 'myriads yet in embrio', but also by the three-part structure of the
ode itself. From timidity born of concern for oneself and one's nearest
relations, it passes through a series of questions and answers to arrive at
a renewed commitment to the cause of 'Sentient Nature'.

As 'Ode II' suggests, the *Confinement* poems aim to provoke a turn to 'Sentient Nature' as much by their language and symbolism as by their forms. Thelwall regarded the poems as his 'first published attempts [...] at correct composition', and in 1821 he would republish them in his newspaper the *Champion* after being charged with seditious libel for an 'entirely unexceptional' article on the Peterloo crisis.[45] What makes the poems 'correct' compositions, however, is not their respect for convention; rather, they are 'correct' insofar as they bear out Thelwall's belief that poetry, the 'nursling of intellectual freedom', should not be shackled by 'the chains of former precedent' but left free to soar. In an essay of 1792 on the English sonnet he explains that provided the basic criteria of 'vivid painting, numerous harmony, sublimity of thought and expression, and pathos of sentiment' are met, then questions of length, rhythm and rhyme scheme should be left to 'the genius of the writer; or at least to that of the language'. This belief made Thelwall a great admirer of the 'illegitimate' elegiac sonnets of Charlotte Smith, whose variations on rhythm and rhyme scheme within the limits of convention he thought even more accomplished than those of Milton.[46]

Putting these views into practice, the *Confinement* collection makes an important but underappreciated contribution to what Stuart Curran describes as the Romantic period's 'revolution in poetry', anticipating by several years the analogy between the prison cell and the 'cell' of the poem more familiar to us from Wordsworth's sonnet 'Nuns fret not at their Convent's narrow room'.[47] A case in point is the opening sonnet, 'The Feelings of a Parent':

> Aн! who yet conscious of the social glow
>> Of Nature—or whose generous breast can feel
>> An offspring's future woe or future weal,
> The cause of sacred Freedom would forego,
> For aught luxurious Grandeur can bestow,
>> Or Tyranny inflict? Who that can view
> In Meditation's glass the scenes of woe
> The darling issue of his loins must know
>> Beneath the Despot's rod, but would pursue
>> (To Nature, and to Patriot virtue true)
> The glorious chace of Liberty, and scorn
>> Each fierce opposing danger—the fell steel
>> Of ruthless Janissaries—the stern Bastille—
> Its bars, its iron doors, and caves forlorn,
> Ere leave a trampled Realm in chains to mourn?[48]

Tagged with the place and date of its composition – '*Tower, 12th July, 1794*', that is, two days before the fifth anniversary of the fall of the Bastille – 'The Feelings of a Parent' suggests that Britain is on the verge of a comparable revolution as those of 'generous breast' rebel against the 'despot's rod' in the name of their children's liberty. The necessity of such rebellion is expressed by the sonnet's rhetorical questions, which imply that no one who genuinely feels the 'social glow / Of Nature' can resist the imperative to action. This defence of political liberty is matched by poetic liberties that make the sonnet representative of the whole collection, notably an irregular fifteen-line rhyme scheme (*abbaacaaccdbbdd*), whereby it simultaneously approximates the 8-6 structure of the Petrarchan (and Miltonic) sonnet and the 4-4-4-2 structure of the Shakespearean. The poem reinforces its assertion of unwavering commitment by omitting the volta or turn characteristic of the form and using recurrent 'o' rhymes – glow, woe, forego, bestow, know – to express unrelenting ardour rather than mournful complaint. Its iambic regularity is interrupted by pronounced caesuras at lines 6 and 12 and by the liberal use of enjambment, features that enhance the declarative speech rhythms which would become a hallmark of Thelwall's prosodic system after 1800. Yet even while asserting liberty in the very form of his sonnet, Thelwall avoids the alternative of complete license. In fact, in no poem does the man accused of plotting treason attempt a revolutionary overthrow of the system he has inherited. Instead, we find him taking regulated liberties such as he would later advocate in a series of essays about lyric poetry in his newspaper the *Champion*, declaring, 'We disclaim all anarchy of rhythmus, as we do all other anarchy: our liberty must be a liberty of order and of law'.[49] As 'transcripts of the heart', the prison poems are decidedly moderate.

The collection as a whole finds an equally fitting emblem in the opening lines of Sonnet IV, 'To Simplicity of Manners':

> O for the Spartan Fife, to pierce the ear
>   Of slumbering Virtue, and again restore
> Those ancient Manners—simple and severe,
>   That aw'd encroaching Tyranny![50]

The lines allude to the opening of William Collins's 'Ode to Liberty', as David Fairer has noted:

> Who shall awake the Spartan fife
> And call in solemn sounds to life

> The youths, whose locks divinely spreading,
> Like vernal hyacinths in sullen hue,
> At once the breath of Fear and Virtue shedding,
> Applauding Freedom lov'd of old to view?[51]

Thelwall likewise wishes for a martial instrument to carry his voice beyond the confines of his cell, into earshot of his fellow inmates and the wider patriot community. His longing is supplied by the prison poems themselves, which, like Percy Shelley's revolutionary clarion, are conduits for his inspiring breath, as well as transcripts of his heart. In the mid-1790s they allowed him to sustain radical vitality in himself and his readers from behind the prison walls until his triumphant acquittal in December 1794.[52] Within a few years, however, a more psychologically devastating experience of public repression and personal loss would threaten to extinguish that vitality completely.

'The channels of vital sustenance have been dried up'

Although for a brief period it seemed as if the widely publicized failure of the Treason Trials would ensure the survival of the radical movement, its resilience only increased the government's determination to silence it for good. It found a welcome pretext that October when a mob demanding peace and bread attacked the royal carriage as it made its way to Parliament for the opening of the new session, pelting it with stones and breaking a window, the sound of which the king mistook for gunfire. Just a few days earlier, the LCS had held a mass public meeting at Copenhagen Fields, on the outskirts of London, to reassert its commitment to parliamentary reform. Although the meeting dispersed without incident, in tandem with the attack on the king's carriage it presented an opportunity for the government to introduce the Treasonable Practices Act, which extended the law of treason to include any verbal or written acts tending to promote contempt for the monarchy, and the Seditious Meetings Act, which gave magistrates the power to dissolve meetings of more than 50 people for the discussion of political or social grievances. The second of the two 'Gagging Acts' was intended to prohibit precisely the kind of mass popular lectures for which Thelwall was famous, but with its passage in December 1795 he merely switched the topic of the lectures to classical history and continued to declaim by analogy against warmongering, political corruption and monopoly land ownership.[53] This open defiance, of which even the king was informed,[54] combined with Thelwall's notoriety as an 'acquitted felon'

to make him a prime target of anti-Jacobin satire: he featured in carica-
tures as a rabble-rousing demagogue and in novels as 'Mr. Rant', 'Citizen
Ego' and 'John Bawlwell'.[55] Thelwall took it in stride, asking Thomas
Hardy in May 1797, 'Do the people of London talk of me at all—what
is the lie of the day? [...] am I gone over to France on a treasonable
embassy? am I teaching the United Irishmen the use of Arms? (the
great Gun, you know, I learnt to work in the Tower!!!) or have I got a
pension for preaching moderation?'.[56] He was less worried about these
libels than about the actual sticks and stones of the loyalist mobs that
greeted his lecture-tour of East Anglia in 1796. In several towns gangs
of armed 'banditti' interrupted his lectures and dispersed his audiences.
There were several attempts to murder him and one to impress him into
the navy on a ship rumoured to be bound for Siberia. At Yarmouth he
extricated himself from his aggressors by holding a pistol to the head
of the nearest, exclaiming, 'Offer the least violence, and you're a dead
man!'.[57] The authorities repeatedly failed to intervene in defence of the
lecturer or his 'Thelwallite' sympathizers, and his only recourse was to
make the crown of his hat cudgel-proof and carry a short tuck-stick.[58]

Threatened with physical violence, unable to earn a living by lecturing and suffering from a lingering illness contracted in prison, a beleaguered Thelwall finally withdrew from public life in the fall of 1797 and
relocated his family to a farm near the Welsh village of Llyswen, at 'one
of the most beautiful, tho least visited, parts' of the Wye river.[59] The
retreat of this 'most indomitable of all the radical leaders' is often seen
as emblematic of the demise of the British reform movement in the second half of the 1790s.[60] E. P. Thompson has been particularly attentive
to what he calls 'the story of the silencing of Thelwall', arguing that by
the turn of the century '[n]othing survived of the Patriot except his fad-
ing notoriety'.[61] That story would appear to find support in Thelwall's
1801 collection *Poems, Chiefly Written in Retirement*, which opens with
the declaration that '[i]t is The Man, and not The Politician, that is here
delineated. The disciple of the Muses; not the Lecturer and Leader of
Popular Societies now no more'.[62] In the midst of the anti-Jacobin backlash it would have been reckless to claim otherwise. Implicitly, however,
the collection does just that. Challenging the idea that the Romantic
poetry of retirement is 'emphatically not Jacobin',[63] it draws on the
model and metaphors of animal vitality to trace, in meditative blank
verse, a path from crisis to cure – voicelessness to voice regained. As in
the *Confinement* collection, moreover, this recovery involves the poetic
interpellation of a reformist community, but not only the one centred
on Wordsworth and Coleridge to which criticism often refers. While

this was certainly a period of lively intellectual exchange among the trio, new documentary evidence allows us to appreciate the equally vital influence of Thelwall's networks beyond Nether Stowey and Alfoxden.

The importance of those alternative networks and the radical-materialist optimism they rekindled can be cast into relief by turning briefly to the poem at the heart of the *Retirement* collection, 'Lines, Written at Bridgewater, in Somersetshire, on the 27th of July, 1797; during a Long Excursion, in Quest of a Peaceful Retreat'.[64] Composed at the end of Thelwall's ten-day visit to Coleridge and Wordsworth, the poem is typically read as an expression of his ardent hope of join-ing their circle.[65] Days spent with the poets amid the lush scenery of the Quantocks, 'pass[ing] sentence on the productions and characters of the age – burst[ing] forth in poetical flights of enthusiasm – & philosophis[ing] our minds into a state of tranquility [*sic*]', had given Thelwall 'serious thoughts' of taking a cottage in the area.[66] The story of his ensuing rejection is now well known: a month after his depar-ture Coleridge wrote to break the news that, with the neighbourhood already unsettled by the arrival of the democrat Wordsworth (and the spy who famously followed him to Somerset), Thelwall's return was ill advised: 'I say it with a very sad, but a very clear conviction—at *present* I see that much evil & little good would result from your settling here'.[67] That rebuff is surely on Thelwall's mind when he writes in the preface to the *Retirement* collection that,

> The channels of vital sustenance have been dried up: and Friendship (the last stay of the human heart)—even Friendship, itself (a few instances of generous perseverance alone excepted) wearied and intimidated with the hostilities to which it was exposed, has shrunk from its own convictions, and left him in comparative insulation.[68]

'Lines, Written at Bridgewater' suggests that on some level Thelwall anticipated the desiccation of those 'channels of vital sustenance'. Composed on what he hailed as the day of his 'double birth', his thirty-third birthday and sixth wedding anniversary, the poem opens with apprehensive questions about whether the day is a 'harbinger of woes, / Precursor of a Year of miseries' – a year in which 'a World most scorpion-like' will 'Wound, with venom'd tooth, the fostering breast' – or whether it brings 'cheering prophecy of kindlier times [...] / Of hours of sweet retirement, tranquil joys / Of friendship and of love'.[69] Loath for the first scenario ('not for aye / In hermit-like seclusion would I dwell [...] / Forgetful and forgotten'), Thelwall spins the memory of his recent visit with the poets into a hopeful vision of shared intellectual and physical labour. He describes himself and Coleridge ('My Samuel') sharing 'sweet converse' as they delve their Voltairean garden plots:

> while, eager, one propounds,
> And listens one, weighing each pregnant word,
> And pondering fit reply, that may untwist
> The knotty point—perchance, of import high—
> Of Moral Truth, of Causes Infinite,
> Creating Power! or Uncreated Worlds
> Eternal and uncaus'd! or whatsoe'er,
> Of Metaphysic, or of Ethic lore,
> The mind, with curious subtilty, pursues—[70]

Sitting by the fireside encircled by their wives, as well as by Wordsworth ('Allfoxden's musing tenant'), Dorothy ('the maid / Of ardent eye, who, with fraternal love, / Sweetens his solitude'), and their friend Thomas Poole ('swain of happier age'), they will

> unbend awhile,
> Winging the idle hour with song, or tale,
> Pun, or quaint joke, or converse, such as fits
> Minds gay, but innocent[.][71]

This idyll of fireside community and 'sweet converse' about 'Metaphysic' or 'Ethic lore' echoes a letter of December 1796 in which Coleridge had expressed eagerness for just such communion: 'I would to God we could sit by a fireside & joke vivâ voce, face to face—Stella & Sara, Jack Thelwall, & I!'. Together they would recite

> Such Verse as Bowles, heart-honour'd Poet, sang,
> That wakes the Tear yet steals away the Pang,
> Then or with Berkley or with Hobbes romance it
> Dissecting Truth with metaphysic lancet.[72]

While this might seem to be an enchanting vision of 'pantisocracy at Stowey',[73] we should note that Coleridge originally addressed these lines to Poole, not Thelwall, to whom he gives them second-hand, as it were. By echoing them in 'Bridgewater', Thelwall seems to imply that despite his most ardent hopes to 'realize this vision' of sociable retirement, already on his departure from Stowey he is cherishing only an echo of the longed-for Somerset community. His remark that 'it would be / A Golden Age reviv'd!' underscores the unlikelihood that he will realize it any time soon.[74] Nor does that realization seem altogether desirable. On the contrary, notwithstanding Thelwall's claim that his soul 'Is sick of public turmoil', his concluding wish to 'yield my soul / (Unshar'd, unharrass'd, by a thankless world) / To the domestic virtues' and sleep on the 'soft pillow [...] / Of envyless Obscurity' can be read as a subtle critique of those who trade public duty for the cosy sense that '"Being is a Bliss!"'.[75]

Thelwall's dawning sense in 'Bridgewater' that 'channels of vital sustenance have been dried up' was mitigated by the abiding friendship of those 'few instances of generous perseverance' whom he mentions in a cryptic parenthesis in the 'Prefatory Memoir' that opens the *Retirement* collection, and whose influence has not yet been examined.[76] Chief among these was the physician, philanthropist and Dissenter Peter Crompton, who in May 1796 stood as an independent candidate in the Nottingham election on an anti-war platform.[77] Thelwall had made Crompton's acquaintance after his acquittal in 1794, and during his peripatetic excursion of 1797 may have been introduced by him to Erasmus Darwin, founder of the Derby Philosophical Society to which Crompton also belonged.[78] In a letter of 1805 to Thomas Hardy, Thelwall would praise Crompton as 'one of the few grains of salt that preserve this else-putrefying carcase of the world from corruption'.[79] They remained in contact as late as 1822, when Thelwall addressed to him the unpublished poem 'Auto-Biography', recalling an occasion when they were attacked by a loyalist mob: 'A stone, thrown at his head, / Miss'd him, 'tis said, / And had well nigh brain'd "dear Doctor"'.[80]

Crompton's importance to Thelwall and the *Retirement* collection comes to light in two hitherto unremarked documents. The first is an unpublished letter from him to Thelwall dated 11 September 1800 (Appendix 1). Together with Thelwall's extant letter to Crompton of two years earlier, which thanks him for a gift of £15, the September 1800 letter attests to Thelwall's abiding links to the overlapping provincial communities of reformers to which Crompton was central.[81] Among the mutual acquaintances named in it are 'Miss Hawes' – no doubt Maria Hawes, the daughter of Thelwall's friend and Humane Society founder William Hawes, and wife of John Gurney, junior counsel for the defence at Thelwall's trial in 1794[82] – as well as the Derby industrialists William and Joseph Strutt and their sister Elizabeth Evans; the scholar and religious controversialist Gilbert Wakefield; and the Liverpool Unitarian minister and politician William Shepherd.[83] Crompton explains that during Shepherd's visit to him the night before they discussed the most lucrative way for Thelwall to publish one of his poems – perhaps his epic *The Hope of Albion*, then in progress – and notes that Shepherd has passed the poem on to William Roscoe, the Liverpool historian and abolitionist. Crompton ends the letter by asking for news of Thelwall's family. His apparent ignorance of the death of Thelwall's daughter in December 1799 suggests that the two of them have been out of touch for at least ten months.[84]

Thelwall nonetheless felt strongly enough about their friendship to address Crompton in a second telling document: the page-and-a-half-long dedication of the *Retirement* collection, which is not reproduced in the 1989 facsimile edition (Appendix 2).[85] Writing in 1800 from Hereford at the conclusion of his Welsh retirement, Thelwall insists that the dedication is motivated not by any hope of 'future Favours', but only by a 'disinterested' wish to acknowledge Crompton's friendship and support: 'Tho on You it can bestow no Honour, some, perhaps, it may reflect on me'. Thelwall singles his friend out from among 'that Class of the Community so successfully enflamed against me' and expresses confidence that he 'will not shrink from this public acknowledgement'.[86] He is implicitly contrasting Crompton with Coleridge, who had asked Thelwall not to mention his name in the 'Prefatory Memoir'.[87] The contrast is more marked in the reference to Crompton as 'at once "My Benefactor and my Brother Man"'. The quoted phrase harks back to Coleridge's 'Reflections on Having Left a Place of Retirement' (1796): 'And he that works me good with unmoved face, / Does it but half: he chills me while he aids, / My benefactor, not my brother man!'. Ventriloquizing Coleridge to praise Crompton, Thelwall expresses a palpable resentment for the hypocrisy of one who had publicly proclaimed his choice of political life over retirement (Coleridge's poem was first published in the *Monthly Magazine*), but soon after became indistinguishable from those 'Who sigh for wretchedness, yet shun the wretched, / Nursing in some delicious solitude / Their slothful loves and dainty sympathies!'.[88] Crompton, by contrast, has severed neither his political nor his personal ties with the now-wretched Thelwall. On the contrary, he has proven instrumental to Thelwall's recovery from the deep depression that followed the death of his daughter:

> when the last of Human Miseries had fallen upon me—when Reason was prostrate, and the Heart was broken, [Crompton] poured into my Wounds the only Balm of which they were susceptible; and, with a solicitude, that neither the distance of Space nor of Circumstances could chill, aroused me (as far as I was capable of being roused) from unavailing Remembrances to more Vital Duties; and restored me to my Family, and to my Muse.[89]

At this moment of acute crisis, Crompton seems to have supplied not only the 'Balm' of friendship – fit antidote to the 'venom'd tooth' of a world that proved 'most scorpion-like' after all – but also the encouragement to write a series of ten 'Paternal Tears' elegies in which Thelwall would work through a double loss: that of his daughter, and that of the ideals that had flourished with her.[90] Coleridge would later remark that the title 'Paternal Tears' was 'a quaint & at the same time, trite conceit. To call a poem *a Tear* is quite Italian—Milton was young enough to be your Son when he used the phrase "melodious Tear"'.[91] For Thelwall, however, allusions to *Lycidas* serve to underscore the distance between these elegies and the prison poems, with their stoic allusions to *Comus* and *Samson Agonistes*. Comparing the *Confinement* and *Retirement* collections in the latter's preface, Thelwall remarks, 'He will there be seen in his strength, and in his weakness'.[92] He can also there be seen en route to recovery.

'Apoplectic whirl'

The thought that his children might escape their father's trials had been a constant source of comfort to Thelwall in the late 1790s, as several poems in the *Retirement* collection attest. In 'To the Infant Hampden', he contrasts his hardships with the imagined future of his son, thereby prompting Coleridge's subtle response in 'Frost at Midnight' about the possibilities for preserving or transforming one's dream of justice in the repressive atmosphere of the late 1790s, as Judith Thompson has shown.[93] In 'The Woodbine' Thelwall likewise finds comfort in imagining his daughter Maria in adulthood: 'my heart, / Turning from retrospects to dreams of hope— / Paternal hope! can dwell on thee, sweet flower!'.[94] Writing to his brother-in-law in 1794, Thelwall had expressed a hope that Maria would 'some time or other be the happy mother of a fine hardy race of Republicans, & Sans Culottes'.[95] The fragment-poem 'Maria' recalls his anticipation of her and her mother's visits to his prison cell in 1794,

> When, thro' my grated dungeon I have gaz'd,
> With straining eye unmov'd, upon the gate
> Thro' which the partner of my soul should pass—
> And this, my only babe:——my only, then,
> And still my best beloved![96]

When on 28 December 1799, just a few days after her sixth birthday, Maria suddenly died of the croup, a disease of the larynx and trachea, Thelwall's state of mind 'equally out of humour with itself and with all the world' turned to despair: 'she, alas! is gone, in whom I liv'd— / In whom all hope was center'd'.[97] So begins the sequence of ten blank-verse elegies that Thelwall composed over the following year, about which Wordsworth remarked that 'though they have great merit, one cannot read them but with much more pain than pleasure'.[98]

Although Thelwall contested the surgeon John Hunter's theory that the blood was the principle of life, as noted Chapter 1, he nonetheless considered it an appealing poetic metaphor.[99] In Effusion I it serves to describe a grief so intense that it threatens the mourner's very life:

> Dim swims the sight;
> The vital spirits languish; and the blood,
> No more obedient to the order'd course
> Of self-preserving Nature, refluent oft
> Turns on her o'ercharg'd fountain; or, impell'd
> By wildering Anguish, rushes to the brain,
> And whelms the sense in apoplectic whirl,
> That Nature's chain seems bursting.[100]

According to this quasi-medical explanation of mourning, the 'vital spirits' – refined substances once deemed responsible for the maintenance of life – have changed course under the impulse of grief and now flow backwards, 'o'ercharging' the heart and engulfing the brain. This 'refluence' brings on apoplexy, an illness that impairs the powers of sense and motion.[101] The sensibility that Thelwall had celebrated in the prison poems thus becomes a painful burden:

> Ah! what to *him* avails the sentient power
> To whom all sense in pain? Who reft of joy—
> Reft of each solace—reft of all that fed
> Hope's vital lamp, benighted, droops, appall'd,
> Amid the horrors of sepulchral gloom—
> A conscious maniac?[102]

By contrast with the 'patriot' of 1794, who within the 'Dungeon's noxious gloom' could 'smile—in conscious Virtue blest', Thelwall now fulfils his own definition of mania as 'distempered imagination intensely coherent to the fantom of its creation; so that present realities cannot divert it from its imaginative object'.[103] As in *The Peripatetic,* he attributes this condition to the mind's powers of association: during Maria's early years they wrought 'round the [father's] heart / [...] links of adamant'; now they confine his thoughts to that one object, leaving him 'unconscious' of any other.[104] Anticipating Thelwall's elocutionary insights into the links between mental and bodily forms of impairment, the man whom Coleridge had described in the mid-1790s as the 'voice of tens of thousands' can now articulate only the sighs, cries and groans of a bereaved father:

> Maria! Oh, Maria! thy lov'd name,
> While Nature yet is vocal—while this heart
> To this sad tongue can dictate, thy lov'd name
> The rocks and conscious echoes shall repeat,
> And murmuring Vaga mourn no loss but thine.[105]

Thelwall's heart communicates with his tongue in a sort of closed circuit that transmits a single signifier, 'Maria', which is echoed by his surroundings, rendering him deaf to everything but the 'lov'd name'. The sinuous enjambment of the lines, like the sinuous, S-shaped meanderings of the river Wye near Llyswen – here called 'Vaga' after the nymph once said to inhabit it, and linked etymologically with vagabondage – help express this rebarbative state of mind and body: even nature and poetry seem to replicate Thelwall's inward turn. This effect is heightened throughout the poems by the recurrence of the 'lov'd name' in various forms – 'Maria', 'thy', 'thine' – and the echoing of the name or its initial 'm' sound by the murmuring, mourning landscape.

Effusions II and III emphasize the gravity of the crisis with allusion to Thelwall's *Monthly Magazine* essay 'The Phenomena of the Wye, during the Winter of 1797–8'. There he demonstrates a fine painterly sensibility to the river's 'intricate meanders [...], and the eternal diversity of its bed and current', as well as to the play of light and shadow on the surrounding mountains, fields and sky. He gives vivid accounts of a wintertime flood that threatens the valley with 'universal deluge', creating a 'sublime picture of desolation', and of a later icicle frost that turns the landscape into a frozen 'fairy land'.[106] Revisiting these enchanting scenes in the months following Maria's death, Thelwall finds in them 'nought but vacancy' – 'Nought, but the dire remembrance of thy loss'.[107] Scenes that formerly 'nurse[d] / Romantic vision' and 'invite[d] the skill / Of imitative effort' now leave him cold:

> All that once,
> With grace or mingled harmony, could thrill

Sight or the list'ning sense, unheeded meets
The unconscious organ[.][108]

The healthful sensory responsiveness on display in the Wye essay has
given way to monomania as the 'echoing Wye' becomes the bereaved
father's echoing 'why', his struggle to comprehend his loss. Thelwall
describes himself in Effusion III as beset by 'afflictive trance' at a spot
where Maria used to play.[109] The phrase evokes the cases of suspended
animation that so fascinated the Humane Society, of which Thelwall was
a keen follower. As editor of the *Biographical and Imperial Magazine* a decade earlier he had published excerpts from the Society's reports on topics
including suspended animation and the resuscitative uses of electricity
and a double-bellows.[110] In the 'Paternal Tears', by contrast, the vitalizing agent is poetry itself, which provides not only an outlet for grief, but
also an occasion for addressing the distinction between 'The Man' and
'The Politician' on which the *Retirement* volume is based – a bisection of
Thelwall's identity under repression that compounds his sorrow.

Sociopolitical reflection makes a cautious reappearance in Effusion VI:

It is the doom of man with toil to earn,
With toil and care, the bread of his support;
Nor must I claim exemption[.][111]

Thelwall is explaining the reason for his recent journey to Merthyr Tydfil,
from which, as the poem's subtitle informs us, he has just returned. He
is noticeably silent about the journey's motive or the nature of his 'toil'
there, but we can infer from the reference in Effusion VII to the 'magic
of Vulcanian art' by which Merthyr has '[g]rown populous' that his visit
may have had some connection with the town's booming ironworks
industry.[112] In October 1800, following popular disturbances in the town,
the ironmaster Samuel Homfray had reported to the Home Secretary,

I have very little doubt but political Principles have in some degree
influenced the Minds of the lower Class of People. [...] When
the cryer proclaimed in the public Markett [*sic*] a Meeting of the
Workmen of the four Works near Merthyr for taking into consideration the high price of Provision Mr. Thelwall was at no <u>very great</u>
distance.[113]

Homfray's letter can be taken to confirm E. P. Thompson's remark that
although in the late 1790s Thelwall had reason to be in retreat, 'he

was not in retreat all that *much*'.[114] Nicholas Roe points out that just a few days after leaving Nether Stowey, Thelwall had tried to organize a Corresponding Society meeting at Bristol.[115] We know, too, that he remained in contact with radical circles in the provinces: his 1798 letter to Crompton sends regards to Liverpool's radical community, while another letter of the same year addressed to the Welsh radical Edward Williams (a.k.a. Iolo Morganwg) expresses regret at their failure to meet the previous summer.[116] Moreover, the addressee of Effusion I, 'J—— G——', was almost certainly the barrister John Gurney, junior counsel for the defence at Thelwall's trial in 1794, son-in-law of Humane Society founder William Hawes, and a friend of Crompton's. The partial elision of Gurney's name is emblematic of Thelwall's cautiously muted interpellation of the reformist community beyond Nether Stowey whose friendship is instrumental to his poetry and the recovery of his 'vital spirits'.

Effusion VI strengthens the case for the reformist subtext of the 'Paternal Tears' by more directly invoking the political causes of Thelwall's distress. While at Merthyr he dreams that he sees his dead daughter standing at the foot of his bed, looking both accusatory and compassionate:

> not lifeless now
> Seem'd'st thou, tho pale: the look, the mournful air
> Was vital; and thine eye's expressive glance,
> In silent eloquence, upon my face
> Reproachfully thou turned'st; but yet fond,
> And full of pitying drops[.]

The 'mournful air' cast by the dream-image of Maria is 'vital' in the sense of being lifelike, but also in the sense of sparking her father's recovery. He understands it to articulate a paradox:

> 'treasuring that
> 'Thy soul so little values, thou hast lost
> 'All that thou deem'd'st worth treasuring.'

The positioning of 'values' between the mercenary and the paternal conceptions of 'treasuring' encapsulates Thelwall's predicament: preoccupied with trying to support his family as a farmer after having been forced out of public life, he overlooked the gravity of his daughter's illness. The closing stanza reveals that the roots of his remorse run deeper:

> Thou, my sweet babe! art to my hostile stars
> Another sacrifice—another fine

> (Heavier than all the past) that I have paid
> For love of human nature—for the crime
> Of universal brotherhood, that, thus,
> Dooms me, in exile from the social sphere
> Of humaniz'd fraternity, to weep
> Thy early loss—in whom myself am lost.[117]

The logic of this closing stanza is clearly ironic: only in a corrupt society could the 'love of human nature' be deemed a crime. The real crime is the forced exile of the friend of humanity. With this self-exculpation, Effusion VIII represents the climax of an ongoing negotiation between public and private identities at heart of the 'Paternal Tears'. At last, Thelwall gives the lie to his prefatory distinction between 'The Man' and 'The Politician', conflating them in his attempt to make sense of Maria's death and his own living-death in retirement.

The dream-encounter with Maria thus marks a restorative turning-point, especially if we consider the term 'effusion' in this pathological sense of extravasation, the 'escape of any fluid out of its natural vessel, and its lodgement elsewhere'.[118] As Thelwall would have known from his attendance at medical lectures and demonstrations in the early 1790s, bloodletting was a common cure for apoplexy – the suspension of sense and motion that metaphorically besets him – routinely practiced by Hunter and others.[119] This medical connotation emerges in the description of the mourning father as 'pierc'd, at last' by Destiny's 'barbed shaft', evoking both the loss of a blood relation and the loss of lifeblood or vitality.[120] Over the course of the sequence, however, 'effusion' also comes to mean sacrifice: a loss incurred to some higher or more pressing claim, in this case the 'love of human nature' and 'the crime / Of universal brotherhood'. 'Effusion' in this sense harks back to classical literature, in which the ritual spilling of blood was a means of conjuring the shades. This connotation is especially appropriate to poems that conjure the ghost of Maria. By framing her death as a 'sacrifice' for his 'love of human nature', Thelwall in a sense reverses the fatal inward flow that he described at the outset. In keeping with the alternative definition of 'effusion' as outpouring rather than influx, the refluence of the first effusion turns outwards once more, spilling forth in 'Paternal Tears'. By the end of the sequence, then, the effusion is no longer pathological but potentially restorative. The path out of mourning is becoming clearer.

The sequence ends with Effusion X, 'Cerrig-Enion' ('Enion's Tomb'), composed in August 1800 on Pen-Heol-Enion in Brecknockshire. The Welsh place-name translates loosely as 'the top of Enion's road' and memorializes the chieftain Einion Glyd, killed by the Normans in 1177.[121] This is a suitable setting for the last effusion, which finally leaves behind the psychologically and topographically depressed landscape of its predecessors and brings Thelwall to a hilltop overlooking the unmarked site of Maria's grave.[122] Although his thoughts are still 'ben[t]' mournfully towards that site, he is now also conscious of other features of the landscape – 'lonely hut[s]' and 'the wrecks / Of prostrate palaces' – which call to mind heroic feats of 'ancient prowess' during past epochs of tyranny. Were he not grieving, Thelwall muses, he would make Enion's tomb his 'thoughtful couch' and meditate on the causes of rural depopulation and decay.[123] Although he does not do so immediately, his incipient 'turn / From *Self* to *Sentient Nature*' suggests that the period of his mourning is passing and that, as he puts it in Effusion IX, echoing *Lycidas*, he is returning to work 'With love of sacred Freedom, yet unquench'd' to

> 'build the lofty rhyme,' and twine the wreath
> Of civic virtue, for the honour'd brow
> Of Albion's earliest Hope[.][124]

Thelwall alludes to his epic *The Hope of Albion; or, Edwin of Northumbria*, which was intended to celebrate the establishment of the British constitution on the basis of civil and religious liberty. Fragments of the poem were published at the end of the *Retirement* collection in 1801, and that same year saw the publication of his abolitionist, feminist novel *The Daughter of Adoption*, followed by the launch of his career as an elocutionist and speech therapist dedicated to 'the enfranchisement of fettered organs' – literally, free speech.[125] Far from remaining silent, Thelwall found new ways of adapting his voice and those of his pupils to the discourse of the times. He did so, however, with a heightened awareness of the limits of radical and materialist optimism in times of repression, one that finds expression as much in his elocutionary venture as in his turn-of-the-century experiments with the genres of romance, epic and the novel.

4

Between Hope and Necessity

The Fairy of the Lake, The Hope of Albion and
The Daughter of Adoption

> [T]here are phenomena enough in almost every life to
> justify an occasional suspicion that we are nothing but
> mere machines – speaking automatons[.][1]

In a brief but fascinating essay of 1820 'On Human Automatonism',
inspired by a 20-year struggle to complete his epic poem *The Hope of
Albion*, Thelwall admitted the possibility that his faith in individual
rational agency was misguided:

> Say what we choose on the self-satisfying subject of free-will, there
> are phenomena enough in almost every life to justify an occasional
> suspicion that we are nothing but mere machines – speaking automa-
> tons, whose very words are breathed thro' us, as thro' an organ-pipe,
> inflated by some exterior agency, and stopped or played upon by
> the finger of a capricious destiny. We reason, it is true, or appear to
> do so; but how seldom is the practical result a consistent part of the
> syllogism? We resolve, or persuade ourselves that we have done so;
> but how frequently our actions gainsay our pretended resolutions: –
> nay, fly in the very teeth of them, and shew that we know nothing
> of ourselves.[2]

Although Thelwall is acknowledging only an 'occasional suspicion' that
free will is meaningless, the essay nonetheless points to a fundamental shift in his thought, from an enthusiastic belief in the possibility
of rational self-guidance, individual and collective, to a heightened
awareness of the limitations imposed by 'exterior agency' or material
circumstance. In his 1796 treatise *Rights of Nature, against the Usurpations
of Establishments*, by contrast, he had answered Burke's arguments for

political precedent and inheritance with a fervent defence of change founded on the common will. '[N]*o man* can pull down a government', he conceded,

> But, when, not a Man, but a *People*, wills a grand revolution, to feel the *will* is also to be conscious of the power; and, when the will and the power cooperate, sophists may string syllogisms, like beads upon a rosary; but while they are reasoning, the thing is done.

Thelwall considered that 'this will is not lightly inspired. It is not to be produced by declamation or logic', and he attributed this inertia to the fact that for most people 'that which *is* will generally appear to be best; merely because it is'.[3] This was in fact 'fortunate' because, as he maintained in *Sober Reflections on the Seditious and Inflammatory Letter of the Right Hon. Edmund Burke, to a Noble Lord* (1796), questions of government should be decided by the 'aggregated *reason* [...] of society', rather than by the opinions or whims of a few.[4] Thelwall nonetheless believed that the will to change could be summoned if a generalized state of discontent were coupled with 'some extraordinary provocative'.[5] As the notion of a 'provocative' suggests, underlying this assertion was his understanding of political vitality as dependent, like animal vitality, on the conjunction of suitably organized matter and a quasi-electrical stimulus.

We have seen how in trying to use language as just such a stimulus, Thelwall confronted the challenges of solipsistic self-interest (Chapter 2), political repression and personal loss (Chapter 3). A recurrent feature of his poetry and fiction of the 1790s is a self-reflexive preoccupation with the limits of appeals to the sympathetic imagination when measured against the force of 'actual feeling and present experience'.[6] In the aftermath of the 'Revolutionary Decade', Thelwall's concern with the deterministic implications of embodied perception and response – or what Coleridge once celebrated as 'the Automatonism of Man'[7] – moves to the centre of his materialist imagination. It finds expression notably in three works that he composed in 'retirement' as he contemplated a return to public life: his Arthurian romance *The Fairy of the Lake* and fragmentary epic *The Hope of Albion* – both published in *Poems, Chiefly Written in Retirement* in 1801 – and his novel of the same year, *The Daughter of Adoption; A Tale of Modern Times*. Largely overlooked by scholarship, all three works feature radical heroes reduced to the status of mere automatons by the reactionary forces of their respective worlds. In *The Fairy of the Lake* the beleaguered would-be-king Arthur achieves victory over his foes chiefly through the intervention of a benevolent *deus ex machina*, while in *The Hope of Albion* the exiled prince Edwin's restoration is challenged by the ability of his supernatural antagonists to enflame the people against him, and further undercut by the poet's inability to bring his epic to fruition. The headstrong heroine of *The Daughter of Adoption* succeeds against the odds in living out her egalitarian 'new philosophy', but only by reconciling her abstract Godwinian idealism with the realization that 'in the moral, as the physical world, action is more frequently decided by the stimuli of custom than the boasted volitions of reason'.[8]

In their various ways, Thelwall's dramatic romance, fragmentary epic and tale of modern times all pursue the strategy initiated in his anti-imperialist plays *Incle and Yarico* (1787) and *The Incas* (1792) of displacing social and political critique to remote times and places. This chapter presents them as instances of the genre of 'historical romance' theorized by Godwin in his 1797 essay 'Of History and Romance', published posthumously. On the assumption that the aim of history is 'to enable us to understand the machine of society, and to direct it to its best purposes', Godwin dismisses the narratives of teleological progress that he finds in the Scottish philosophical histories of David Hume and William Robertson as merely 'romance under a graver name'.[9] As an alternative he proposes 'historical romance', 'a composition in which, with a scanty substratum of facts and dates, the writer interweaves a number of happy, ingenious and instructive inventions, blending them into one continuous and indiscernible mass'. By contrast with the period's standard definition of romance as 'an heroic fable, which treats of fabulous persons and things', Godwin's version encompasses any fictional reconstruction of the past for radical purposes.[10] In view of this ideological dimension, Jon Klancher renames the genre 'republican romance', noting that it 'seeks imaginatively to reopen that possibility in English history – the moment of 1642 [when Parliament defeated Charles I] – which the Scottish philosophical historians, and most notoriously Hume in the first volume of *The History of England* (1763), had been especially anxious to close'.[11]

If Godwin was the first to theorize this 'new, reflexive, and progressive [...] mode of historical knowledge', Thelwall was surely among the first to attempt it multiple times.[12] As this chapter will show, his 'republican romances' adopt and eventually set aside the supernatural machinery of traditional romance to reopen moments of alternative historical possibility and envision the advent of political justice in the post-revolutionary era. In so doing they engage what Raymond

Williams described as the materialist question of 'the real relation between projects of human liberation cast in collective and epochal terms and the physical conditions which determine or affect actual individual human lives'. Without presuming definitively to answer such a question, Williams maintained that while 'physical-material' circumstances are unavoidably 'constitutive' of our experience, they do not render us merely passive, and can in fact be enabling.[13] Thelwall, too, holds fast to a belief in the possibility of reform, even while demonstrating an acute awareness that the circumstances for it must be propitious. To achieve the rational self-direction that he deemed characteristic of a healthy republic, rather than mere automatonism that he associated with tyranny, the body politic must be predisposed with susceptibility to the vitalizing stimulus.[14] Failing that, even the most heroic efforts necessarily prove impotent.

Freezing spirits: *The Fairy of the Lake*

Thelwall's 1801 *Retirement* collection opens with *The Fairy of the Lake*, a 'Dramatic Romance' in three acts based on the legend of King Arthur. At once a psychodrama and a stageable romance, as its performance in 2009 demonstrated, *The Fairy* reworks the story of Arthur's succession to the throne as a lively allegory of the impediments to radical agency in the late 1790s.[15] Taking up themes of psychophysical debility and suspended animation that are central to the 'Paternal Tears' elegies, which figured in the same collection and were composed at roughly the same time, Thelwall depicts Arthur in a quasi-automaton state of 'senseless torpor' and makes his recovery and triumph contingent on the intervention of a benevolent *deus ex machina* and the 'politic valour' of his Welsh companion Tristram.[16] Critics have therefore regarded the would-be king as symbolic of the historical contingency of human action and of the dramatist's own predicament in exile.[17] In a characteristically self-reflexive move, however, Thelwall has Arthur play a decisive, if unconventional, part in his liberation by resisting the lure of apostasy while incapacitated, suggesting an abiding optimism about the powers of 'patriot' virtue in a world of 'double visag'd Fate'.[18]

The action of *The Fairy* centres on the Saxon sorceress Rowenna's plot to murder her husband Vortigern and marry Arthur, eventually sharing his rule over Albion and uniting the warring Saxons and Celts. Rowenna finds an opportunity to strike in Act 2, as the hero and his companion wander lost in a forest, lamenting the desertion of their one-time friends and allies. Closely re-enacting Comus's assault on the virtuous Lady in Milton's masque, Rowenna ties Arthur to the spot 'Charm-bound from voice or motion', while an 'icicle devil' in her command lays hands on Tristram, causing even his words to freeze. "Tis in vain Your lungs you strain', warns the fiend, as Tristram stammers for help.[19] The dramatic forced silencing of the future 'patriot King' and his companion had a clear parallel in the gagging of British radical reformers in the previous decade, and specifically in Thelwall's prosecution and exile.[20] The parallel is reinforced by his decision to relocate the action of the legend to Wales, a choice no doubt suggested by his Llyswen retreat – a 'sort of enchanted dormitory' on the banks of the Wye – and by the 'fairy land' spectacle of an icicle frost during the winter of 1797–98.[21] The many autobiographical allusions invite a mode of reading that Damian Walford Davies, referring to Thelwall's 1793 anecdote 'King Chaunticlere', calls 'historicist psychobiography': the interpretation of imaginative works and symbols for their interrelated historical and psychological significance.[22] On such a reading, Rowenna embodies the spirit of conquest and corruption that had become synonymous among reformers with the government of William Pitt. In his political lectures and pamphlets of the mid-1790s, Thelwall had repeatedly denounced Pitt and his ministers as magicians of state who employed 'tricks and antics' to exert 'a sort of witching charm' over the deluded populace.[23] Rowenna likewise exercises her 'sovran power' with the help of dark enchantments and a crew of supernatural spies and informers, her 'shapeless spirits of the impassive air'.[24] The foremost of these is the icicle devil Incubus. From his comical conversation with Rowenna's attendant Agga we learn that some 50 years earlier he was banished to 'The Frozen Regions' (or Scandinavian hell) for having 'slunk from the ranks' in the hour of battle – specifications which suggest that this duplicitous freezing spirit is modelled on the spy James Walsh, who was present at Thelwall's arrest in May 1794 and lurked at Nether Stowey in the summer of 1797.[25] Rowenna's husband (and Guenever's father) Vortigern, meanwhile, evokes the increasingly feeble George III: he remains offstage until his death, allowing Rowenna to wield sole power over 'prostrate' Britain and plot Vortigern's attempted rape of his daughter, the Britannia-figure Guenever.[26]

Beset by this devilish cast, Arthur represents the diminished vitality of radicals like Thelwall, who just a few years earlier had expressed scepticism about the possibility that his 'sinews of patriotic exertion' might one day 'relax'.[27] Likewise evoking the disempowered hero Hamlet, Arthur excoriates himself for 'war[ring] with women's weapons',

'senseless brawl' and 'rage'. Rather than resolve to act at the first opportunity, however, he welcomes the onset of his morbid symptoms:

> Come then, thou sullen Calm
> Of conscious desperation, thro my soul
> Breathe thy narcotic influence – steep each nerve
> In opiate dews, and o'er each maddening sense,
> Bewilder'd, from their chilling urns pour forth
> Thy inanescent torpors, till no more
> Reflection wakes, and dull Oblivion drop
> The vail [*sic*] by Fancy lifted.[28]

Arthur invites the state of suspended animation that Thelwall had experienced at Llyswen, when the brave patriot of 1794 became a 'conscious
maniac' following the death of his young daughter, as Chapter 3 has
shown.[29] In a gesture of seeming resignation, Arthur throws away his
helmet, shield and enchanted sword, and slumps down on the stump
of an oak, a symbol of 'sapless' British valour.[30] His arm 'Sinks palsied,
and [...] / Hangs powerless' by his side – a direct echo of the prison
sonnet in which Thelwall had described the people's hearts 'Sink[ing],
palsied, in degenerate lethargy' under a corrupt regime.[31] Thelwall also
reuses the prison poems' lexicon of 'fell opiate[s]' and 'detested drugs',
ascribing Arthur's loss of volition to the 'narcotic influence' and 'opiate
dews' of desperation (the coinage 'inanescent' seems to mean 'capable of rendering inane' or senseless). Thelwall may well be alluding to
Coleridge's addiction to the most notoriously will-destroying of those
drugs, opium – his *'free-agency-annihilating* Poison'.[32] In advance of
Thelwall's November 1803 visit to Grasmere, Coleridge would ask him to
stop by 'the best druggist in Kendal' to buy 'an Ounce of crude opium,
& 9 ounces of Laudanum', and Thelwall would later insist that '[r]eal
genius [...] has little obligation to the Tuscan Bacchus, or to the Turkish
Poppy'.[33] According to his second wife and biographer, during his imprisonment Thelwall found hidden in a delivery of books and writing materials an unsolicited 'large lump of opium', but refused to use it.[34] That
his Arthurian alter-ego succumbs to a quasi-opiated stupor suggests some
sympathy with Coleridge's condition, a 'conscious desperation' that
Thelwall shared in retirement. But Thelwall is at the same time critical
of Arthur's passivity insofar as he makes his triumph dependent on the
intervention of a benevolent *deus ex machina*, the Fairy of the Lake. An
allegory of the principles and rights of 'Nature' that Thelwall had cham-
pioned throughout the 1790s, the Fairy arises from her lake to liberate

Arthur and his knights so that they can lay siege to Vortigern's castle.[35] It is Rowenna, meanwhile, who ultimately kills her tyrant-husband. Arthur in fact condemns the act – not one, he, to 'compass or imagine' the king's death![36] Equally ineffectual, at first, is the hero's companion Tristram. Whereas Arthur lapses into a stupor of despair, Tristram seeks 'spiritual' sustenance in a cask of ale, leaving it 'Hollow as a false friend'.[37] Yet, as Judith Thompson points out, Tristram ultimately redeems himself by protecting another 'vital fountain' of 'Hope', the virtuous Guenever: he infiltrates the castle where she is prisoner, diverts the seneschal with his witticisms about the benefits of feasting before fighting and keeps Guenever from harm until the arrival of Arthur and his knights.[38]

If Tristram's wordsmanship is essential to the play's romantic resolution, Arthur also displays an unconventional and equally self-reflexive sort of heroism after all. Despite appearances, he is not ultimately the 'mere machine' that Thelwall describes in the 'Human Automatonism' essay. Unlike Rowenna's minions, 'Mechanic instruments – / Unconscious pivots in the state machine', when Arthur realizes his danger, he puts up a struggle worthy of Milton's virtuous Lady: 'in these bonds / Powerless I stand, yet can my soul disdain / Thy blandish'd witcheries'.[39] Like *Comus*, too, *The Fairy* defines heroism not in terms of action, but in terms of 'constancy', the 'appalling' trait for which Rowenna threatens to make Arthur witness Vortigern's attempted assault on Guenever.[40] And it is only at this juncture, when Arthur has proven himself true to his cause, that the Fairy of the Lake intervenes to secure his triumph, albeit with the gentle rebuke, 'Your weak despair yourself will freely blame'.[41] Should he – could he – have done more for his cause? Thelwall must often have wondered this of himself as he grappled at Llyswen with 'intellectual proscription', an unyielding soil, hostile neighbours and parental heartache.[42] The answer was hardly a simple yes. Certainly, around 1800 he had dwindling reason to believe that the beleaguered patriots of the 1790s would ultimately vanquish their foes in an exchange of 'Fire for […] fire', as Arthur's cohort vanquish theirs.[43] Accordingly, the forms of rational exhortation whose effect Thelwall had once compared with the 'alchymist's fire' have been superseded in *The Fairy* by the delusive enchantments of corrupt power.[44] What, then, was the would-be hero's role in a realm thus enthralled and over-mastered? Only, it seems, to act when the time was right and await that moment with 'constancy', without presuming that one's fate was sealed.[45] And this is precisely what Thelwall did during the late 1790s in retirement, as the previous chapter has shown. By 1800, however, he was beginning to recover his spirits, resuming work on *The Hope of Albion* and planning a return to society as a professor of elocution and speech therapist. In his epic he is correspondingly more sanguine about the possibility of renewed radical agency, but this returning optimism is severely qualified by a newly ambiguous attitude to the power of verbal communication and an inability to bring the poem's action to fruition.

'Contagious wrath': *The Hope of Albion*

The Hope of Albion; or, Edwin of Northumbria was to be Thelwall's greatest literary achievement. The idea of a national epic had apparently occurred to him in the late 1780s, but he did not begin writing one until 1798 when, 'in the depths of solitude and irksome seclusion from all active life, the mind recurred to its former projects'.[46] Then he set to work with gusto, composing and partially correcting more than 4,000 lines ('the matter of the first six books') in 15 or 16 weeks. Soon after, he embarked on his career as an elocutionist and found no time to add more than a few cantos.[47] He was apparently still working on the epic as late as 1822, when he wrote the unpublished poem 'Auto-Biography' that describes 'evening hour[s]' when

> the Muse guides him on thru the story
>   Of 'Albion's Hope',
>   The aim & scope
> Of his dreams of <u>posthumous</u> glory![48]

We can glean a sense of the poem's 'aim & scope' from the fragments that concluded the *Retirement* volume of 1801 and those published over the next two decades in newspapers and elocutionary compilations. Its subject was the emancipation of Northumbria in the seventh century by the exiled prince Edwin, whose triumph over the tyrant Adelfrid paves the way for the establishment of the British constitution on the basis of civil and religious liberty.[49] Although Hume's *History of England* was a crucial source for the poem, Thelwall was not satisfied with the historian's 'superficial and imperfect' version of events, whereby Edwin's accession is secured by the East-Anglian king Redwald.[50] He must also have objected to Hume's rejection of the notion of Anglo-Saxon liberties and emphasis on the influence of external political forces, which seemed to relieve individuals of moral responsibility for their actions.[51] Thelwall, by contrast, wants to present Edwin as the earliest champion of British constitutional liberties, the very existence of which had been called into question by the political debates of the 1790s. By weaving into his narrative 'retrospective and prophetic views' of history, Thelwall intended to trace the influence of Edwin's triumph

> thro' the whole of the ultimate limits of the British empire; and embrace, in fact, the prominent events of the history of that empire, from the arrival of the Saxons to the period of the Revolution [of 1688], which re-asserted the principles of Anglo-Saxon liberty, and placed the Dynasty of the Brunswicks on the British throne.[52]

Thelwall thus takes advantage of the 'obscurity and ambiguity' of the historical record to develop a radical version of events that charts the progress of liberty from Edwin to the seventeenth-century republican heroes with whom 1790s' radicals strongly identified. In seeking imaginatively to recover the original Anglo-Saxon 'purity' of the constitution from subsequent corruption, he makes *The Hope* as much a 'republican romance' as *The Fairy*.[53]

As in that earlier work, too, the imaginative reconstruction of the past is an opportunity for a radical critique of the present. *The Hope* has strong allegorical ties with the anti-Jacobin reaction of the second half of the 1790s, particularly as it alienated Thelwall from his former mentors. A fragment entitled 'The Shipwreck', published in the *Champion* in 1820 alongside the 'Essay on Human Automatonism', opens with an account of the hero's hope of triumph: 'High of heart, / In Esperance, I bid the morning hail / Should give me to my wish'.[54] With nothing to identify the first-person speaker of this passage as Edwin, readers could be excused for taking him to be Thelwall, the narrative of whose own frustrated ambitions prefaces the fragment. (Thelwall even named a son born in 1802 Edwin Northumbrian.) The rest of the passage consolidates the identification. The hero returns from exile, where he was 'with unremitting ills / Hemm'd and pursu'd'.[55] Worn out by 'toil and expectation', he retires to his cabin and has a prophetic dream:

> Methought mine arm
> Wielded the misson'd thunder should avenge
> My bleeding country [...].
> ....
> And now, from urns
> Transparent as the crystalline heaven, I pour
> (For living and apparent streams they seem'd!)
> Justice and peace and mercy thro' the realm, –
> And blessings like the dew.[56]

With its lexicon of blood and streams, the passage calls to mind what Nicholas Roe describes as Thelwall's efforts in the mid-1790s to diffuse political information through the communicative networks of the body politic just as the vital principle was diffused through the vascular networks of the animal body.[57] The passage suggests, moreover, that vitality will be restored to the country not by further bloodshed, but by the salutary transfusion of 'Justice and peace' through the medium of language. The 'urns / Transparent as the crystalline heaven' from which Edwin pours forth these blessings contrast markedly with the 'chilling urns' that poured 'inanescent torpors' on the hero of *The Fairy*.

Such visionary optimism is severely qualified, however, when Edwin's dream is interrupted by a visit from the 'tutoring angel' Moseroth, who warns that 'hours of sharper trial' are in store.[58] Sure enough, the hero wakes to find his ship caught in a terrible storm – a recurrent symbol in Thelwall's corpus for the violent anti-radicalism of the 1790s – from which only he and his mentor Albert escape alive. A 'doubtful' dawn reveals the wreckage and 'the floating carcasses / Of our disastrous mates'.[59] We learn from the argument of Book I that Albert is later assassinated but returns as a ghost to warn the hero of plots for his destruction. The hero's 'former Tutor and preserver' evokes Thelwall's one-time 'intellectual and political father' John Horne Tooke, with whom he had a permanent falling-out in 1795.[60] Likewise, Edwin's subsequent protector Redowald, whose 'love of Justice' needs 'firm example, to sustain / In virtuous daring',[61] calls to mind another wise but cautious East-Anglian philosopher-king, Godwin. Having rebuffed Adelfrid's multiple requests to deliver up the fugitive Edwin, Redowald weighs the enemy's alternatives of 'War or alliance'.[62] Meanwhile, Adelfrid's ambassadors Hermanric and Ossa attempt to 'rouse / The sullen passions' of the populace – 'scorn, and deadly hate / Of alien tribes' – much like the loyalist 'banditti' who interrupted Thelwall's East-Anglian lecture tour of 1796. (The miniature epic catalogue of their verbal weaponry includes 'sordid speech, / Quaint idiom, and obscener mirth, disguise / Insidious malice; [...] and martial strain'.[63]) This rabble-rousing is abetted by Woden's 'ministering furies', who take human form to mingle with the crowd. In a passage about the 'subtile sophistry' of one named Beornulph, Thelwall dramatizes his own vilification by Burke and other anti-Jacobin writers and orators. Like them, the fiend deploys

> hell-instructed eloquence, to goad
> Delirium on to madness; and the wrath,
> Kindled by wiles demoniac against

> The race of Cambria, on the head divert
> Of Edwin – erst so favour'd: popular love
> (Ah, boon precarious!) to the deadly gall
> Of hatred turning.[64]

The fiend eventually dissolves into a dark and menacing cloud, but continues to hover over the nation as a symbolic counter-revolutionary spirit.[65]

Thelwall's description of the effect of Beornulph's powers of incitation turns on a metaphor of electricity that carries a very different charge from earlier instances in his oeuvre:

> The fierce throng
> Kindle with martial rage. All join the peal,
> And swift, from man to man, contagious wrath
> Spreads, direful: as, from group to group, expands
> The electric fire, when to the crystal jar,
> Or sphere excited, the hermetic hand
> Applies the tried conductor, and relieves
> The imprison'd elements, whose subtile flames
> Dart thro' the languid nerves, the fibres brace,
> And with encreas'd pulsation urge the heart.[66]

The passage probably refers to the Leyden jar, a discovery of the Leyden professor Pieter van Musschenbroek, who solved the problem of how to capture the electrical 'fire' by coaxing it from water contained in a glass jar. The jar was placed on an insulated stand and electrified by a conductor consisting of a gun barrel charged by a rapidly spinning globe.[67] As Noel Jackson remarks, in Thelwall's allusion to the experiment it is unclear whose 'hermetic hand' wields the electrifying conductor and whether it will 'contain or redistribute' the surge of popular opinion it gathers. However, rather than presenting 'a model of incendiary language as transmitted most effectively through [...] the press', Thelwall's extended electrical metaphor seems to register an acute consciousness that the popular imagination can be kindled both for and against the cause of reform, orally and in print.[68]

Consciousness of the challenge to reform posed by the 'contagious wrath' of counter-revolutionary discourse, Edwin's friend Reynier urges him in Book IV to abandon his cause: 'Ah! fly, disastrous prince'.[69] But Edwin refuses, resolved to try 'what Energy can do' on his behalf.[70] His eloquent reasoning inspires a correspondent resolution in his friend, and together they lay plans to reclaim the people's allegiance. While dramatizing Thelwall's own return to public life around 1800, this passage also confirms that his attitude to reformist exhortation has undergone a significant change. Edwin muses that the 'fickle throng' needs 'able leaders' to guide its 'headlong passions'; if such leaders are 'weak and wavering', those passions can be easily 'enflam'd to action' by some malignant power. The people, he concludes, 'are but limbs and passions: who would rule / Must find pervading reason!'.[71] Only a decade earlier, Thelwall had insisted against Burke that the people could be trusted to lead themselves: 'a sort of Socratic spirit will necessarily grow up, wherever large bodies of men assemble'.[72] Now, however, he nearly echoes Burke on the 'swinishness' of the multitude and Godwin on the need for an enlightened elite to guide it.[73] The devastating political and personal storms of the late 1790s have shaken his faith in the common people's capacity for virtuous self-direction, as his elocutionary works would confirm. *The Hope of Albion* thus marks another critical moment of self-reflection in Thelwall's oeuvre, comparable to *The Peripatetic*'s awareness of the limits of the sympathetic imagination in the service of reform. Far from demonstrating that he considered enthusiasm – in the negative sense of a violent and disruptive state of mind transmitted by the mob – to be 'steadily retreating in the face of the inevitable progress of truth and reason', as Jon Mee suggests, *The Hope* testifies to a heightened sense of the 'uneasy tension' between rational and fanatical forms of enthusiasm that Mee attributes to Romantic culture more broadly.[74]

The poem's final fragments suggest that if the nation's patriot heroes still hope to triumph, they must fight counter-revolutionary incitation with more effective forms of communication. Having resolved not to flee, Edwin turns his attentions from 'graphic toil' to leadership. Moving through the crowd with a look that 'Beams with majestic ardour', he inspires comparison with the Anglo-Saxon leaders Hengist and Horsa. The sentiment spreads 'From mouth / To mouth [...] / Reverberate', countering the 'contagious wrath' of his enemies.[75] By Book V, he is no longer a mere peon in the contest between Adelfrid and Redowald, but a heroic agent in his own right. Echoing the title of one of Thelwall's pamphlets of the mid-1790s, he defies the tyrant powers to 'strike, then; strike!'[76] knowing that martyrdom will advance his cause almost as much as continued struggle. Yet his fiery oratory gains only a partial victory, and it becomes clear that an assembly of the Wittena-gemot – the 'soveran voice of congregate East Anglia' – is necessary to secure his triumph.[77] Meanwhile, Adelfrid's agents

Hermanric and Ossa denounce the 'plotted treason' and conspire to prevent it.[78]

And here the narrative ends abruptly, leaving the nation's and the hero's fates hanging in the balance. We know that Adelfrid will eventually be overthrown and Edwin 'elected' to the crown of Northumbria. Yet the mechanics of this denouement remain unclear. Perhaps Thelwall was planning to preserve 'a degree of historical fidelity' in this regard, despite having availed himself of poetic 'latitude' in many others.[79] Or perhaps the hero's fate was to reflect Thelwall's own, in keeping with so much of the action. Judith Thompson follows Thelwall in claiming that the demands of his elocutionary career prevented his completion of the work, and she suggests that it found a sort of continuation through its recitation at the elocutionary institutes and societies in which he became active.[80] For Stuart Curran, by contrast, the unfinished state of Thelwall's epic suggests that '[a]s political repression deepened, [...] it became more difficult to celebrate a constitutional accord whose true existence was in doubt, and difficult even to praise anything resembling a revolution without threat of penalty'.[81] The proliferation of epics in the period may also have been a factor, notwithstanding Coleridge's remark to Thelwall in a letter of April 1801: 'I suspect, that in a very short time the London Booksellers will be marvellously shy of Epic Poems'.[82] While all of these explanations seem plausible, reading *The Hope* in the context of *The Fairy* and *The Daughter* suggests another: Thelwall's growing dissatisfaction with the reliance of epic and romance on a supernatural machinery. Originally he had considered that such a 'great and beneficent design – the concentration of a mighty empire' could not adequately be represented as 'the mere result of human agency', and he therefore chose to make his epic hero 'the elected instrument of Heaven, [...] superintended by a particular providence'.[83] In *The Peripatetic*, he prefaced the fragments of an unfinished mock-epic poem on British print and visual culture with a discussion among the characters about whether a Greek or Christian machinery would have been more suitable for John Dryden's intended epic about King Arthur or Edward the Black Prince.[84] In *The Hope*, however, the question seems to be not *which* supernatural machinery to prefer, but whether any can be reconciled with an abiding faith in individual rational agency. This doubt helps explain Thelwall's decision to do away with a supernatural framework by pursuing questions of agency and necessity in the genre of the novel. In *The Daughter of Adoption*, Thelwall finds greater scope for restaging the debates at the heart of radical-materialist theory and practice.

'The necessity of treason': *The Daughter of Adoption*

In the course of its 12 books (more than 1,200 pages in the first edition), *The Daughter of Adoption; a Tale of Modern Times* tells the story of the philosophical and sentimental education of Henry Montfort, the only son of the English slave trader Percival Montfort.[85] In the early chapters we watch Henry grow up under the contradictory influences of his domineering father and meekly benevolent mother, and then follow him to the French colony of St. Domingue – referred to as 'St. Domingo' in the novel[86] – where his father sends him at age 20 to remove him from the corrupting influence of his Oxford companions. On arrival in Port-au-Prince, Henry is witness to the injustices of colonial slavery and the depravity of the local population. He observes the women, 'whites as well as mulattoes', to be 'little better than masses of inanimate affectation'.[87] Bodies seemingly deprived of conscious agency, these slaves to the island's commercial and sexual economies instantiate one of the novel's central themes, the power of the 'stimuli of custom' to prevail over the 'boasted volitions of reason'.[88] The exception is Seraphina, a white Creole who is the adopted daughter of a reclusive Godwinian philosopher named Parkinson. Seraphina and Henry fall in love amid the horrors of a slave rebellion and promptly sail for England, consummating their relationship en route. The second half of the novel follows the pair in London, where the social and philosophical differences between them become apparent. Henry resumes a prodigal lifestyle in the expectation of inheriting his father's fortune and even contemplates marriage to another woman, while Seraphina finds her radical principles compromised by the mercenary values of a society where women are bartered like the slaves in her native West Indies. A true daughter of the 'new philosophy' of Godwin and Wollstonecraft, she considers herself to be Henry's de facto wife and balks at being treated like a courtesan. These differences combine with various adventures – a kidnapping, a near rape, an attempted murder, four potentially incestuous relationships and several mistaken identities – to thwart the marriage of the hero and heroine, who are reconciled during the novel's convoluted dénouement.

The Daughter sums up its own genesis when Henry's companion Edmunds – a radically minded, working-class, expatriate Englishman based to a large extent on the author – reassures Seraphina that he will support her if Henry does not:

'I would write for the booksellers, madam (for I have been thinking that I could compile a history, or a book of travels, or teach a German ghost or an incubus to talk English, as well as some of those who get a very good livelihood by it); or I would write your history, madam, under some fictitious name, and call it a novel; and I am sure every body would read it; for every body would weep over it.'[89]

Like Edmunds's proposed novel, *The Daughter* appeared under the fictitious name 'John Beaufort, L.L.D'. By its connection with the buildings where Thelwall lived and lectured in the mid-1790s, the transparent pseudonym evoked a period of political activism cut short by repressive laws and loyalist mobs, and Thelwall's subsequent retreat to Wales.[90] His experience there was certainly matter to 'weep over': *The Daughter* was partly a response to a threat of 'pecuniary ruin' provoked by the disastrous harvest of 1799, and partly a distraction from the frustrations of political exile and the devastation of his daughter Maria's untimely death that December, shortly after he had finished writing the novel's first chapter.[91] Set aside for many months and then resumed in haste, *The Daughter* is in many ways a surrogate daughter, a fantasy of what Maria might have become had she lived to be educated according to radical principles of equality and benevolence.[92] Henry, 'sole memorial' of his mother's youthful idealism, is just six years old when the novel opens, the age at which Maria died.[93] In giving new life to Maria, *The Daughter* also keeps alive the legacy of another Mary, Wollstonecraft, whose reputation was in ruins following the publication of Godwin's *Memoirs* of her life that incautiously disclosed details of her sexual relationships and suicide attempts.

Like Edmunds's hypothetical work, moreover, *The Daughter* was a popular novel of the day destined for the circulating libraries. E. P. Thompson considered that although the first volume 'contains some passages of social criticism', the last three are 'mere conventional money-spinners'.[94] While profit was certainly a concern for the struggling farmer Thelwall, Thompson's assessment underplays the novel's combination of 'astute sociopolitical analysis with psychological insight, maudlin melodrama, and flat-out farce',[95] and especially its interrogation and development of key aspects of Thelwall's materialism. Like the 'Jacobin' novels of the 1790s, *The Daughter* expresses social dissent, advocates humanitarian reform and bases its structure on the principle of necessity, linking character and incident 'like the parts of a syllogism'.[96] Yet if we consider that the Jacobin novel 'was born, flourished, and died with English Jacobinism itself', it seems more appropriate to think of *The Daughter* as its radical progeny, a second-generation or post-revolutionary work that is markedly aware of its formal, philosophical and historical inheritance.[97] Like *The Fairy* and *The Hope*, *The Daughter* is even more fittingly described as a 'republican romance', one that systematically foregrounds the relationship between necessity, agency and genre. (Klancher in fact defines the 'republican romance' as a descendant of the 'Jacobin' novel.[98]) Setting aside the supernatural machinery and variously incapacitated heroes of his drama and epic, Thelwall creates a memorable female heroine who confronts the limits of radical idealism and arrives at a more pragmatic version of political justice rooted in a materialist understanding of 'that complicated machine of the human heart'.[99] He also carries forward the debate begun in *The Peripatetic* about the conditions under which a fictional appeal to the sympathetic imagination might succeed in promoting 'the moral duties and social charities of life' – that is, in giving a reformist 'turn' to the 'brains' of its readers just as Seraphina's is said to have been 'turned' by her reading of poetry.[100]

The Daughter's dramatization of the conflict between agency and determinism within materialist philosophy begins in its opening account of Henry's upbringing under the contradictory precepts of his parents. Amelia's 'rational system' of 'theoretical and practical lessons' intended to 'nerve the intellect and ameliorate the heart' strikes her authoritarian husband as the 'foolish jargon and mock morality' of 'petticoat philosophers' designed to turn the boy against him.[101] Only when Montfort threatens to achieve his 'counter-revolution' by force does Amelia reluctantly yield 'general principles' to 'particular expediency', convinced – as Thelwall had become – 'not only of the inutility, but [of] the danger of all further remonstrance'.[102] The question of whether it is ultimately more conducive to reform to yield to one's circumstances or sustain a lone struggle to transform them is at the heart of *The Daughter*, and comes dramatically to the fore when the hero is sent to the West Indies. The ensuing quarter of the novel offers much more than a 'sentimental vignette' of the horrors of colonial slavery.[103] Thelwall had already attempted to rewrite imperial history in two plays, *Incle and Yarico* (1787) and *The Incas* (1792), both of which relate the triumph of indigenous populations – unspecified Native Americans in the first case, Peruvian Incas in the second – over their European aggressors.[104] Likewise in *The Daughter*, the St. Domingue rebellion is the occasion for a reassessment of radical ideology in a geographically and temporally displaced setting: St. Domingue rather than Britain; 1791 rather than 1801.[105] Drawing on accounts of the colony by Bryan Edwards and the Baron de Wimpffen, Thelwall has Henry arrive there on the eve of the slave rebellion of August 1791, when some 100,000 slaves from the northern plantations took a violent revenge on their masters.[106] Henry's sympathy for the slaves and open denunciation of their owners' 'trafficking in human gore' leads his Creole host to suspect that he is a member of the *Amis des Noirs* or Friends of the Blacks, a French abolitionist society established in 1788 to advocate equal rights for free people of colour.[107] Henry defends his revolutionary stance in what is perhaps the novel's most famous scene, a dramatization of an exchange that took place during Thelwall's 1797 visit to Coleridge in Somerset.[108] Henry and Edmunds are wandering through a beautiful part of the Glen of Limbé when Henry remarks (ventriloquizing Coleridge), 'What a scene, and what an hour, Edmunds, [...] to hatch treason in', to which Edmunds replies (ventriloquizing Thelwall), 'What a scene, and what an hour, sir, [...] to make one forget that treason was ever necessary in the world!'. There ensues a short debate in which Henry maintains that to forget the 'necessity of treason', one would also have to forget 'the facts of history', specifically those concerning the oppression of native peoples, which are indelibly engraved on the landscape.[109]

Can one ever forget the necessity of treason? Thelwall stages his own ideological self-debate in 'retirement' at Llyswen by promptly putting Henry's and Edmunds's positions to the test. Soon after their treason exchange they happen upon the cottage of the philosopher Parkinson, an expatriate Englishman who has abandoned his early religious studies to live a sequestered life in the French colony with his wife Amanda and their adopted daughter Seraphina. A utilitarian, a free thinker and a gradualist in matters of reform, Parkinson bears a striking resemblance to William Godwin.[110] Upon learning that the slaves have risen up against their masters, Parkinson is apprehensive rather than elated: 'I would die to emancipate them, but I cannot wish for their revolt', he explains, adding that only the gradual progress of sympathy can bring a lasting improvement of the slaves' condition. Edmunds is appalled at the 'snail-like expedition' of this approach and counters that the slave trade is unlikely to be abolished when so many profit handsomely by it: 'In the meantime, sir, we reason, but the poor negro feels'.[111] Moments later the brutality of the uprising seems to confirm Parkinson's warning that '[t]hough you speak with the tongues of angels, the fury of vengeance is deaf and cannot hear'.[112] But his rationalism founders when he realises that his own wife and daughter might be caught in the fighting: 'Distraction! Amanda! Seraphina! Whither shall we run? What shall we do to save them?'.[113]

Parkinson's panic dramatizes the inadequacy of theory to guide action in the heat of the moment and implicitly refutes Godwin's 'famous fire cause' in *Political Justice*, an argument for actions based on calculations of general utility rather than personal affections.[114] Parkinson's pessimism is further undercut by the heroic actions of the servant Mozambo, a character who, as Peter J. Kitson has noted, embodies the eighteenth-century 'noble negro' tradition as well as the Enlightenment explosion of that myth.[115] Led by Mozambo, the three men try to circumvent the carnage only to end up in its midst. Mozambo carries Parkinson into the fray, leaving Henry and Edmunds caught in a crossfire where '[n]eutrality and retreat were alike impossible'.[116] Henry impulsively throws himself on the side of the planters and Edmunds follows to defend him. They eventually escape the fighting and find their way back to the plantation, where they witness the planters' brutal retaliation against the insurgents, who are hanged, whipped or burned to death. Disgusted with these 'reciprocal horrors', Henry and Edmunds resolve to leave St. Domingue by the first available ship. Henry later justifies their backing of the planters: 'Hurried on by blind necessity; precluded from the possibility of neutrality; we chose between two terrible alternatives: and how could we have chosen otherwise?'.[117] Henry, however, is on the brink of a re-education.

With the relocation of the action to London in the remaining six books, the reassessment of the force of necessity is transferred to Seraphina, who faces comparable restraints on her will and judgement. Taking its pronouncements on marriage chiefly from Wollstonecraft, *The Daughter* presents gender relations in Britain as continuations of master-slave relations in the West Indies. Seraphina proves herself to be a true daughter of the 'new philosophy' when she describes marriages of interest as 'legalised prostitution', echoing Wollstonecraft's phrase 'legal prostitution', and refuses to play the part of Henry's courtesan while he pursues another woman.[118] In defying her society's view of marriage settlements as 'deeds of bargain and sale' and of female chastity as a 'commodity' on offer to the highest bidder, Seraphina – like other heroines of Jacobin fiction, and indeed like Wollstonecraft herself – stands alone.[119] Considering herself to be Henry's *de facto* wife by virtue of their emotional and sexual connection, she is happy to dispense with the formality of marriage and its 'gingle of mystic phrases' provided Henry reciprocates her affection.[120] Henry, however, is 'the slave of forms and ceremonies' and cannot immediately bring himself to view marriage in Seraphina's radical way, as an 'entire and absolute union of soul' that 'annihilates individuality' and, where wealth is concerned, 'considers the blended stock of both [...] as the common property of each'.[121] In one sense, then, *The Daughter* is the story of Henry's moral reformation, his 'adoption' of Seraphina's principles of 'social equality and reciprocal love' over the prejudices of birth and gender that he has inherited from his father, and indeed his sense of being at the mercy of 'blind necessity'. Like the concept of automatonism in Thelwall's 1820 essay on that subject, Henry's enslavement to 'forms and ceremonies' is a metaphor for a condition of diminished or impaired volition that is not confined to a particular race or gender, but afflicts all those who – whether compelled by whips, apathy or self-interest – are passive in the face of injustice.

But although Seraphina's view of marriage ultimately prevails, her high-minded principles also undergo a profound transformation. When Henry proves fickle she resolves to live in seclusion in Somers Town, the area of London where Wollstonecraft lived with Godwin in 1797, and she gives birth to a daughter who dies almost immediately – an allusion to the death of Thelwall's daughter Maria and symbol of Henry's failed moral rebirth or 'regeneration'.[122] Thereafter, like the 'new Recluse' of Llyswen farm (as Thelwall called himself), Seraphina soon feels a renewed yearning for society.[123] Her sense of isolation compels her to re-examine her convictions in a pivotal passage:

> Alas! educated, as it were, in abstraction, she had considered every question of morality only in an abstract point of view. With a system of action deeply engraved upon her heart, that consulted only the happiness of others, she had not considered how essential to the permanency of our exertions for that happiness, it is to provide for the security of our own; and, with feelings alive to every generous sympathy and emotion, she had never considered that generosity may become bankrupt from too inconsiderate a profusion; and that, when the heart has not wherewithal to support its tranquillity, its benevolence to others must expire in a wish and a sigh.
>
> She mourned therefore alike over her lost utilities and her hopes; and reproached herself, in the bitterness of [her] heart, for having despised too much the prejudices and false opinions of the world, without considering how much opinions (while established,) how-ever false in themselves, must necessarily operate upon the moral and intellectual capabilities of the individuals to whose conduct they may attach.[124]

The heroine thus awakens to the fundamental flaw of Godwinian philosophy: its failure adequately to weigh the influence of domestic affections and public opinion in the balance with individual rational judgement.[125] Her discovery that no woman is an island – symbolized later in the novel by her rescue from a coastal shoal where she is trapped at high tide – is part of the novel's case for a more pragmatic version of political justice.[126]

The Daughter's reassessment of radical ideology culminates in Henry's long-awaited moment of reformation. Having stood by patiently as he failed to act on his virtuous resolutions, Seraphina finally puts him to the test. Will he finally marry her, even if it means incurring the scorn of the fashionable world? Henry deliberates, and then has an epiphany:

> 'The world! – the world!!' repeated he [...]. 'How many of those petty circles we call *worlds* are there upon this little sphere?'
> The thought struck him like electricity.
> His doubts were ended. He rushed to Seraphina. He seized her in his arms; and strained her throbbing heart to his –[127]

Henry experiences a galvanic rebirth, internalizing at last the electrical charge of radical ideology. Yet it has not been because of Seraphina's rational appeals or exemplary conduct, as Arnold A. Markley claims, but because of the conjunction of those appeals with his own experiences that he finally comes to adopt a more judicious world-view.[128] This is in fact the case with many characters in the novel. Montfort's garrulous doctor Pengarron, for instance, recounts 'tales and anecdotes of former times' in a bid to correct anomalies in 'the texture or temporary disposition of the heart' of his patient.[129] Meanwhile, Edmunds and Seraphina at various moments try to reform Henry and his father by means of exhortation. All subscribe (sooner or later) to the belief that expressions of sympathy – whether in stories, tears or conversation – can serve to heal the minds and even the bodies of others. As the narrator asserts,

> They know little of the nature of man, physical or moral, who are sceptics upon this question; – little of the affinities, reciprocations, and dependencies that exist between the corporeal mass, and what is called the intellectual essence! – little of the power of fancy, of sentiment, of passion over the circulation of the fluids, and the tone or relaxation of the fibres.[130]

And yet, if mind-body reciprocity holds out the possibility of effecting radical 'regenerations' by means of language, verbal and bodily, it also reveals them to be highly contingent on a material susceptibility to the transformative stimulus. Indeed, none of the attempted reformations occurs until circumstances are right – until, as Pengarron observes, 'the state of [... the] pulse indicate[s] a predisposition in the constitution'.[131] The novel thus casts into question its own power to catalyse the sorts of reforms that it dramatizes, the 'adoption' of new ways of thinking and acting.

The contingency of such reformations is the subject of an exchange among Henry, Edmunds and Seraphina en route from St. Domingue to England. Edmunds entertains his friends with a poem about the twelfth-century Old Provençal troubadour Jaufré Rudel of Blaye (or 'Jeffrey Rudell') who is credited with creating the theme of *amor de lonh*, or love from afar, after falling in love with the Countess of Tripoli based solely on reports of her beauty and virtue.[132] Edmunds tells of how the poet set out to meet the countess but fell gravely ill on the journey, reaching Tripoli in time to gaze on her once before dying. These events so closely resemble the circumstances of Henry and Seraphina's relationship that, we are told, they cannot help but be moved by the poem:

> Numbers were not requisite, in this instance, nor the embellishments of fancy, to awaken their sympathy. They sympathised relatively, as it were – as the mother sympathises over the sufferings of her child; merely because it does suffer; not like the stranger, who must be tricked into pity by the exaggerations of eloquence and the plaintive harmony of well-arranged syllables.[133]

The passage echoes Adam Smith's definition of sympathy as the sharing of another person's feelings when imagining oneself in the other's situation. Smith illustrates this definition with reference to 'the pangs of a mother, when she hears the moanings of her infant that during the agony of disease cannot express what it feels'. In Smith's view, the mother joins to the infant's suffering her own terror of the unknown consequences of that suffering, and thus forms 'for her own sorrow, the most complete image of misery and distress'.[134] In *The Daughter*, however, the mother who sympathizes with her infant 'merely because it does suffer' is distinguished from the stranger who 'who must be tricked into pity by the exaggerations of eloquence and the plaintive harmony of well-arranged syllables'. The distinction is reinforced by Henry's remark about the story of Rudel that 'as [...] an undoubted truth, it is not incurious. As a fiction, it would be too wild and extravagant to interest the hearer'. Edmunds disagrees: 'Not if the hearer had our experience'.[135] The exchange suggests that a fictional tale is more likely to elicit this kind of spontaneous sympathetic response if its subject intersects with the personal experiences of its audience, or as Thelwall put it in *The Peripatetic*, if the audience is in the grip of 'actual feeling and present experience'.[136] There is, however, an alternative to first-hand experience: that of 'tricking' the audience into sympathy by 'the exaggerations of eloquence and the plaintive harmony of well-arranged syllables'. How far this actually constitutes trickery, and how far it is only a sort of enhanced 'truth to nature', would become one of Thelwall's main preoccupations in the years following the publication of *The Daughter*, when he returned to society as a self-made professor of elocution, prosodist and speech therapist who taught his pupils how to achieve eloquence and harmony in speech and writing.

While calling attention to Thelwall's doubts about rational agency and the power of literary appeals to the sympathetic imagination, I have not meant to suggest that the anti-Jacobin backlash deprived his radical theory of its empirical foundation, thus reducing it to the status of an impossible ideal that was readily assimilable into the 'Romantic ideology' of the canonical poets.[137] Thelwall stands by his belief in human agency within a materialist framework: in a few years he would unambiguously reassert that such agency is indispensible to intellectual, literary and historical progress.[138] But in *The Daughter*, as in *The Hope* and *The Fairy*, he also demonstrates a heightened awareness that the circumstances for such progress must also be propitious. Far from charting an increasing distance from his former activism, Thelwall's turn-of-the-century 'republican romances' dramatize the need to adapt the vitalizing stimulus to the conditions of the body, human and political. In this respect they prefigure his interest over the next three decades in the material dynamics of elicitation and response, and his literary and critical efforts to develop a physiologically informed aesthetics and theory of the imagination.

5

The Language of Nature
Elocutionary Writings and *Poems, Chiefly Suggested by the Scenery of Nature*

> I know of no such distinction as a *verse mouth* and a *prose mouth:* I want only a distinct, a sonorous, an artic-ulative mouth – a mouth that 'is a parcel of the mind'.[1]

On account of his political lectures and speeches at the open-air meet-ings of the London Corresponding Society in the 1790s, Thelwall was widely regarded as one of the most powerful public speakers of the age. Wordsworth thought that he had 'extraordinary talent' and Coleridge regarded him as 'the voice of tens of thousands'.[2] William Hazlitt described him more ambiguously as '[t]he most dashing orator I ever heard', 'the model of a flashy, powerful demagogue – a madman blessed with a fit audience' and 'a volcano vomiting out *lava*'.[3] In James Gillray's iconic depiction of a mass meeting of reformers at Copenhagen Fields in the fall of 1795, Thelwall towers over the crowd from a podium in the foreground, fist pumping the air, lips parted mid-sentence – a posture that recalls his invitation to audiences for his weekly lectures in the Strand to 'take my lungs for a pair of bellows to blow an alchymist's fire withal'.[4] (Figure 5.1) Thelwall prided himself on such spontaneous over-flows of powerful feeling. Rather than compose lectures in tranquillity he spoke from notes and outlines, asserting that 'the clothing and embel-lishments ought to be left to the time of delivery: for that language will always be most emphatic, which the warmth of the moment supplies'.[5]

To his critics, however, the result was merely hot air. Thomas Amyot, a friend of Henry Crabb Robinson, remarked of Thelwall's lectures at Norwich in 1796 that '[h]e raves like a mad Methodist parson':

> the most ranting Actor in the most ranting Character never made so much noise as Citizen Thelwall; his voice tho' sufficiently loud, is

96

coarse & unpleasant & his action seems to have been learned at the School of Mendoza [a renowned boxer] & Co. If it had not been for the feebleness of his Person, I sho.[d] [should] almost have been led to suspect he was going to beat his audience out of doors.[6]

In Isaac D'Israeli's satirical novel *Vaurien; Or, Sketches of the Times* (1797) Thelwall appears as the incendiary 'Mr. Rant', 'the successful rival of orator Henley' – a reference to the eccentric London preacher John Henley (1692–1756) who combined sermonizing with show-manship.[7] Other anti-Jacobin novels portray him as 'Citizen Ego' or 'John Bawlwell'.[8] By contrast, the antiquary and topographer John Britton insisted that '[u]nlike many of the unprincipled and reck-less demagogues of the time, [...] Thelwall, even in the midst of his most eloquent speeches and writing, was select and cautious in his phraseology'.[9]

Paradoxically, it was only once the anti-Jacobin backlash had effec-tively 'gagged' the reform movement – placing a 'padlock [... on] the mouth of an injured people'[10] – that the foremost 'Jacobin' orator turned his attention to the material dynamics of speech, prosody and oratorical performance. Writing in December 1801 to his friend Joseph Strutt, Thelwall remarked,

You would smile to see me in my metamorphose – for I am really quite transformed. [...] In dress, in manners &c. I assimilate myself with all possible diligence to the fashion of the times; assume ~~to myself~~ the pride & port of a man of some importance; & aspire to the reputation of every aristocratical accomplishment. In short as persecution would not suffer me to crawl upon the earth, I am try-ing what can be done by soaring into the clouds. Hitherto I like the experiment vastly. Flying is certainly a more salubrious exercise than creeping – I was not formed to creep.[11]

The notorious radical-turned-farmer was casting off the trappings of rural exile for the accoutrements of respectability. Within a few years he would have sufficiently overcome his dread of honorifics to style himself 'John Thelwall, Esq. Professor of the Science and Practice of Elocution'.[12] Although Thelwall's new aura of respectability and quick-ness to style himself 'Esquire' smack of 'incivism' – as George Saintsbury noted decades ago and others have re-iterated since – he was not aban-doning his principles for profit and 'bourgeois' public acceptance.[13] Just as in 1795 he had responded to the passage of the 'Gagging Acts' by enlisting '*Socrates* and *Plato*, *Tully* and *Demosthenes*' to speak on his behalf, so after 1800 he found in 'that republican talent, eloquence', a new means of promoting democratic principles by teaching his pupils to speak impressively for themselves.[14] A 'correct and impressive elocution is attainable by all', he maintained.[15] Scholarship has called attention to Thelwall's 'logopaedic' aim to reform the body politic by reforming its habits of oral expression.[16] However, the continuity of Thelwall's career before and after 1800 has not only to do with his reformist end, but also with his materialist means.

Around the same time that elocutionists and physiologists were developing a theory of the body's 'natural language',[17] Thelwall was reviving his medical training of the previous decade to investigate the material basis of effective utterance. Elocution, he asserted, was not simply the art of public speaking, but also its science: a 'branch of Natural Philosophy'.[18] A more direct link with his speculations about the principle of life a decade earlier is apparent in his extended metaphor for the various components of verbal expression. Eloquence – the 'Art of expressing our thoughts and feelings, with precision, force, and elegance' in speech or writing – is 'the Soul, or animating principle of Discourse', while elocution – 'the Art, or the Act' of effectively communicating our thoughts and feelings orally – is its 'embodying Form, or representative power'. Oratory, or 'Oral Eloquence', is 'the complicated and vital existence, resulting from the perfect harmony and cooperation of the two'.[19] Therein lay oratory's power, but also its danger. Like Frankenstein's creature, a contemporaneous 'vital existence' remarkable for its powers of speech, oratory had the potential to be sociable or destructive. As this chapter will show, Thelwall's elocutionary teaching, speech therapy and poetry of the early nineteenth century all attest to his awareness of this ambiguous power of oral discourse, as well as to his continuing belief that its pathologies, whether in the form of impairment or intemperance, were the results of error and miseducation, and therefore treatable. In his elocutionary writings as in his unpublished collection *Poems, Chiefly Suggested by the Scenery of Nature*, recovered as part of a three-volume faircopy of his poetry in Derby, England, Thelwall cultivates 'restrained vehemence', a careful coordination of semantic and extra-semantic modes of expression intended to elicit 'a correspondent sympathy in one's audience' without giving way to either 'absurdity' or 'fanaticism'.[20] Notwithstanding Thelwall's emphasis on self-restraint, however, the persistence of his materialist science and radical politics soon threatened to obstruct his newly recovered powers of utterance.

Organic action and reaction: 'Rhythmus' in speech and verse

The physiological underpinnings of Thelwall's elocutionary career are the subject of his *Letter to Henry Cline, Esq. on Imperfect Developments of the Faculties* (1810), a treatise addressed to the long-time friend and fellow democrat whose lectures on anatomy he had attended in the early 1790s. The *Letter to Cline* begins with an account of how Thelwall discovered the 'efficient sources of the melody of the language' while reading, scanning and 'resounding' the poetry of Dryden and Milton before resuming work on *The Hope of Albion* during his residence in Wales.[21] Around the same time, Thelwall made his first therapeutic experiment when a Brecknock hatter, having heard the local gossip that Thelwall was an orator and 'a bit of a conjuror', asked him to cure the speech impediment afflicting his two sons. After determining from an examination of the boys' mouths that their impediment was not anatomical, Thelwall gave them an exercise in recitation that transformed their 'strange and unintelligible jargon' into clear speech.[22] These insights into voice production and prosody, which occurred just as Thelwall was ending his 'retirement', laid the groundwork for his professional self-reinvention. In November 1801 he delivered an inaugural series of lectures on the 'theoretical and practical' foundations of elocution in the north of England, and the following month announced his 'metamorphose' to Strutt.[23] Within a few years he would have cultivated a professional network spanning England and Scotland that included the Glasgow physician and educationist George Birkbeck (after whom Thelwall would name his son Weymouth Birkbeck, born in 1831) and the Edinburgh literary scholar and former surgeon Robert Anderson. Writing to the latter in February 1804, Thelwall announced that his and Birkbeck's 'respective operations & cooperations for spring and summer are projected – & the ensuing winter will witness, I hope, the establishment of both in London'.[24] The following year, inspired no doubt by Birkbeck's mechanics' classes in Birmingham and Glasgow, Thelwall established at Liverpool an Institution for the Cure of Impediments and the Cultivation of English Elocution, relocating it to Russell Square, London, in 1806 – a homecoming of sorts after a decade-long exile from the metropolis – and then to Lincoln's Inn Fields in 1813.[25] The Institution served as a clinic for the treatment of speech defects and a school for children and adults of both sexes.[26] It was also home to the Historical and Oratorical Society, which met weekly for speeches and debates on subjects from English history and literature. Attendees included Godwin, Holcroft, Coleridge, Hazlitt, Robert Southey, Charles Lamb, John ('Major') Cartwright, Thomas Noon Talfourd and Henry Crabb Robinson. So great was the success of Thelwall's Institution that he was eventually able to purchase a carriage, stock a library with some 4,000 volumes and take over the *Champion* newspaper in 1818.[27] His tireless programme of study, lecturing, teaching, therapy and writing ended only with his death in 1834 while on an elocutionary lecture-stop at Bath.

A comprehensive assessment of Thelwall's system has long been complicated by the scattered state of his elocutionary corpus, a vast patchwork of essays, treatises, anthologies and marginalia. His first works on the subject were the multiple editions of *Selections and Original Articles* that he sold at the door of his lectures.[28] These were followed by frequent contributions to the *Monthly Magazine*, his 'usual channel of communication' on elocutionary matters,[29] and four major treatises: *Introductory Discourse on the Nature and Objects of Elocutionary Science* (1805), *A Letter to Henry Cline* (1810), *Illustrations of English Rhythmus* (1812), and *Results of Experience in the Treatment of Cases of Defective Utterance* (1814). Additional essays appeared in the *Medical and Physical Journal*, the *Retrospective Review*, and the *Panoramic Miscellany*, the latter having been launched by Thelwall in 1826 on the model of the *Monthly Magazine*. He also composed nine entries on elocutionary topics for Abraham Rees's *Cyclopaedia; or, a New Universal Dictionary of Arts, Sciences, and Literature* (1819–20).[30] Thelwall claimed that his eight-to-six working day left him no time to consolidate these 'detached portions' of his system into a single work that would allow them to be 'justly appreciated in their connection as a whole'.[31] Of the hundreds of lectures that he delivered across the country articulating many of his core principles, we retain only the outlines.[32] His widow planned to give a 'slight sketch' of his elocutionary system in the second volume of the *Life of John Thelwall*, but that volume was never published and possibly never written.[33] Some of Thelwall's precepts nonetheless lived on in the teaching and publications of his son, the Rev. Algernon Sidney Thelwall, who became the first lecturer on public reading at King's College, London, in 1850, as well as in the phonic primer compiled by Thelwall's daughter Sara Maria.[34]

The phonetician Robin Thelwall (a distant relative of Thelwall's) has found too little detail in the available publications to offer a comprehensive evaluation, while the speech therapist Denyse Rockey has concluded that the key to Thelwall's 'logopaedic' system is missing.[35] There can be no doubt, however, about the importance of what he called the 'principle of rhythmus'. Although the *Oxford English Dictionary* defines 'rhythmus' as a synonym for rhythm deriving from the Latin *rhythmus* (meaning 'a sequence of sounds forming a pattern', especially in speech, verse and music), for Thelwall the term also refers to a conjunction of physiological and prosodic principles.[36] His epigraph to *Illustrations of English Rhythmus* quotes Anthony Ashley Cooper, the Third Earl of Shaftesbury's praise for the 'true Rhythmus, and harmonious Numbers' of Milton and Shakespeare.[37] He was no doubt also familiar with the medical uses of the term, notably to describe modulations of the pulse, and he was probably right to single himself out as one of the few elocutionists of his time to explain rhythmus in terms of 'the indispensable necessities of organic action' rather than attribute it solely to 'election and voluntary taste'.[38] In the *Letter to Cline* Thelwall credits his friend's lectures on anatomy in the early 1790s with instilling the 'habit of thinking and of reasoning physiologically' that he applied to elocution.[39] He ascribes the production of voice to the action of the 'primary organ of speech', the larynx, on streams of air expulsed from the lungs. Modulations of tone, pitch and loudness result from the actions of 'secondary organs' – such as the roof of the mouth, the nostrils, the skull and the chest – with the cooperation of the 'enunciative organs' – the tongue, uvula, lips, gums and teeth – which turn sound into speech.[40] Like all 'reiterated' (as opposed to 'continuous') actions, those of the vocal and enunciative organs are subject to the 'universal law of action and reaction' or 'principle of pendulation':

> for as the pendulum when it has made its full swing in one direction must re-act in the opposite direction, before the primary action can be repeated [...], so when the tongue, lip, or uvula have acted in any given direction for the formation of any given element, it must react silently or expressively either upon the primary, or in some new direction, before the same element can be repeated, or any other element, requiring a similar line of action can be formed.[41]

Following the ancient Greek grammarians, Thelwall designates this 'pulsation' and 'remission' in the speaking body as the 'thesis' and 'arsis', symbolizing them Δ and ∴ respectively. The syllables thus produced are either 'heavy' or 'light' according to their degree of emphasis or what Thelwall calls their 'poise', which he distinguishes from the attributes of quantity, accent, breath and percussion.[42] Whereas the latter can be altered at will, poise is a matter of physical necessity. Any contraction of the organs for the sounding of a 'heavy' syllable must be followed by an expansion that manifests itself as a 'light' syllable or a silent pause.

Thelwall considers this 'law of vocal progress' from heavy to light to be the single most important principle of elocution and the least understood. On the basis of this insight he became one of the period's foremost proponents of 'music-verse' or 'temporal' prosody, an alternative to the long-dominant syllabism that applied classical quantitative metrics to the stress-based rhythms of English. Unlike 'foot-verse' prosodists, who regarded the poetic line not as a fixed number of syllables but as a series 'feet' that admitted of substitutions and vowel elisions, 'music-verse' prosodists like Thelwall defined the poetic line as a sequence of time units or 'bars'. These bars could be composed of a variable number of syllables provided they were isochronous, that is, provided they could all be delivered in the same amount of time.[43] Thelwall calls this the 'law of measured cadences', defining cadence as 'a portion of tunable sound, beginning heavy and ending light'.[44] Many of his strictures and notations approximate those of Joshua Steele, whose *Prosodia Rationalis: or, An Essay towards Establishing the Melody and Measure of Speech* (1779) introduced the concept of a musical rest to account for irregularities in the alternation of stresses in English poetry.[45] Although Thelwall claimed not to have read the *Prosodia* until 1802, when the foundations of his system were already in place,[46] like Steele he places a bar division before each heavy syllable in a line, and he solves the problem of the opening unstressed syllable in iambic pentameter by adding rests to the beginnings and ends of lines, marking them ". His scansion of two lines from Dryden illustrates the result:

```
"  | Arms and the | man, I | sing | who    | forc'd by | fate,  | "
     Δ     ∴    ∴     Δ   ∴   Δ∴    Δ  ∴      Δ     ∴    Δ∴
"  | Aus|picĭous | prince |    at | whose na|tivity  | "  –
   ∴   Δ   ∴      Δ ∴   Δ ∴      Δ    ∴ Δ∴∴ ∴.[47]
```

Each line is thus shown to contain not five iambic feet but a variable number of isochronous cadences, in this case with marked pauses on 'sing', 'who', 'fate', 'prince' and 'at'.[48] In theory, Thelwall contends, a line of English blank verse might contain innumerable cadences so long as they remained isochronous.[49] He instilled these two core principles – the law of measured cadences and the law of vocal progress from heavy to light – through a form of close reading.[50] First he taught his pupils to scan selections of poetry with attention to the 'abstract rhythmus' of each piece, that is, to 'the mere inherent poise and quantities of the syllables'. Next he had them tackle 'rhetorical rhythmus', taking account of 'rhetorical emphasis, or grammatical pause'.[51] Finally he guided them in the analysis of prose, which, in prosodic terms, differed from verse only by the more erratic arrangement of its cadences. Through this process his pupils learned the 'plain principle' that 'heavy poise, always, pertains to the potential significance'.[52]

Thelwall's use of a time-beater to accompany his pupils' recitations (as on the occasion of a staged recitation of *Comus* by a group of stutterers) has led some to describe his system as 'metronomic', while his dictum 'read as you would speak' has led others to think that he was insensitive to the effects of poetic metre.[53] The misapprehension seems to have originated with Wordsworth, who in a letter of January 1804 addressed what he conceived to be the key difference between his and Thelwall's systems. Referring to an untraced letter from Thelwall he wrote, 'I must correct one error you have fallen into, [ov]er verse mouth and prose mouth. I never used [such] phrases in my life, and hold no such opinions'.[54] The distinction actually originated with Francis Jeffrey's scathing attack on Wordsworth's Preface to *Lyrical Ballads*, which formed part of his review of Robert Southey's *Thalaba the Destroyer* (1801). Jeffrey had attributed to Southey the remark that even the dullest reader could not distort his poem's versification: 'he may read it with a *prose mouth*, but its flow and fall will still be perceptible'. Quoting a few stanzas of *Thalaba*, Jeffrey remarked that it was doubtful 'whether even a *poet's mouth* could turn these passages into good verse'.[55] In responding to Thelwall's query about these remarks, Wordsworth took the opportunity to remark of his friend's prosody,

> [Y]our general rule is just that the art of verse should not compell [*sic*] you to read in [tone? some?] emphasis etc that violates the nature of Prose. But this rule should be taken with limitations for not to speak of other reasons as long as verse shall have the marked termination that rhyme gives it, and as long as blank verse shall be printed in lines, it will be Physically impossible to pronounce the last words or syllables of the lines with the same indifference, as the others, or to follow them with a pause, not called out for by the passion of the subject, but by the passion of metre merely.[56]

Wordsworth is not wrong about Thelwall's 'general rule', but his inference that his friend had no notion of the 'passion of metre' as distinct from the 'passion of the subject' is misleading. Thelwall in fact discouraged 'artificial and measured formality' in favour of 'flexure and harmonic variety'. His dictum 'read as you would speak' was based on the belief that

> [w]hat is connected in the mind, must be connected with equal intimacy by the voice; and what, in the mind, is transposed, interrupted, or suspended, must be separated, interrupted, or suspended, in the mode of articulation.

The dictum applied as much to verse as to prose. Alluding to Wordsworth's letter and Jeffrey's review of Southey, Thelwall observes in *Illustrations of English Rhythmus*,

> I know of no such distinction as a *verse mouth* and a *prose mouth:* I want only a distinct, a sonorous, an articulative mouth – a mouth that 'is a parcel of the mind', and of a mind that can identify itself with its author, or its subject, and modulate its tones and motions accordingly; so that the manner may be a comment upon the matter – whether that matter be in verse or in prose.[57]

Thelwall's call for 'a mouth that "is a parcel of the mind"' recalls Sir Hugh Evans's remark in Shakespeare's *The Merry Wives of Windsor* that 'the lips is *parcel* of the *mind*', and also evokes the reference to those lines in John Horne Tooke's materialist treatise on language *The Diversions of Purley*. Towards the beginning of this Socratic dialogue, the author's mouthpiece 'H' and his interlocutors 'B' and 'T' are discussing Locke's theory of language when 'B' asks what difference it would have made if Locke had been more cognizant of the inseparable connection between words and knowledge – that '"the lips is *parcel* of the *mind*"'.[58] Although Thelwall did not share Tooke's opinion that the operations of the mind could be explained strictly in terms of the operations of language, a point addressed more fully in the next chapter, his allusion to Tooke's materialist linguistics reminds us that what is missing from existing assessments of his prosody is a sense of its connection with his own materialist views on the coordination of mind and body in the elicitation of 'passion'.

Speaking one's mind

Thelwall's notion of the mouth as 'parcel of the mind' serves to describe an ideal of oral communication that depends on 'the law of universal sympathy between the executive and perceptive organs', which manifested itself in 'all the phenomena of vital action and vital perception'.[59] His views on the treatment of impaired speakers help clarify the implications of this 'law'. Although Thelwall required the assistance of an artificial set of teeth to correct the impediment that had earned him the nickname 'Lisping Orator', he considered that the vast majority of speech impediments were the results not of anatomical defects, but of 'mental and moral maladies' such as 'embarrassment of mind' or 'irritability of temper', which misdirected or 'overstrained' the speaker's volition.[60] Noting that 'medicine was never yet radical in the removal of diseases of the mind', and that '[t]he imagination, the judgment, and the passions, require other physicians than the pupils of Galen and Hippocrates',[61] Thelwall recommended a programme of re-education:

> Remove the mental and moral maladies [...] that are, in reality, the immediate causes of so many serious impediments; restore, or produce those essential links of association, between the physical perception and the mental volition, and between the mental volition and the organic action, which either have some how been broken, or have never properly been formed – and the stammerer, the stutterer, the throttler, the endless reiterator, and almost the whole order of unfortunate persons, whose impediments consist in *obstructed* utterance, are relieved from their affliction[.][62]

Squarely contradicting the notion that Thelwall's system 'suffered the limitations of a mechanistic philosophy' and 'was concerned with only the externals of delivery, with physiology and not with psychology', the passage articulates his system's underlying materialist premise: the interdependence of the mind and body by way of the 'essential links of association' that coordinate perception, volition and muscular action.[63] A break in those links produces a form of 'idiotcy' or 'derangement', for, as Thelwall puts it to Cline, 'what but derangement can it be called, to be constantly doing a thousand things that we neither intend to do, nor are conscious of doing? nay, that are the very reverse of all that is in our intention!'.[64] Impairment is thus figured as a form of automatonism in which the body takes control of the mind, turning the speaker into a stammering, stuttering, throttling or reiterating machine. The analogy anticipates Thelwall's 'Essay on Human Automatonism' of 1820, discussed in Chapter 4, in which he speculates semi-facetiously that we are all 'mere machines – speaking automatons, whose very words are breathed thro' us, as thro' an organ-pipe, inflated by some exterior agency, and stopped or played upon by the finger of a capricious destiny'.[65] The metaphor may have been inspired by Erasmus Darwin's invention of a speaking machine consisting of 'a wooden mouth with lips of soft leather, and with a valve over the back part of it for nostrils, both [of] which could be quickly opened or closed by the pressure of the fingers'.[66] By contrast, Thelwall's ideal orator is at once orchestra and conductor of his own performance, his voice a 'concert of many instruments, whose respective powers and characteristic tones are exceedingly different from each other'.[67]

As speech therapist and elocutionist, Thelwall thus offered a radical and materialist re-articulation of some of the core assumptions and objectives of the eighteenth-century 'new elocutionary movement', which had begun in the 1760s with the aim of rescuing public speaking from a perceived state of decline.[68] For all its leading contributors – namely Thomas Sheridan, Hugh Blair, James Burgh and Joseph Priestley – spoken language was superior to written language (or 'secondary speech') because of its greater affective power.[69] Sheridan asserted that spoken language was a 'gift of God' which had the power of creating bonds of sympathy among individuals provided it was delivered 'naturally', that is, without the 'false pauses and rests' that modern punctuation had introduced.[70] According to this 'natural' view of elocution, a speech-like delivery was democratic because it facilitated mutual understanding; by contrast, an elevated and incantatory style was potentially anti-democratic because it could serve to overawe or enchant listeners rather than communicate openly with them.[71] Sheridan and others in the 'natural' school insisted on the persuasive force of genuine sentiments: rules of accentuation, pronunciation and emphasis were useful as guides to public speaking, but the speaker's natural inclinations were paramount.[72] Thelwall, too, inveighs against all forms of monotonous or 'chaunting' delivery, including what he called the 'bellman' style (after Andrew Bell, a contemporary elocutionist who encouraged chanting), the 'Clerical Drawl' and the 'Cathedral Chaunt'.[73] With these labels Thelwall is criticizing orthodox Anglicanism and its endorsement of the mesmeric potential of elocution, as Lucy Newlyn has noted.[74] He is probably also obliquely criticizing the recitation styles of Wordsworth and Coleridge, whose 'chaunting' was described by Hazlitt as 'act[ing] as a spell upon the hearer, and disarm[ing] the judgment'.[75] (Thelwall would likewise later remark in the margins of the *Biographia Literaria* that Coleridge's recitation was 'frequently contaminated by his own abominable singsong drawl of delivery'.[76]) Thelwall's principal target, however, is the obfuscating use of language that he had once associated with 'aristocratical declaimers' like Burke.[77] Reviving the terms of his mid-1790s disputes with Burke about the competing claims of natural rights and 'Gothic' custom, Thelwall compares educators who 'flog their pupils into an arbitrary mode of scanning' with 'drowzy monastics' of the past who clung irrationally to the 'pedantic technicalities of established usage' and *'the wisdom of their ancestors'*.[78] He maintains, moreover, that learning to speak one's native tongue fluently and impressively is the duty of every Englishman who wishes to participate in the 'great business of life':

> when we have seen this mighty nation, wielded, almost despotically, for twenty years, by a flow of swelling periods, rendered impressive and captivating, by the force of a well-cultivated voice, and the harmony of a well-regulated cadence, – surely, we may expect – that, some time or other, the Measure and Melody of English Speech will be thought as worthy of comprehension and cultivation, as the Prosodies of Greek and Latin authors[.][79]

By becoming better attuned to the mechanisms of speech and the affective power of cadence – cultivating what Thelwall once called 'practical fluency'[80] – Britons might equip themselves to resist the 'flow of swelling periods' that held them captive. If he was now helping to 'assimilat[e]' his pupils to the institutions of 'bourgeois' public life[81] – parliament, the church and the law courts – he was also equipping them to reform those institutions from within, through eloquent, impressive speech.

While Thelwall follows the 'natural' elocutionists in insisting that a speaker's delivery will be all the more effective if he actually feels the passions that he wishes to convey, he nonetheless allows a role for 'art' in the management of those passions.[82] The object of exciting 'a correspondent sympathy' in one's audience justifies the recourse to tone, look and gesture, which some deem '[t]heatrical affectations, and meretricious artifices'.[83] No doubt glancing at critiques of his own performative oratory, Thelwall maintains that tone, look and gesture are 'essential parts of the original language of Nature':

> when really actuated by any strong and genuine emotion, the tone becomes affected; the physiognomy assumes a sympathetic expression; and, bursting through the boundaries of fashion, and the chains of unnatural torpor, each limb and muscle struggles with inspiring passion; and, with efforts, rude and imperfect (because untutored

and unaccustomed,) endeavours to enforce upon the eye, what the words of the Orator are labouring to communicate to the ear.[84]

Thelwall's defence of performative oratory as consistent with the 'natural' or instinctive impulses of the body exemplifies what Jay Fliegelman and Patricia Howell Michaelson have described as the paradox of the 'new' elocutionists' recommendation of acting naturally.[85] He approvingly cites Sheridan's assertion that the 'passions and fancy have a language of their own' that is 'utterly independent of words'.[86] He likewise echoes ideas about the body's 'natural language' put forward by the physician Matthew Baillie (nephew of John Hunter), who in a lecture of 1794 had explained that the

> different emotions of the mind are also conveyed along nerves to different muscles of the body [...]. Each emotion [...] sets in action its appropriate muscles, producing a change in the countenance and attitude, which is expressive of emotion. This becomes a natural language, and is not connected with any arbitrary customs of society.[87]

For Thelwall, too, elocution is a matter of re-learning what 'nature' has imparted and society has failed to nurture. Vocal and physical 'bursts of action' appear ridiculous only because 'the Dulness [*sic*] and Indolence of modern Elocutionists', combined with a faulty education system, have prohibited their cultivation. When properly managed, however, they can be 'temperate, graceful and expressive' – indeed, virtually natural.[88] This is especially true of spontaneous speech. Taking issue with the schoolmaster William Cockin's recommendation of different styles of delivery for reading, recitation and spontaneous speech, Thelwall argues that the first two should aim for the naturalness of the third, which alone can produce the 'warmth, ease, and flowing energy' necessary to 'awaken the genuine sympathies of the soul'.[89]

In the 1790s the 'genuine sympathies of the soul' had been the basis for Thelwall's appeals to a mass plebeian public, whom he expected to regulate their conduct by their inherent benevolence, as Jon Mee has observed.[90] After 1800, however, Thelwall expresses a heightened sense of the potential for the enthusiasm of the orator and his audience to go astray. This change of emphasis within an otherwise consistent commitment to 'the enfranchisement of fettered organs' has been underestimated in criticism to date.[91] We saw signs of the shift in *The Hope of Albion*, where Thelwall describes reactionary mob enthusiasm using the same metaphors of electrical communication that he had applied to radical discourse in the 1790s. He is even more explicit about the possible consequences of a too-warm delivery in his *Cyclopaedia* entry for 'emotion', where he observes that is it not always 'safe and proper to throw the reins on the neck of feeling, and leave it to make its way to the goal, by its own independent energies'. One risks affecting one's audience too little by displaying 'frigid affectation', or too much by fall-ing into 'coarseness, indecorous vehemence, or bombast'.[92] Similarly, in his entry for 'enthusiasm', Thelwall notes that this 'species of rapturous elevation and fervour' is capable of producing the 'highest impressions' of elocution, but also its worst excesses. Among the 'enlightened and educated portions of the community', a mismanaged enthusiasm will prove impotent or absurd, while among the uneducated, the mere semblance of enthusiasm will tend to inflame the passions, producing 'bigotry and fanaticism'.[93]

Such remarks betray a definite unease about the elicitation of the passions: an anxious sense of how easily they can misfire, giving way to 'absurdity' or 'bigotry and fanaticism'. Enthusiasm, in particular, is 'a state of feeling, at once so potent and so evanescent' that only 'persons of superior genius' should attempt to communicate it. Doing so effectively is a matter of 'restrained vehemence': the orator 'spreads the undulations of sound through an extended circle' without giving leeway to 'any of the disgusting effects of vociferation'. In terms of voice production, enthusiasm calls for 'a deep and powerful aspira-tion' and 'an increase of quantity in all the syllables'; in terms of gesture, it is typically accompanied by 'a considerable dilatation of the nostrils, a protrusion of the eye-balls, and great tension and rigid-ity of the whole muscular system'. The result of this combination of power and restraint is an enthusiasm 'allied' to 'genuine sublimity' that is capable of producing 'the highest impressions that can result from human eloquence'.[94] In such passages, Thelwall sustains his reformist interest in the communication of enthusiasm, but with new emphasis on the need for 'restrained vehemence' in speakers and audiences alike – an emphasis that can be traced to the revolution-ary and counter-revolutionary excesses of the previous decade. This is the case not only in his elocutionary writings, however, but also in his prolific poetry of this period. In those little-known compositions we see Thelwall applying the principles of rhythmus and 'restrained vehemence' to spread 'undulations' of sound and sympathy among readers; we also see how, even in that seemingly innocuous form, the persistence of his reformist and materialist convictions threatened to obstruct his new career.

Poetry and the 'pulse of thought'

Thelwall's remarks on 'restrained vehemence' in the *Cyclopaedia* apply just as much to speech as to poetry, the 'very soul and essence' of which he identifies as enthusiasm.[95] Its ubiquity in his elocutionary works and methods suggests that he regarded it as an oral art form that partook, like speech, of the advantages of 'promptitude – accommodation to active purposes – impressive force – sympathetic excitement'.[96] His renewed interest after 1800 in using poetry as a stimulus of such excitement are on display in the unpublished collection *Poems, Chiefly Suggested by the Scenery of Nature*. Although he mentions the collection in his newspaper the *Champion*, where some of its contents eventually appeared, it was not known to exist until 2004, when it came to light as part of the three faircopy volumes of Thelwall's poetry in Derby.[97] Comprising revisions of earlier works and at least 25 new poems composed around 1803 to 1805 as Thelwall launched his elocutionary career, the *Scenery of Nature* collection has been read as an attempt to recapture his early 'peripatetic' muse and rival Wordsworthian nature poetry.[98] Whatever the intention, the result was to showcase his formal and prosodic ingenuity. A note in the Derby manuscript probably added near the end of Thelwall's life calls for a 'twofold arrangement' of the poems, 'first as to their respective classes or species; & then the individual poems of each class chronologically'. The 'classes' were to centre on Thelwall's odes and sonnets, 'Beginning for an obvious reason with the Anacreontics; then the Paphiads; then perhaps the Blank verse odes [...]; then the Odes in General; then the Sonnets'. The chronology was to range from his juvenilia of 1787, through the poetry of *The Peripatetic* and the *Confinement* collection, to the new compositions of 1803 to 1805.[99] In addition to meditations 'on the scenery of nature' properly speaking (for instance, 'Mirfield', 'A Farewell to the Dale of Kent'), the new compositions would have included conversational addresses to friends and family ('Ode to Paley', 'Ode to Edward Rushton', 'Hannah's Eye', 'Sonnet to Stella'), playfully erotic addresses to his wife (the Anacreontic odes and 'Paphiads'), reflections on ageing ('The Stormy Voyage of Life', 'The First Grey Hair'), and comic light verse ('Epistle from an Orator to his Dentist', 'Pegasus O'erladen', 'Draw Your Yellow Stockings On').

While the collection as a whole merits wider attention, in the context of Thelwall's attempts after 1800 to demonstrate and elicit affective responses through performances of virtuously self-regulated sympathy, a few poems are especially noteworthy. One is the 'Proem' that was to open the collection. Thelwall later described it as offering a 'faithful history not only of the dawn and progress of a poetic mind, but of the means by which the moral and intellectual energies of such a mind may be nursed and nurtured'.[100] As such a history, the 'Proem' invites comparison with *Lyrical Ballads* (especially the contemplative 'Tintern Abbey') and *The Prelude*, as Judith Thompson has shown,[101] but it bears a distinctly materialist stamp. It appears in two versions in the Derby manuscript, an earlier version probably composed around 1804 (like many of the adjacent poems), and a later version dating from around 1820, when Thelwall published it in the *Champion* under the title 'Sylvanus; or, the Pupil of the Groves'.[102] The earlier version revises a poem from *The Peripatetic* about Thelwall's youth ('Me, from my infant years, the inspiring Muse'), to which it adds some 50 blank-verse lines that present the *Scenery of Nature* collection as a tour through Thelwall's poetic corpus, emphasizing the constancy of his fascination with the operations of sympathy in the natural and social world. Readers will first revisit Thelwall's 'young mellifluous warblings' about 'Love', 'Friendship' and 'Philanthropy' – an allusion to his 1787 collection *Poems on Various Subjects* and *The Peripatetic*. Next they will turn to scenes of 'riper manhood' when the Muse, her voice 'half-untuned / By the soul-racking woes that long supprest / Her tuneful cadenza', still sang the 'strain of Nature' and 'social sympathy' – an allusion to the *Confinement* and *Retirement* collections. The reader will then discover 'sprightlier measures' and 'tales of Merriment, to chace the gloom / Of agonis'd remembrance' – no doubt a reference to the 'attempts at humour' that were to form part of the *Scenery of Nature* collection.[103] In the later version of the 'Proem', Thelwall shifts to the third person and prefaces the review of his poetic corpus with some 100 lines that recount how love of nature leads to love of man through the intermediary of a bardic imagination acutely responsive to the material stimuli of sight and sound. In childhood, the muse speaks to him 'Not in smooth sounds, but secret influences' of the natural world: 'The wild rack of clouds, / The meteor, or the morning's glittering dew, / [...] Such were to him visions of rapture – things / That clinging to his childish fancy / Begat strange after thoughts'. In youth, such scenes awaken the 'social thoughts and kindred sympathies / That link us to our kind'. In adulthood, he begins to hear the Muse whisper of the 'eternal consonance of sounds and things'. There follows the chronological account of Thelwall's poetry, as per the earlier version, and the 'Proem' concludes with an invitation to the reader to retrace these paths and 'draw from social sympathy the lore / Of soul-expanding science'.[104]

The materialist valence of Thelwall's 'science' of sympathy is apparent in the essay 'On the Influence of the Scenery of Nature on the Intellectual and Moral Character, as well as on the Taste and Imagination', which accompanied the version of the 'Proem' that Thelwall published in the *Champion* in 1820. The essay defends an associationist understanding of cognition whereby 'it is from without that we have imbibed whatever is within us; and present scenery and present associations have always a certain influence on the current of our feelings'. On this basis Thelwall asserts that urban and rural scenery tend to affect the mind in different ways. Although our 'principles' remain unchanged in the country, 'the pulse of thought beats differently' there: 'we are not less patriotic, [...] but we are more philosophical, [...] as well as more poetical'. Thelwall's striking phrase 'the pulse of thought' suggests an awareness of recent insights into the complex structure and capacities of the brain. In a lecture of 1817, for instance, the surgeon Astley Cooper – Thelwall's friend and prospective post-mortem recipient of his heart – described the 'small but very numerous' blood vessels that nourished the brain.[105] The 'pulse of thought' captures this sense of how brain and body are connected by the arterial networks of the body. Thus, while continuing to endorse an associationist approach to cognition, Thelwall also shares the emergent brain science's sense of that organ's dynamism and creativity.

A recurrent motif for the embodied mind in the *Scenery of Nature* collection is the passionate body of the poet-orator. The motif has a decidedly erotic inflection in the Anacreontic odes and 'Paphiads' that were to feature prominently in the collection. The name of the latter alludes to the mythical birthplace of Aphrodite, while the former were convivial and often erotic poems or drinking songs in the manner of the Greek poet Anacreon, popularized in the eighteenth century by Thomas ('Anacreon') Moore.[106] Whereas in the prison collection of 1795 the Anacreontic ode had figured as a song of defiance, in the *Scenery of Nature* collection Thelwall plays on the form's erotic conventions in amorous addresses to his wife Susan, trading the intoxication of drink for that of desire:

> Let others press the maddening grape,
>   And quaff the vintage, blushing red;
> Be mine the soft bewitching shape; –
>   The blush o'er yielding beauty spread.
>
> The kindling joy, the thrilling pain,
>   Alike to every sense are dear,

> Nor, Venus, – would I break thy chain,
>   For all Silenus' group revere.[107]

Although Thelwall's subsequent addition of stanzas addressed to his second wife Henrietta Cecil, more than thirty years his junior, make it tempting to read the Anacreontics and 'Paphiads' as expressions of unbridled libido and attempts to rekindle a diminishing sexual and political vitality,[108] Thelwall is keen to stress that his mind remains firmly in control of the potentially intemperate responses of his body:

> But <u>temper</u> me the Teian bowl!
>   And chasten me the Teian shell!
> The visions that in memory roll
>   Are such as Nature's bosom swell.
>
> Nor, lawless, thro the realms of Love,
>   Where native Venus lights the way,
> Shall yet excursive Fancy rove, –
>   Inebriate with the wanton lay.[109]

Beyond the Anacreontic odes and 'Paphiads', we find performances of virtuous self-restraint in the various poems addressed to Thelwall's female pupils and friends. In 'To Miss Grahame' – composed in Glasgow on 23 January 1804 and possibly addressed to the daughter of the lawyer and poet James Graham – Thelwall's 'tale of woes' elicits from his young listener a sympathizing look that rouses 'warm' erotic feelings, but he promptly turns away to think instead of his wife and young daughters:

> Enchanting maid! as o'er thy form.
>   In holiest rapture, roves my eye,
> I feel the father – struggling – warm,
>   And (homeward glancing) heave the sigh.[110]

Similarly, in 'To Miss Bannatine', also composed at Glasgow in March 1804, Thelwall laments his falling out with a mutual friend of theirs, which hinders the deepening of their acquaintance. Miss Bannatine reminds Thelwall of a younger version of his wife, but, lest she doubt his motives, he promptly assures her, 'I could love thee, with a father's heart'.[111]

A more prosodically complex expression of virtuous sympathy is Thelwall's 'Sonnet to Stella (in the Style of Ossian)', composed in 1803 as he travelled through the Scottish borders to lecture at Edinburgh. Later publishing the poem as 'Ode from the Land of Mountains' in *The Vestibule of Eloquence*, he describes it as a 'metrical experiment' in 'methodizing the incoherent rhythmus of Ossian', the third-century Scottish Highlands bard whose works were fraudulently 'translated' by James Macpherson in 1760–63, and whose style was thought to epitomize the 'plain and venerable manner' of ancient poetry and 'rapid conciseness' of its images.[112] The result is 'one of the most complicated illustrations [of rhythmus] that can come within the ascertainable limits of versification'.[113] In *The Vestibule of Eloquence* Thelwall uses notations of long and short (¯ and ˘) to indicate syllabic quantity, together with marks of 'grammatical pause' (Figure 5.2).[114] In teaching pupils at his Institution, Thelwall used an even more complicated system of musical notation 'from the minim to the semiquaver, or from the semibreve to the quaver', to indicate 'the respective proportions of every syllable'.[115] A version of such notation is preserved in the Derby manuscript (Figure 5.3).

In both presentations, 'Ode from the Land of Mountains' attests not only to 'the precision with which Thelwall's ear was accustomed to work', but more specifically to his development of prosody that can be described as 'organic' if we bear in mind Alan Richardson's point that, before Coleridge connected the term with a transcendent psyche, it referred to the body and its material organization.[116] From the ambiguous first word 'It', the poem effects a three-way association among possible antecedents: the 'voice of songs' that Thelwall hears in the mountains, the voice of his wife as she mourns his absence at their home in Kendal and the voice of the poem itself, a poetical and prosodic re-enactment of the other two. Like the voices of Stella and the mountains, the poem 'whisper[s] of delight and peace' with rich internal rhymes (e.g., sounding/wing), assonances (wing/wind) and alliterations ('murmur the soft message'). The alliterations involve mainly 'liquids' (especially M, V and W), to which Thelwall attributed gracefulness of composition, and 'semi-liquids' (especially B), to which he attributed energy.[117] Given his belief that the most passionate or expressive music has the most varied cadences, and the most peaceful has the most regular, his ode apparently aims for a middle effect: it is regular in its alternation of lines of five or six 'heavy' syllables and lines of only three, and it is varied in the number of cadences per line and of syllables per cadence.[118] In all of these ways the ode seeks to achieve what Thelwall would later describe as 'a liquid melody capable of all diversities of expression – a music of its own'.[119] Its 'pulse of thought' beats in unison with the speaker's heartfelt

IT is the | voīce of | sōngs, |ĕchŏïng frŏm thĕ |Lānd of | Mŏuntāins; |
 Its | warblings ăre thĕ | brēath of | Lŏve. | | |
It | calleth, ĭn ĭts | speed,⌐ fŏr thĕ | soūndĭng | wĭngs of | eagles; |
 It would | rival the | trăck of | wĭnds. | | |
It | flē-eth to the | faithful | bōsŏm | ⌐ of the be|loved : |
 To the | pillow ŏf | tēndēr | thōughts : | | |
There | fain would it | mūrmūr |⌐ the soft | message ŏf thĕ | hēart; |
 There | whisper ŏf dĕ|light⌐ and | pēace. | | |

Thou art the |sunbeam ŏf thĕ|wintĕry |sōul,⌐| mōurner of | absence! |
 Even | thou⌐ the be|loved ŏf mў | hēart ! | | |

The | sunbeam of | jōy⌐ | scattĕring thĕ | stōrmў | clouds, |
 And il|lumĭning thĕ | mountain | path. | | |
Thy | image ĭs bĕ|fore me⌐ ĭn thĕ | lōvelў | trăck of | light, |
 And thy | vōice⌐ ĭn thĕ | mōanĭng | wĭnd. | | |
For | sad⌐ are the | moanings ŏf mў | Lŏve,⌐| lonely | lingĕring ! |
 And | mournful⌐ the | lustre ŏf hĕr | eўe. | | |

When—|when will ye | cēase, ⌐|storm clouds of | wāywārd | destiny ! |
 En|veloping our | jōys no | more ? | | |
Ah!—|when shall the | dark-chilling | vapours,⌐| lightly | scattĕring, |
 Dis|perse from the | hĭlls of | distance ? | | |
When,⌐| welcome tŏ thĕ | wāy-wōrn | fōot of the | lōnely | wandĕrer |
 Shall the | vale of de|light ex|pand ? | | |
Oh! | sunbeam ŏf thĕ | hēart !⌐ |⌐ shine | forth ŭpŏn mў | dreams ! |
 And be | present⌐ ĭn thĕ | visions ŏf thĕ | day ! |

Figure 5.2 Thelwall, 'Ode from the Land of Mountains', in *The Vestibule of Eloquence*, pp. 160–1. Reproduced by permission of the HCL Widener Library

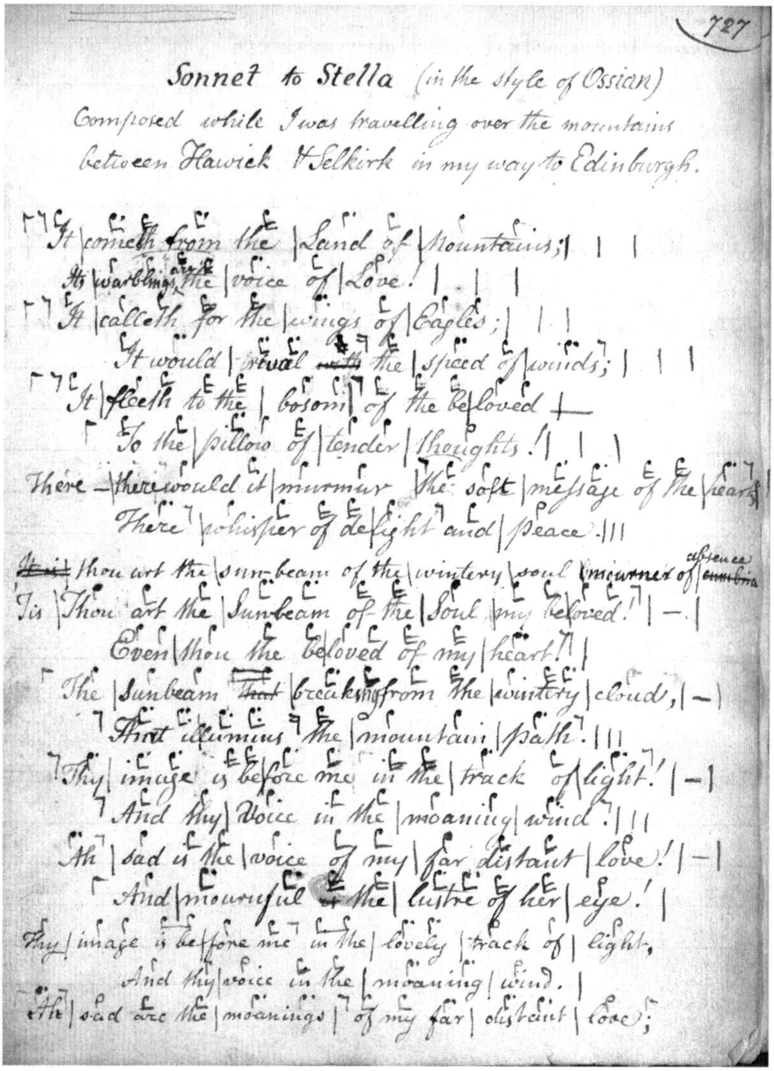
727

Sonnet to Stella (in the style of Ossian)

Composed while I was travelling over the mountains between Hawick & Selkirk in my way to Edinburgh.

It cometh from the Land of Mountains;
Its warblings are the voice of Love!
It calleth for the wings of Eagles;
It would rival with the speed of winds;
It fleeth to the bosom of the beloved +
To the pillow of tender thoughts!
There — there would it murmur the soft message of the heart
There whisper of delight and peace.
~~Tis~~ thou art the sun-beam of the wintery soul mourner of absence
'Tis Thou art the Sunbeam of the Soul, my beloved! —
Even thou the beloved of my heart!
The Sunbeam ~~that~~ breaking from the wintery cloud, —
That illumines the mountain path.
Thy image is before me in the track of light! —
And thy Voice in the moaning wind.
Ah sad is the voice of my far distant love! —
And mournful the lustre of her eye!
Thy image is before me in the lovely track of light,
And thy voice in the moaning wind.
Ah sad are the moanings of my far distant love;

Figure 5.3 Thelwall, 'Sonnet to Stella (in the Style of Ossian)', in Derby manuscript, vol. II, p. 727. Reproduced by permission of the Derby Local Studies Library

wish that the storms of 'wayward destiny' will yield place to the domestic warblings of 'delight and peace'.

It was Thelwall's hope that the *Scenery of Nature* collection as a whole would inspire such 'delight and peace' in readers, thanks partly to its themes of love, sympathy and social harmony, and partly to its respect for the organic necessity of action and reaction in the speaking body. Yet, notwithstanding the emphasis on virtuously 'restrained vehemence' in Thelwall's poetry and elocutionary career in the early 1800s, both would prove deeply suspect – as the very journey that produced the 'Ode from the Land of Mountains' revealed. On the first night of his elocutionary lectures in Edinburgh, Thelwall was interrupted by raucous laughter from several parts of the room. Although he could not see the instigator, who apparently cued his 'confederates' from behind a screen at the end of the lecturer's platform, he blamed the 'conspiracy' on Francis Jeffrey, whose acerbic review of *Poems, Chiefly Written in Retirement* had appeared in the *Edinburgh Review* the previous year.[120] (In fact the instigator was Walter Scott's friend William Erskine, who regarded Thelwall as a 'traitor'.[121]) Thelwall was so confident of Jeffrey's guilt that in January 1804 he published *A Letter to Francis Jeffray* [*sic*], which accused him of orchestrating the interruptions to hinder Thelwall's professional self-reinvention. Yet it becomes clear from the ensuing pamphlet war between them that what irked Jeffrey even more than Thelwall's pretension to gentility was the still-beating materialist 'pulse' of his thought and poetry.

In *A Letter to Francis Jeffray* Thelwall explains that the disturbance took place on the night of his inaugural lecture 'On the Importance of Elocution in a Moral and Intellectual Point of View'.[122] A first interruption occurred when he remarked that the power of induction – 'the power of remembering, comparing, and drawing conclusions' – was shared by even the lowest forms of animal life. A few more minor interruptions culminated in the 'grand assault' at the 'climax' of his argument, when he asserted that the capacity for discourse made humans uniquely capable of moral improvement because it triggered their sympathetic imaginations:

> Hence from the central throb of individual impulse, the feeling expands to the immediate circle of relative connections; – from relatives to friends and intimate associates; from intimate association to the neighbourhood where we reside – to the country for which we would bleed! – from the patriot community to civilized society – to the human race – to posterity – to the sentient universe: and wherever

the throb of sensation can exist, the Virtuous find a motive for the regulation of their actions.
Such are the expanding undulations of virtuous sympathy.[123]

Thelwall's account of how individual feeling inevitably leads to universal benevolence by way of discourse directly echoes his earlier 'Jacobin' assertions about the powers of the sympathetic imagination to connect the individual with 'the whole intellectual universe', as well as his confidence in the powers of his own words to catalyse that process.[124] In a letter of September 1795 to his wife Thelwall had noted with pride that his lectures in the Strand had 'shaken the pillars of corruption, till every stone of the rotten edifice trembled. Every sentence darted from breast to breast with electric contagion[.]'[125] His remarks on the 'expanding undulations of sympathy' merely swap the overtly political metaphor of 'electric contagion' for the seemingly anodyne but nonetheless materialist ones of 'throb[s]' and 'undulations'.[126]

The radical-materialist connotations of Thelwall's ideas about speech and sympathy were not lost on Jeffrey. In an earlier review he had taken issue with Thelwall's 'undisguised [...] defence of materialism' in the 1793 paper 'On the Origin of Sensation'.[127] Now, in his anonymous *Observations on Mr. Thelwall's Letter to the Editor of the Edinburgh Review* (1804), Jeffrey refuses to retract his allegation of materialism and explicitly yokes that position to radical politics, designating Thelwall as 'The Champion of Materialism, the Orator of Chalk Farm, and the Committee Man of the London Corresponding Society'.[128] Equally telling is Jeffrey's distaste for two of the works that Thelwall recited at his lectures: William Collins's ode 'The Passions' and Thelwall's own 'Massacre of Bangor', an excerpt from *The Hope of Albion* that includes the electrical 'hermetic hand' metaphor for political discourse discussed in the previous chapter.[129] Jeffrey remarks that anyone who has heard Thelwall recite these passages will understand that the disruption of his lecture was a result not of political malice but of the 'irresistibly ludicrous' nature of the performance.[130] In fact, it seems likely that Jeffrey singles out these works because they both describe the process of expansive sympathetic response that was the focus of the accompanying lecture.[131] In an indignant *Reply to the Calumnies, Misrepresentations, and Literary Forgeries Contained in the Anonymous Observations on His Letter to the Editor of the Edinburgh Review* (1804), Thelwall responds in particular to Jeffrey's charge of materialism against his 1793 paper 'On the Origin of Sensation', insisting that 'it was not the *Essay* that was objectionable to the [*Physical*] Society, but the *Essayist* who had become obnoxious to *certain individuals*[.]'[132] Yet he is clearly protesting too much. As this chapter has tried to show, Thelwall's elocutionary teaching, speech therapy and poetry of the early nineteenth century all had roots in a materialist understanding of the actions and reactions of the (embodied) mind and body, and also shared the aim of propagating 'undulations' of sympathy throughout the body politic to the whole 'sentient universe'. No wonder, then, that what Thelwall described as a 'diseased association' between his name and 1790s' 'Jacobinism' remained incurable.[133]

Aware that his perfectibilist faith in the power of the correctly trained mind to regulate the speaking body might lead him to be more widely 'suspected of the horrible crime of materialism', and also conscious that his livelihood was at stake, Thelwall is careful in the aftermath of the Edinburgh debacle to emphasize the pragmatism of his elocutionary system.[134] He finds a counter-model in the idealist epistemology and metaphysics of Immanuel Kant, which he first learned about when attending lectures on the subject delivered in London in 1796 by Kant's disciple Friedrich August Nitsch.[135] Thelwall alludes to his debates with Nitsch when he notes in the *Letter to Cline*,

> I do not go the lengths I have heard ascribed to Professor Kant. – I do not mean to say – that 'Speech in a faculty purely mental; and that a man might become an orator, tho he had neither teeth nor tongue, by the mere action of the mind'. I am no such *intellectual philosopher*. I trust, alone, to the facts of *physical experience*, and the inferences of *logical induction*; and leave the visionary theories of metaphysicians to those who imagine that they understand metaphysics.[136]

With this dig at Kant and other 'intellectual philosophers', Thelwall establishes a continuity between his elocutionary and prosodic systems and the staunch empiricism of his *Animal Vitality* essay of 1793, while also anticipating his defence of that position in his renewed poetic and philosophical debates with Coleridge. As the next chapter will show, in response to Coleridge's *Biographia Literaria* and Burke's theory of the sublime, Thelwall extended the physiological premises of his elocutionary career in an attempt to develop a materialist account of affective response and the poetic imagination, and in so doing articulated the principles that had underpinned his theory and practice all along.

6

The Materialist Imagination
Late Poetry and Criticism

> [M]aterialism & immaterialism are but a strife of words.[1]

In April 1801, five years to the month since first striking up a correspondence with Thelwall, Coleridge wrote describing the gulf of mutual understanding that had formed between them:

> we are so utterly unlike each other in our habits of thinking, and we have adopted such irreconcilably different opinions in Politics, Religion, & Metaphysics, (& probably in Taste too) that, I fear— I fear—I do not know how to express myself——but such, I fear, is the chasm between us, that so far from being able to shake hands across it, we cannot even make our Words intelligible to each other.[2]

The rupture (or continental drift) that was carrying Coleridge away from his former friends and philosophies finds expression in his broken syntax, which seems to convey particular distress at his distance from Thelwall – until we turn to the *Biographia Literaria* (1817) and find Coleridge repudiating the one-time reformer James Mackintosh's associationist psychology in precisely the same terms:

> So wide indeed is the chasm between this gentleman's philosophical creed and mine, that so far from being able to join hands, we could scarce make our voices intelligible to each other: and to bridge it over, would require more time, skill and power than I believe myself to possess.[3]

Coleridge takes issue with Mackintosh's lectures of 1799–1800 'On the Law of Nature and Nations', in which he renounced his former radicalism but continued to defend the doctrine of association. Mackintosh's effort in those lectures to trace the doctrine to Thomas Hobbes informs Coleridge's rebuttal of it in the *Biographia*, where it becomes clear that associationism, like the larger materialist tradition to which it belonged, is synonymous for Coleridge with radicalism, republicanism, atheism and Godwinism – all the 'isms' he now abominated. Conversely, materialism's radical connotations were precisely what continued to make it attractive to Thelwall.

Forced to silence his political opinions for the sake of renewed public utility, Thelwall turned not only to a theory and practice of elocution rooted in embodied cognition, but also to a materialist understanding of the imagination. One result was the unpublished collection *Poems, Chiefly Suggested by the Scenery of Nature* discussed in Chapter 5. But the Derby volumes, in which that collection is preserved, also give us access to a range of other previously unknown poems that demonstrate the consequences of materialist philosophy for Thelwall's theory of the imagination. Of particular relevance are the unfinished satire on contemporary poets *Musalogia: or The Paths of Poesy* (1827) and the nightwalk poem 'The Star' (1825). This chapter examines them alongside late critical writings by Thelwall that have likewise not yet received substantive attention, notably an essay on the poetry of Letitia Elizabeth Landon, marginal annotations on the *Biographia Literaria* and on a volume of poetry by William Lisle Bowles that was a gift from Coleridge, and a hitherto unremarked essay that responds to Burke's theory of language and aesthetic response. All together these works demonstrate to what extent Coleridge's sense of an unbridgeable chasm between his and Thelwall's 'opinions in Politics, Religion, & Metaphysics, (& probably in Taste too)' was overstated. As this chapter will show, Thelwall's late poetry and criticism challenge the dichotomy between materialism and idealism, and by extension between passive subjectivity and voluntaristic creativity, propounded by Coleridge and still vital in criticism today. In so doing they offer a compelling alternative to the paradigmatic understanding of the Romantic imagination as a faculty of transcendental vision theorized on the ruins of eighteenth-century materialist thought, and can even shed light on the influence of that thought on Thelwall's contemporaries.

The materialist sublime and beautiful

Although Thelwall's works brim with encomiums on the imagination, they do not address its workings in the substantive way one would expect from this 'Champion of Materialism'.[4] For the first time, however, we can begin to understand the nuances of his theory thanks to an essay that appeared in two instalments in the *Monthly Magazine* in October and November 1803 under the title, 'Observations upon the Theory Adopted by Mr. Burke in His Examination of the Effects Produced upon the Mind by Words'.[5] The essay contributes to Romantic-era efforts to develop a materialist science of the mind and clues us in to what was probably the gist of the lost paper of 1793 in which Thelwall sought to explain mental phenomena 'upon principles *purely Physical*', the controversy over which spurred his departure from the Physical Society.[6] Signed 'J. T.' in the second instalment, the essay refutes Burke's claim in *A Philosophical Enquiry into the Origin of Our Ideas of the Sublime and Beautiful* (1757) that a certain category of words – 'compounded abstract words' such as virtue, honour and persuasion – operates by evoking the 'good or evil' impressions produced on the occasions when one first heard them used, rather than by raising images in the mind of the things they stand for.[7] In Burke's terms, compounded abstract words operate by 'sympathy' rather than 'imitation'.[8] Historians of language point out that Burke thus sought to establish a specific area of language that was exempt from Lockean 'picture theory', or the idea that words bore a 'quasi-pictorial' relation to thought.[9] Burke's assertion of the sympathetic, non-mimetic power of language is a step towards his concluding claim in the *Philosophical Enquiry* that poetry affects the passions precisely because it fails to raise distinct images in the mind. Milton's description of a 'universe of Death', for instance, is not in his view a 'clear expression', that is, a description of 'a thing as it is' addressing itself to the understanding; but it is nonetheless a 'strong expression', one describing a thing 'as it is felt' and addressing itself to the passions. Burke compares these effects to those produced in speech by 'naked description' on the one hand, and by the tones, looks and gestures that accompany it on the other, crediting the latter with communicating the speaker's 'strong and lively feeling' like a 'contagion' or 'fire'.[10]

Although Thelwall on the whole admires the *Philosophical Enquiry*, quoting William Shenstone's injunction, 'Of all books whatever, read Burke on the Sublime', he regards Burke's denial of the representational power of compounded abstract words as 'sophistry in the extreme'. He agrees that words are only sounds, as opposed to material 'essences', but he considers it impossible for them to operate on the mind without raising any 'annexed notion' whatsoever: 'unless we comprehend the things they stand for, no *intellectual* impression can be produced'.[11]

Thelwall grants that not all words have the power to raise 'clear' or 'determinate' images, but he insists that all words must raise some image nonetheless. Responding to Burke's examples of blind men who are able successfully to use language denoting things they have never seen, Thelwall observes that he has never seen the Egyptian pyramids, but he can nonetheless form an idea of them from verbal description. Blindness, in other words, is beside the point; what matters is the writer's or speaker's power to impress the imagination with vivid images. Thelwall refers to this as the power of 'making even hearing sight', taking the phrase from the ancient Greek treatise *On the Sublime* attributed at the time to Longinus, which Burke also claimed as a source of authority.[12] Against Burke's claim that the rapidity of speech makes it impossible for the mind to form an accurate notion of the sound of a word and the thing or idea it represents, Thelwall asserts that the mind can in fact 'form and receive images quicker than the ordinary exertion of the organs of speech'. He also rejects Burke's analogy between the seemingly 'unconscious' operations of the mind in conducting certain bodily actions and its operations in receiving the impressions produced by language. In the first case, Thelwall notes, the mind is not actually unconscious, but only distracted by more immediately 'interesting' ideas.[13] His insistence that this inattention is not equivalent to an absence of thought recalls Godwin's contention in *Political Justice* that while thought is essential to animal motion, it need not be voluntary or conscious. Three more of Godwin's premises resurface in Thelwall's essay: first, that the mind can have only one idea at a time; second, that the succession of ideas in the mind must be 'infinitely rapid'; and third, that more powerful ideas tend to drive out weaker ones.[14]

Like Godwin, Thelwall grounds his claims in the associationist psychology of David Hartley. In his influential *Observations on Man* (1749), Hartley had combined Locke's notion of the mind as a blank slate susceptible to sensations with Newton's theory of vibrations to argue that all mental phenomena were results of the mind's association of ideas derived from sensory impressions communicated by vibrations along the nerves. Words, by this logic, were sensory impressions on the eye or ear that raised pictures in the mind of the things they represented.[15] In the 1803 essay Thelwall adheres closely to these propositions, as, for instance, when he explains of the sense of feeling that 'the impression is conveyed along the course of the nerves to their common origin, the brain'. The resulting perception 'is not that of an indeterminate feeling, but the very figure of the body making the impression is also communicated; we know whether it is square, round, rough, or smooth'. For

Thelwall, '[t]his seems [...] actually to prove, that the very *image* of the body is presented to the mind; if it is not, I know not how to account for the effect, and may safely defy any reasoner to do so'.[16] In the same spirit he explains that in the act of seeing, 'the object first is painted upon the retina, the expansion of the optic nerve; [and] the same nerve conveys it to the brain', while in the act of hearing, 'the mere sound having made its impression upon the organs of the ear, it is presented, by means of the auditory nerve, to the mind, which is affected only by the *idea* annexed to that sound'.[17]

Thelwall had endorsed this associationist theory of perception in earlier works, notably *The Peripatetic*, which bases its digressive structure and hybrid genre on the narrator's associative responses to his changing surroundings and encounters on the road, as discussed in Chapter 2. Only in the second instalment of the *Monthly Magazine* essay, however, does he develop the implications of associationism for the imagination and affective response. The provocation is Burke's claim in the *Philosophical Enquiry* that intelligible images diminish the affective force of poetry. If we 'attend coolly' to the sensible images raised by Virgil's description in the *Aeneid* of the formation of thunder, for instance, we will think them as 'wild and absurd' as 'the chimeras of madmen'.[18] For Thelwall, conversely, the sublimity of Virgil's description depends precisely on the intelligibility of its images: 'I understood not the passage at first, because I did not comprehend its images; I learned the propriety of those images, and enjoyed its sublimity'. Yet even while defending the criterion of intelligibility, Thelwall agrees with Burke that clarity can diminish poetry's sublime effects and emphasizes the role of suggestion in stimulating the imagination and giving it an active role in aesthetic response. Echoing Burke's examples, he notes that Homer's avoidance of 'particulars' in his description of Helen 'put it out of the power of any mind to conceive a more beautiful woman', while Milton's representation of death evokes a form whose very indistinctness augments the horror of the subject.[19]

Although recent scholars have criticized Thelwall for failing to achieve an equivalent to Paine's 'intellectual vernacular', the *Monthly Magazine* essay confirms that Painite transparency is not his foremost criterion for imaginative writing.[20] Far from sharing Paine's or Godwin's suspicion of performative language, Thelwall articulates a materialist aesthetics of suggestion that bears out Tom Furniss's remark that 'the discourses of tradition and revolution become mirror images of one another to the extent that they exploit the same linguistic resources for different ends'.[21] At the same time, however, he dismisses Burke's distinction between a 'clear' expression addressed to the understanding and a 'strong' one addressed to the feelings. The literary sublime is not, in his view, predicated on the failure of language, but on the creation of intelligible ideas in the mind, whether by clarity or suggestion. For Thelwall, the 'true excellence of a poet' consists in 'his observation of nature, and his application of those observations'.[22] What he calls for, in short, is 'truth to nature' in the sense of vivid language capable of stimulating the inductive powers of the mind. (Such language must also respect the laws of physical nature, including the laws of the speaking body discussed in Chapter 5.) The general principle, as expressed in a later essay, is that, '[e]ven poetry, when it pretends to argue, should have something that looks like premises, as the bases of its inductions. Imagination itself is not without its logic, whatever may be the case with the mere distemperature of *fancy*'.[23] As the distinction between fancy and imagination suggests, the violations of this materialist aesthetics are at the root not only of Thelwall's disagreement with Burke, but also of his and Coleridge's 'irreconcilably different opinions in Politics, Religion, & Metaphysics, (& probably in Taste too)', which began, innocuously enough, as a dispute about the poetry of William Lisle Bowles.

'A strife of words'; or, 'Ha! Ha! Mr S.T.C. ! ! !'

What Coleridge memorably called his and Thelwall's 'sparring about Poetry' began in April 1796, when the 24-year-old aspiring radical addressed the 31-year-old 'acquitted felon' with overtures of friendship: 'Pursuing the same end by the same means we ought not to be strangers to each other'.[24] Coleridge wrote in the first instance to clear up a misunderstanding about his reference to an 'unsupported Malcontent' in *The Plot Discovered*, his pamphlet against the Two Acts. Having heard that Thelwall felt targeted by the phrase, Coleridge insisted that his only reference to Thelwall in the pamphlet was a description of him as the 'voice of tens of thousands'. As evidence of goodwill, Coleridge enclosed a copy of his *Poems on Various Subjects*, calling Thelwall's attention to 'Religious Musings' and possibly inscribing the volume with his sonnet 'To John Thelwall'.[25] The misunderstanding cleared up, Coleridge and Thelwall embarked on a candid and affectionately combative correspondence that ranged across poetry, politics, philosophy and religion. In the only one of Thelwall's letters to Coleridge to have been preserved, he objects to the obscurity and artifice of his friend's verse, remarking that more than half of 'Religious Musings' consists in 'abstruse, metaphysical, mistical [*sic*] rant'.[26] Many of Thelwall's remarks anticipate his later elocutionary objection to the 'Della Cruscan' placement of adjectives and other such 'weak words' in relation to the nouns that they modify.[27] Coleridge, for his part, accepts many of Thelwall's criticisms but disagrees that 'Christian poetry [... is] very vile stuff', asking, 'Why so violent against *metaphysics* in poetry?'.[28] He in turn offers qualified praise of Thelwall's works, remarking of *The Peripatetic*, for instance, that, 'the poetry is frequently *sweet* & possesses the *fire* of feeling, but not enough (I think) of the *light* of Fancy'.[29] At once piqued and amused by Thelwall's disdain for his 'mistical rant', Coleridge sent Thelwall's wife a copy of the fourth edition of Bowles's *Sonnets, and Other Poems* (1796), remarking in the accompanying letter: '(Shall I give it thee, Blasphemer? No. I won't—but) to thy Stella I do present the poems of my [Bowles] for a keep-sake'.[30]

Copiously annotated by Thelwall, yet largely overlooked by critics, the Bowles volume offers a fascinating record of Thelwall and Coleridge's differences of poetic opinion while gesturing towards the larger philosophical and political 'chasm' across which Coleridge would eventually find it impossible to converse. The annotations repeatedly take issue with Bowles's forced inversions, clichéd diction, misused prepositions and incongruous imagery. Beneath the 'Elegy, written at the Hotwells', for instance, Thelwall writes: 'Lawn of early life, and spring tide plains, and transports bland, [...] – Drivelling enough for one page at any rate'.[31] A poem particularly replete with vague similes about things that 'seem' provokes the rebuke, 'What a <u>seeming</u> poet this is'.[32] Thelwall's objections coalesce in his note on Bowles's 'Verses on Reading Mr Howard's Description of Prisons', a reference to the prison reformer John Howard, to whom Thelwall had also addressed an early ode.[33] He is especially struck by a passage that ventriloquizes the sentiments of an anonymous prisoner:

> 'What pitying spirit, what unwonted guest,
> 'Strays to this last retreat, these shades unblest?
> 'From life and light shut out, beneath this cell
> 'Long have I bid hope's cheering sun farewell.[']

As a former prisoner, Thelwall is understandably provoked; as a poet, he is even more deeply vexed:

> How did the prisoner get <u>beneath</u> his cell to bid farewell to anything? But I forgot he tells us in the same line that he is shut out from life (i.e. <u>is dead</u>) & then to put him (i.e. to bury him) under the cell was a cheap way of disposing of him: but after being so disposed of it was very civil of him to make such a speech to Mr Howard?[34]

On one level, Thelwall is having arch fun, mocking both the cliché of describing death as the shutting out of life and the prepositional choice of 'beneath', which sacrifices sense to preserve metre. Both are anathema to Thelwall's creed of poetic enfranchisement from the tyranny of convention. On another level, however, Thelwall is targeting the naivety of a poet who, unlike him, has never known the living-death of imprisonment as anything more than a hackneyed metaphor.

Admittedly, Thelwall's notes here and throughout the volume smack of intransigence. Yet David Fairer, in the only critical commentary on the annotations to date, is perhaps too hasty in deeming Thelwall's remarks bluntly literalistic. While he acknowledges that Thelwall 'delights in subjecting Bowles's melancholy to gleeful burlesque', he also claims that 'Thelwall strongly resists anything that sacrifices clear description to vague evocation, and he particularly dislikes images of evanescence, liminality, or transience'.[35] Citing Thelwall's definition of 'qualities' in the *Animal Vitality* essay of 1793 as 'solely and purely, modifications of matter', Fairer concludes that 'Thelwall aims for something like Paine's "transparency" of meaning', stripping away all 'non-material modifiers of mood, colour, and sound, to expose the no-meaning behind the elegiac tinges, the gleams and glimmers, the hushed sighings'.[36] We get a strikingly different sense of Thelwall's attitude in the marginalia, however, when we connect it with the materialist aesthetics articulated in the essay on Burke, where it is apparent that clarity and transparency are less important to his definition of good poetry than intelligible truth to nature. Thus, when he wonders what Bowles means by 'the distant turret's gleamy fan' – asking, 'Does he mean the sail of a windmill?' – he is not being naively literal but coyly suggesting that the poet tilts at windmills of sense. The same is true of his sarcasm about lines in which 'Heaven's beauteous bow / Beams on the night-storms [*sic*] passing wings below'. Thelwall transcribes the offending lines beneath the poem, underlining 'night' and following it with three exclamation marks. Mocking the poem's garbled imagery he notes, 'This must have been a lunar rainbow in spite of the bright sun'.[37] It is not, then, the lack of transparency in Bowles's (and by implication Coleridge's) poetry that bothers Thelwall, but the failure to create vivid images capable of stimulating the associative mind.

The wider aesthetic and ideological stakes of Thelwall's position begin to emerge when we consider that he probably annotated the Bowles volume not contemporaneously with the publication in November 1797 of Coleridge's 'Nehemiah Higginbottom' sonnets, to which his notes allude, but around 1819 when, after 'an interval of 23 Years', he re-read the letter from Coleridge that had accompanied the volume and responded in the margins to passages that he thought misinterpreted his views on poetry and religion.[38] The later dating is corroborated by annotations that identify lines of seven or nine 'heavy' syllables in Bowles's pentameter, an idiosyncrasy which is consistent with Thelwall's view after 1800 that a blank-verse line could contain more than five such syllables provided they occurred in isochronous cadences. Recontextualized thus, the Bowles marginalia can be seen as part of the crystallization of Thelwall's materialist aesthetics in the early nineteenth century, when the publication of Coleridge's vehemently anti-materialist *Biographia Literaria* in 1817 provoked him to articulate more fully his own theory of the imagination.

Like his remarks on Bowles, Thelwall's marginalia on the *Biographia* demonstrate the deep affinities between his and Coleridge's theories, particularly their fundamental agreement about the material dimensions of perception and imagination.[39] They are more typically cited for their candid responses to Coleridge's denial of youthful radicalism. Alongside Coleridge's claim that his principles had always been 'opposite [...] to those of jacobinism or even of democracy', Thelwall tries to set the record straight about them both:

> If Jacobinism be antisocialism, I have never gone the lenghts [*sic*] in that way which the Pantisocratist went at any rate, nay I may say I never had the slightest tinge of that with which Mr C. was deep died: but that Mr C. was indeed far from Democracy, because he was far beyond it, I well remember – for he was a down right zealous leveller & indeed in one of the worst senses of the word he was a Jacobin, a man of blood –[40]

Similarly, alongside Coleridge's critique of 'the modern jacobinical drama', Thelwall inveighs against his former friend's 'sophistical use of really unmeaning, but yet popular cant nick names'. Coleridge reveals his 'destitution of principle' by applying the damning epithet not merely to 'reformers & *incliners* to republicanism – in short to all who are dissatisfied with the established systems of *legitimate* despotism', but consequently to 'everything that is immoral & detestable in arts literature manners & habits'. Thelwall concludes bitterly of his former friend, 'He does not call those from whom *he has deserted* "spawn of Hell" – He only endeavours to lead the minds of his readers to think (or at least to feel) of them as such'.[41]

The stakes of this quarrel about an already outmoded term of abuse are best understood in relation to the broader philosophical and aesthetic opinions with which they are intricately intertwined in the margins of Thelwall's copy of the *Biographia*.[42] Many of his annotations indicate a coincidence of views, and even hint at unacknowledged borrowing. When Coleridge remarks that philosophy apprehends truth by first 'intellectually separat[ing]' given propositions and then restoring them to unity, Thelwall elaborates: 'And such philosophy must the poet be complete master of'. He also concurs with Coleridge's remarks on the use of language to communicate truth and pleasure, and he attentively draws lines down the margins of passages in which Coleridge describes the poet's power to reconcile opposite or discordant qualities. The points of agreement culminate in Thelwall's expression of strong 'approv[al] and admir[ation]' for Coleridge's chapter on 'poetic power' as elucidated in Shakespeare: 'the doctrines of many parts of it, particularly of the last section (nay sometimes the very illustrations & language[)] seem as if they were but the echo of those I have so long & so frequently inforced in my Lectures'.[43] Thelwall repeats the suggestion of plagiarism alongside Coleridge's assertion that fancy and imagination are distinct faculties, remarking that the distinction has been a 'favourite topic' of his lectures for the past 10 or 15 years and asking why Coleridge makes 'all this pompous display of metaphysical analysis about a discovery which the mere consideration of the passages quoted by the blundering obtuseness of the anti-etimological [*sic*] Johnson under the word Fancy might sufficiently have evinced'. He also rebukes Coleridge for borrowing without acknowledgement, in his famous footnote on the desynonymizing of words, from John Horne Tooke's *Diversions of Purley*, a work that Coleridge professed to hold in 'utter contempt'.[44]

This is not just petty wrangling: Thelwall is repeatedly highlighting the materialist foundation of Coleridge's theory and his abiding debts to Tooke and himself. Coleridge's attempt to repudiate that foundation seems to him as absurd as his denial of former 'Jacobin' sympathies, and he is eager to expose the resulting fallacies. Alongside Coleridge's reiteration of the Priestleyan view that 'body and spirit [...] *may* without any *absurdity* be supposed to be different modes or degrees in perfection, of a common substratum', which in the 1790s Coleridge had endorsed,[45] Thelwall notes:

> That is to say they may be considered as different modifications of one common essence (to which it will then be perfectly indifferent whether you give or deny the name of matter – or what other name you may give it) one dense or gross & therefore confined to locality form & motion; the [other] infinitely rare & subtile & therefore capable of pervading all space & substances. Of this subtile essence of

materiality let us suppose seperability [*sic*], or identified portions, & we have the soul of Men (& of Brutes) – or let us admit (in which there would be no incongruity) constantaneous omnipressence [*sic*], & we have God, the universally pervading consciousness, the source of all volition, order, creation – the soul of the universe: but if this be not materialism, materialism & immaterialism are but a strife of words.[46]

Thelwall expresses much the same idea in an entry on 'Metaphysics' in the *Panoramic Miscellany* in 1826, concluding that the 'distinction [...] between *materialism* and *immaterialism* must always be mere vanity of verbiage, till the difference is intelligibly defined between *immateriality* and *nothingness*'.[47] In both cases Thelwall echoes the basic premise of his *Animal Vitality* essay that the universe must consist of matter or vacuum, something or nothing – a premise that in turn echoes Joseph Priestley's materialist monism in *Disquisitions Concerning Matter and Spirit*, discussed in Chapter 1. In the *Animal Vitality* essay Thelwall had allowed that spirit might form part of the 'animal composition', but he had insisted that however refined or 'subtile' such spirit, it 'must still be material'. Therefore the apparent self-contradiction had vanished – for Thelwall, at least – as dualism was folded back into monism.[48]

By contrast, Thelwall finds the *Biographia* rife with self-contradiction. When Coleridge asserts that the 'dogmatic materialist' tends merely to 'affect the mysterious, and declare the whole process a revelation *given*, and not to be *understood*, which it would be profane to examine too closely', Thelwall can respond only with an incredulous, '! ! ! Ha! Ha! Mr S.T.C. ! ! !'.[49] The fallacy of Coleridge's anti-materialist logic is also the subject of the seemingly trivial anecdote that concludes the marginalia. Alongside Coleridge's remark that Christian faith is rooted in '[t]he sense, the inward feeling' of spiritual longing, Thelwall remarks that some 'cold reasoners' may regard such feelings as 'very ambiguous arguments'. He then alludes to a scene in Henry Fielding's farce *The Tragedy of Tragedies, or, The Life and Death of Tom Thumb the Great* (1731) in which King Arthur feels a sudden chest pain and wonders whether it betokens 'Love, or only the wind collic'. Thelwall quips that Coleridge's metaphysics would put an end to the king's scepticism by explaining the colicky pain as a symptom of love, thus implying that Coleridge is likewise wrong to deny the material sources of the imagination.[50]

Flippancy notwithstanding, Thelwall may well have construed Coleridge's indictment of 'dogmatic' materialism as a personal attack, and with reason. Coleridge's claim that materialism is reducible to a single 'sophism', 'mistaking the conditions of a thing for its causes and essence',[51] recalls the letter of December 1796 in which he remarked that Thelwall's theory of vitality was '[a]s likely as any other' but added, 'you *assume* the thing to be proved—the *"capability* of being stimulated into sensation" *as* a *property* of organized matter—now "the Capab". &c is *my* definition of *animal Life'*. Coleridge favoured the Scottish anatomist Alexander Monro's Neo-Platonic theory of 'a plastic immaterial Nature—all-pervading', which had inspired the portion of his 'Effusion XXXV' ('The Eolian Harp') that he quoted for Thelwall:

> And what if all of animated Nature
> Be but organic harps diversely fram'd
> That tremble into *thought* as o'er them sweeps
> Plastic & vast &c—[52]

Rereading this correspondence after 'an interval of 23 Years', as he annotated Bowles's poetry and the *Biographia*, Thelwall feels particularly called upon to answer Coleridge's contention in the latter that materialist philosophy cannot account for human creativity because '[m]atter has no inward'.[53] Coleridge accuses materialists of reducing complex cognitive processes to 'blind mechanism', the soul to a mere '*ens logicum*' or logical entity, and the self to a 'poor worthless I' defined solely by physical properties, such as 'extension, motion, [and] degrees of velocity'.[54] Eager to redeem the imagination from such reductions, he famously defines its 'primary' form as 'the living power and prime agent of all human perception, [...] a repetition in the finite mind of the eternal act of creation of the infinite I AM'. The 'secondary' imagination is an 'echo' of the primary that differs in degree rather than kind: 'It dissolves, diffuses, dissipates, in order to re-create', and although it is 'essentially vital', its 'objects (*as* objects) are essentially fixed and dead'. Against these two forms of imagination Coleridge sets fancy, a faculty that can operate only on 'fixities and definities' – the impressions of the world it receives from the senses – according to the doctrine of association. Fancy is merely 'a mode of memory, emancipated from the order of time and space; and blended with, and modified by that empirical phenomenon of the will, which we express by the word choice'.[55]

Although Coleridge thought that his theory of the imagination effectively invalidated materialism – 'Doctrine of necessity rendered not dangerous by the Imagination', he observed in a notebook[56] – for Thelwall it only confirmed the need for a fuller defence of the role of embodied cognition in mental creation. Alongside Coleridge's attack in the *Biographia* on the 'dogmatic materialist' who 'reject[s] as *inconceivable* whatever

from its own nature is un*imaginable*', Thelwall admits that the 'imagination cannot travel beyond the limits of time & space', and that 'every
image has necessary locality & is contemplated as present'. But he also
notes that we can transcend this locality 'in the abstract' by a process of
mental 'negation', which allows us to conceive of 'the infinitudes before
which Time & space sink into comparative annihilation'.[57] The idea of
apprehending the empirically unknowable through a sort of negative reasoning not only challenges notions of Thelwall's obstinate literalism, but
also suggests a role for the materialist imagination as a mediator between
the knowable and unknowable, the bodily and the mental – a role that
emerges more clearly Thelwall's subsequent poetry and criticism.

The 'concentric fire' of imagination

Criticism had been one of Thelwall's habitual modes since the late
1780s, when he served as editor of and lead contributor to the *Biographical and Imperial Magazine*; after 1800 it became one of his main
means of reforming public taste and opinion, notably in the *Champion*,
the *Monthly Magazine* and his own short-lived periodical the *Panoramic
Miscellany*.[58] A case in point is the essay about Letitia Elizabeth Landon
that Thelwall published in the *Panoramic* in 1826, roughly around the
time that he was composing the verse satire *Musalogia: or The Paths of
Poesy*. Together, these little-known works show how, in continued dialogue with Coleridge and also Wordsworth, Thelwall's ideas about the
embodied dimensions of perception and aesthetic response crystallized
in a theory of the imagination as a vital power.

The essay on 'The Poetry of Miss Landen [*sic*]' was primarily a
response to her collection *The Troubadour* of 1825, which followed her
highly successful *The Improvisatrice* of the previous year.[59] Thelwall was
struck by Landon's ingenuous talent, but also by what he perceived as
her want of a mentor. After the death of her father in 1824, Landon had
become the protégée of the family neighbour William Jerdan, editor of
the widely read *Literary Gazette*, to which she contributed and made
her fame as 'L. E. L'. Concerned that Jerdan is misguiding his young
protégée, then in her early twenties, Thelwall presents himself in the
Panoramic essay as an alternative mentor and father figure.[60] Although
he admires the 'sparkle' and 'freshness' of Landon's poetry, he finds it
lacking in 'that *concentration* of thought and feeling, which strikes with
deep and durable impression to the heart, instead of playing over the
surface of the fancy'. If Landon aspires to works of 'greater magnitude',
she must achieve the 'unity', 'coherency' and 'intensity of purpose' that

'pervade, as with a living soul, every part and proportion, and render every motion, turn and grace [...] co-operative to some concentric purpose'.[61] Thelwall's advice recalls Coleridge's remark – in a passage of the *Biographia* that Thelwall marked with an X – that 'good sense is the body of poetic genius, fancy its drapery, motion its life, and imagination the soul that is everywhere, and in each; and forms all into one graceful and intelligent whole'.[62] With Thelwall, however, the metaphor of the imagination as a soul or vital principle is closely associated with chemical experiments such as those conducted by Priestley. Referring to the gourd-shaped vessel used in processes of distillation, Thelwall declares that, '[t]he poet's art is the limbec of all sciences: condenses the spirit, and evaporates the aqueous bulk'.[63] Approximating John Keats's poetico-materialist vocabulary – specifically his assertion in a private letter that 'the excellence of every Art is its intensity, capable of making all disagreeables evaporate, from their being in close relationship with Beauty & Truth'[64] – Thelwall suggests that the poet is a sort of chemist or alchemist whose imagination transforms the gross matter of 'science' or knowledge into something vital and sublime. Imagination is 'the steady light, the concentric fire, the plastic vivifying heat'.[65] These remarks also resonate with Wordsworth's ideal of poetry as the 'breath and finer spirit of all knowledge' in the 1802 Preface to *Lyrical Ballads*, which he had urged Thelwall to consult.[66] But whereas Wordsworth's Preface seeks to contain the potential for the 'spontaneous overflow' of poetic enthusiasm to overwhelm the self by insisting that the sources of inspiration be 'recollected in tranquillity',[67] Thelwall's essay on Landon urges just the opposite. For poetry to act as a vital stimulus on the minds of others, it cannot rely on the 'cold researches of memory', but must arise from the immediacy of bodily sensation and mental perception: from 'images vividly floating in the poetic eye' and 'feelings that are actually palpitating at [the] heart'. Whatever its subject, he insists, poetry 'must be felt as passion, pursued as passion, and expressed as a passion'.[68]

Thelwall develops these views and underscores their abiding radicalism in the unpublished satirical poem that has come to light as part of the Derby volumes. Forming part of the third volume, the contents of which date from the mid-1810s to 1827 or later, *Musalogia: or The Paths of Poesy* appears to have been left unfinished at Thelwall's death in 1834.[69] With a satirical tone and comic triple rhymes evocative of Byron's *Don Juan* (for instance, 'chatter all'/'supernatural'), *Musalogia* sets out in the 'rambling song' of iambic tetrameter 'To castigate the scribbling throng'.[70] The poem's critique of the commercialization of literature recalls Thelwall's fragmentary mock-epic on types and pictures in *The Peripatetic*, a revised version of which is also preserved in the Derby volumes as *Typopictoromania*. But *Musalogia* is more pervasively concerned with issues of style, prosody and the moral powers of the poetic imagination. Noting the advent of a 'Poetic Age' when every 'class, age, sex, degree' aspires to write verse, Thelwall envisions the birth of a tenth muse, the Muse of Criticism, 'Before whose searching beam intense, / Perish the flowers of vain pretence'.[71] In the autobiographical 80-line conclusion of Canto II, Thelwall explains that want of such critical guidance was to blame for the 'crude conceit & glittering phrase' of his own early verse. Through dogged self-education – 'Snatching the scanty means to explore / The fountain depths of critic lore' – he eventually achieved renown for his elocutionary and prosodic insights (even 'those of prouder name have hung / Upon the precepts of his tongue').[72] On this basis he puts himself forward as a guide to the younger generation and alternative to those (like Francis Jeffrey) who 'snarl in periodic prose' and those (like Jerdan) who puff and flatter young poets indiscriminately.[73] Thelwall's critic muse is an egalitarian who judges the merits of a poet's verse without reference to reputation or social status:

> Shall Critic censure softer flow,
> To please the Juntas of the Row?
> Make different laws for gnat & griffen?
> And spare a Campbell more than Wiffen?
> Or heed if her free voice affront
> High Walter Scott, or low Leigh Hunt?[74]

While *Musalogia* has something to say about each of these writers and more, it devotes particular attention to Wordsworth, who is singled out in an 80-line passage of the first canto as one who might 'vie with the Miltonian Lyre' were it not for his unnerving tendency to bathos. Capable of attaining the 'mountain highth [*sic*]' of sublimity, he will also deign

> With nursery babes to pule & whine,
> Or in an idiot's slaver shine;
> Of puddles & of Leech-ponds sing,
> And moralize—like any thing!
> While measuring pools from side to side
> Just four-foot long & three-foot wide,
> Or teaching Farmers' teeth to chatter
> When pilfering croans their curses scatter.[75]

In his marginalia on the *Biographia* Thelwall had remarked of 'The Idiot Boy' that he could 'find nothing [in it] that is poetical—To me it is perfect drivelling [*sic*]', and he noted that several years earlier he could not get Coleridge to agree with his criticisms of 'The Thorn', which 'was then an object of unqualified panegyric with him'.[76] Thelwall seems to be suggesting that Coleridge's critique of Wordsworth's 'matter-of-factness' in some parts of *Lyrical Ballads* is indebted to his own prior censure of that tendency.[77] Now in *Musalogia* – a work whose title invites comparison with Coleridge's *Biographia* – Thelwall links Wordsworth's 'maudlin mock moralities' with his political apostasy:

> No marvel then if we deplore
> To hear thee pule in nursery lore,—
> Or sicken if thy nervous line
> To mongrel politics decline,
> Tory at once & Jacobine!
> Painting all noblest highths of mind
> In those to lowliest state <lot> consign'd,
> Yet bidding laud & glory wait
> On those low things the chance-born great;
> And with a moist & pitying eye
> For trampled poor humanity,
> Ranting of grim & blood-smear'd Slaughter
> As God-almighty's darling daughter.[78]

Echoing Coleridge's praise for Thelwall's own 'nervous song' in the 1796 sonnet 'To John Thelwall', this lament for Wordsworth's 'nervous line' and may imply that Thelwall's, by contrast, has not 'decline[d]' or slackened.[79] Like another poet-radical in the early nineteenth century, Percy Shelley, Thelwall sees Wordsworth as a Milton manqué.[80]

Letitia Landon, however, need not suffer the same fate. Thelwall addresses her anew in Canto II, repeating his warning from the *Panoramic* essay against the mentorship of Jerdan – that 'dry-nurse critic winter-sapt' – and urging her to abandon the mode of hasty improvisation: 'scan your fancies & your verse / Till these are chaste, & that is terse'.[81] He extends this advice to the wider community of 'Lady Bards, so throng of late', including 'cold' Joanna Baillie, 'sweet' Felicia Hemans and 'doz[y]' Mary Russell Mitford.[82] All of them mistake 'Fancy's coruscations' for the 'creative beam' of Imagination, which is alone capable of producing poetry that satisfies the ideal of 'vital semblance true' exemplified by Milton and Shakespeare. Thelwall urges all young poets to aim for this ideal whatever their subject:

> whether thou new forms create,
> Or old creation imitate,
> The ideal by the true you scan,
> Congenial with the primal plan,
> And all that you in thought conceive
> Nature avows, & we believe.[83]

As in the essay on Burke and the marginalia on Coleridge and Bowles, Thelwall establishes as the highest criterion of good poetry its ability to 'stamp with prompt energic art / Truth's glowing image on the heart'. As he notes elsewhere, '[e]ven poetry [...] should have something that looks like premises, as the bases of its inductions'.[84] The canto ends with Thelwall's expression of confidence in the power of his own late poetry to achieve such effects: 'future times may not disdain / To listen to his later <evening> strain'.[85] Ironically, that evening strain has found almost no audience until now, when the recovery of the Derby manuscript gives us access to a range of previously unknown late works. Having taken stock of the *Poems, Chiefly Suggested by the Scenery of Nature* in Chapter 5, I conclude with an analysis of a virtually unknown late poem that exemplifies the 'concentric fire' of Thelwall's materialist imagination.

From the visual to the visionary: 'The Star'

'The Star that Shone When Other Stars Were Dim' appeared in the Supplement to the first six issues of the *Monthly Magazine* for 1825 when it was under Thelwall's editorship, and it was included in the Derby volumes with the subtitle, 'A Night-Walk in the Vicinity of Whitehall'[86] (Appendix 3). Consisting of more than 100 lines of irregularly rhymed iambic pentameter, 'The Star' recounts a midnight walk in the neighbourhood of Whitehall, near the seat of the British Parliament. In 1822–23 Parliament had debated the legitimacy of the Continental allies' support for a French invasion of Spain intended to restore the absolutist Bourbon king Ferdinand VII, who had been deposed by the liberal revolution of 1820.[87] Publishing 'The Star' two years after that invasion had succeeded, Thelwall is acutely aware that his poem has lost its main claims to public attention, prophecy and 'local interest'. Yet the fact that Spain remains in turmoil creates a new justification for the poem, which Thelwall dedicates to those who share his lingering hope for the triumph of 'Constitutional Patriotism'.[88]

'The Star' would appear, then, to be a thoroughly political work partaking of precisely the sort of matter-of-fact localism that Coleridge thought alien to good poetry. But the shortcomings of that reading are apparent from the opening lines, in which the Spanish crisis is eclipsed by the poet's attention to his urban and celestial surroundings:

> I WALK'D at midnight in the cluster'd glare
> Of the throng'd street—for, maugre the dull hour,
> The sons of Belial and the sons of care,
> From wine-cup or protracted toil, were there,
> Even yet in throng: nor had the sleep-god's power
> Clos'd half the city's eye.—And while around
> (As 'twould the midnight and mid-noon confound)
> The flaring gas, in implicative shower,
> O'er the blanch'd pavement shed factitious day,
> I gaz'd aloft:—for more I love to view,
> At such an hour, the soft and pensive hue
> Of heaven's blue concave, and the glimmering star,
> That whispers of the myriad worlds afar,
> Lit by the eternal splendours of such car—
> To us though dimly seen,—than to survey
> Whate'er the gorgeous city can display,
> In street or hall, of banquet-revelry:
> Even though the reeling carnival of joy
> Make every window blaze, and every tower.[89]

The contrast between the first-person night-walker and the demonic revellers and weary labourers who throng the streets is replicated between the 'flaring gas' of the street lamps and the 'glimmering star' towards which the poet turns his eye. Unlike the still wakeful half of the city that is blind to the scene overhead, Thelwall gazes aloft in rapt anticipation of a sublime spectacle, but his hope is at first disappointed:

>   All, all on high
> Was Stygian gloom—as though from out the sky
> The vanquish'd stars had fall'n, and lent their rays,
> That should through ever-changing time endure,
> Subservient to that earth-engender'd blaze
> That warr'd on Nature's light[.]

As his eyes adjust from the blinding glare of their former terrestrial objects, however, Thelwall comes to perceive

> one pure—
> One bright ethereal guide—one star of stars,
> That (as with emanation more divine
> His lamp were fed) continu'd still to shine,
> And his essential splendour scorn'd to veil,—
> Tho round he saw the lesser suns turn pale,
> And merge the lustre of their burnish'd cars
> In adventitious beams.[90]

In the prefatory note that accompanied the poem in the *Monthly Magazine*, Thelwall explains that while 'all singular atmospheric or planetary phenomena' tended to impress him deeply, on this occasion he was particularly struck by the appearance of the single star: 'he never remembers to have seen it so conspicuous on any other occasion'.[91] This puzzlement initiates a form of dialogue or internal monologue in which a voice that emanates from the star, the heavens or Thelwall's own mind urges him to make sense of the scene through a terrestrial analogy:

> 'Return to earth. Can that no proof supply
> Of heaven-illumin'd worth, which, even now,
> The high ethereal spirit scorns to bow,
> Or, in a sphere of seeming darkness, quail?['][92]

The voice prophesizes that the 'mimic suns' of earth will come to perceive that the human sphere, too, has its lodestar in the Spanish revolutionary Francisco Espoz y Mina, who in 1823 had led the Liberal army in Catalonia against the French and thereafter sought refuge in London[93]:

> [']Though now Oppression urge its meteor car
> Triumphant in a dazzled sphere below,
> Earth hath its MINA still, and Heaven its Star:
> And they shall shine, and spread their glorious light,
> Victorious o'er the envious shades of night[.']

The poem concludes with the almost jingoistic assertion that

> [']A thousand and a thousand spirits still
> (Though not the dazzled optic hence descry

Their watchful fires) hover o'er stream and hill
Of gloom'd Iberia; and their light shall fill
Even yet again the horizon, and re-shine
(When fade the baser fires—as fade they will!)—
In constellated glory round the shrine
Of Liberty, eternal and divine!
And MINA, with a patriot's joy, shall own—
Though hail'd her brightest star, he shines not all alone.'[94]

If 'The Star' is an epitome of Thelwall's career, this is not so much because it asserts the 'inadequacy of Romantic vision' – of transcendental perspectives on nature and religion that characterize the poetry of Wordsworth and Coleridge[95] – as because it suggests that such vision need not be the exclusive product of an idealist conception of the imagination. As the night-walker gazes raptly on the 'star of stars', his perception undergoes a modal transformation:

Entranc'd I gaz'd.
Those earth-born stars around unnotic'd blaz'd,
Thought-dimm'd; and on the mental eye alone
That isolated beam of glory shone,
Keeping the pauseless tenour of its way,—
Vicegerent of an else-extinguish'd zone[.]

At the same time that Thelwall begins to perceive the single star as an allegory of political freedom in Napoleonic Europe – 'Vice-regent of an else-extinguish'd zone' – he also begins to perceive it as an allegory of his 'mental eye', which alone amid a throng of night-time revellers makes a transition from visual to visionary modes of perception. This transition culminates in a moment of synesthetic revelation:

I gaz'd, and gaz'd, till thought began to climb,
And with that solitary star to stray;
Communing with the attribute sublime,
Which its ethereal progress would not stay
For those false glares, that, in our mole-weak eyes,
Eclipse the lustrous virtues of the skies,
And make heaven's concave dark; when from that beam
A voice—or emanation that might seem,
To the tense-listening heart, an in-voic'd stream
Of more than mortal colloquy, there came:—
A music of the spheres![96]

The fusion of the poet's physical and mental eye, and his consequent ability to perceive more than meets the eye – to *hear* the scene's 'invoic'd stream' – recalls not only the synesthetic logic of William Blake's 'London', of which Thelwall was perhaps unaware, but also the melding of faculties in Wordsworth's 'I wandered lonely as a Cloud'. In the latter, however, the sensory vision of a 'host of dancing Daffodils' is less significant than its recollection in tranquillity: 'I gazed—and gazed—but little thought / What wealth the shew to me had brought'. Recalling the power of 'spots of time' in *The Prelude*, moments of experience whose complex significance defies immediate comprehension, Wordsworth's vision of the daffodils achieves its fullest intensity in later moments of 'vacant or [...] pensive mood', when 'They flash upon that inward eye / Which is the bliss of solitude', transporting him back to the original experience.[97]

Noting that critics have been too hasty in reading Wordsworth's poem as a celebration of the faculty of transcendental vision, Alan Richardson makes a case for recuperating the Romantic period's demand for 'clear, vivid images readily susceptible to recreation' in the mind of the reader.[98] In some poems, he notes, such imagery enables the reader to re-enact the experience of the mind itself. Richardson proposes the phrase 'neural sublime' for this moment approaching 'antitranscendental revelation' when the subject is left marvelling not at the power of reason, but at the complexity and capacity of the brain itself.[99] In a comparable way, the main subject of 'The Star' turns out not to be its political prophecy, but the embodied train of perception and association whereby the night-walker becomes blind to his immediate environment and gains a revelatory star's-eye perspective on himself, discovering that he has been as much prone to 'deluded sight' as his contemporaries: he was too quick to see 'Stygian gloom' and 'semblant darkness' where 'one star of stars' still shone. The poem is thus a meditation on the central concern of Thelwall's entire career: how dissatisfaction with what one sees in the world of things as they are can trigger an imaginative vision that is not perforce reactionary, but can in fact renew hope in the triumph of liberty. Subject to the dual stimuli of his night-walk vision and the proximity of Whitehall, Thelwall effects what in his prison poetry he called a 'turn / From *Self* to *Sentient Nature*', an outward movement of the mind from introspection to consciousness of the sentient world and one's place within it.[100] In this sense, his initial hope of seeing 'the glimmering star / That whispers of the myriad worlds afar' has not been disappointed, but he has had to change his way of seeing to appreciate this, redirecting his gaze from the heavens to the here and now – to what Wordsworth once celebrated as 'the world / Of all of us, the place in which in the end / We find our happiness, or not at all'.[101]

Encapsulating Thelwall's ambition to spark new ways of seeing and responding in his audiences, 'The Star' is thus a fitting capstone to his oeuvre. It asserts and demonstrates the continuity between visual perception and visionary imagination, thus substantiating his remark in the margins of the *Biographia* that even a materialist imagination can exceed the limits of the known by a sort of negative conception; and it shows that the product of Thelwall's materialist imagination is not merely what one critic, referring to the poetry of Mark Akenside, calls 'vague Hartleyan associative verse', but the vivid conjunction of scientific, political and literary modes of perception and expression that Coleridge once praised as Thelwall's 'vigorous song'.[102] Underpinning that 'song' is a quintessentially radical and Romantic faith in the imagination's power to spark new forms of consciousness, as encapsulated by the conclusion of Thelwall's *Monthly Magazine* essay on Burke. The essay quotes at length from a passage in the treatise *On the Sublime* in which the narrator addresses his interlocutor on the subject of images:

'Visions, which by some are called images, contribute very much, my dear youth, to the weight, magnificence, and force of compositions. The name of an image, is generally given to any idea, however represented in the mind, which is communicable to others by discourse: but a more particular sense of it has now prevailed; 'When the imagination is so warmed and affected, that you seem to behold yourself the very things you are describing; and to display them to the life, before the eyes of an audience.'

'You cannot be ignorant, that rhetorical and poetical images have a different intent. The design of a poetical image is surprise, that of a rhetorical is perspicuity. However to move and strike the imagination, is a design common to both.'[103]

Describing a form of prolepsis – the exhibition of that which the speaker wishes to engender in the audience – this passage goes to the very heart of Thelwall's corpus. Whether by means of 'poetical' or 'rhetorical' genres, in speech or writing, Thelwall sought to move and strike the imaginations of his audiences by raising vivid images in the mind of things as they really were in the world, and as they might yet be.

Although this chapter and this book as a whole have sought to recover the materialist underpinnings of that endeavour, the overarching argument has not been that a materialist understanding of Romanticism ought to prevail over an idealist one. Rather, I have tried to bring to view what I referred to in the introduction as the double-helix DNA of Romanticism: the dialogical relationship between materialism and idealism that helps give the literature of the period its vital power. Borrowing a metaphor from Coleridge, we might also think of this relationship as a 'war embrace'. The metaphor occurs in a passage of the *Biographia* annotated by Thelwall that describes the struggle between 'creative power' and 'intellectual energy' in Shakespeare's poems: 'Each in its excess of strength seems to threaten the extinction of the other'; either they are reconciled and fight a mutual foe, or 'like two rapid streams' they repel each other before merging and flowing onwards in a wider channel and 'with one voice'.[104] Given Coleridge's resistance to such a confluence of ideas with Thelwall – his sense, that is, of an unbridgeable aesthetic and ideological 'chasm' across which they could not converse – and given the persistence of such resistance in criticism, a still more fitting metaphor for the relationship that this chapter has been describing is, in the end, Thelwall's own, articulated to Coleridge in July 1797 shortly after his visit to Nether Stowey:

> Ah! 'twould be sweet, beneath the neighb'ring thatch,
> In philosophic amity to dwell,
> Indicting moral verse, or tale, or theme,
> Gay or instructive; and it would be sweet,
> With kindly interchange of mutual aid,
> To delve out little garden plots, the while
> Sweet converse flow'd, suspending oft the arm
> And half-driven spade, while, eager, one propounds,
> And listens one, weighing each pregnant word,
> And pondering fit reply, that may untwist
> The knotty point—perchance, of import high——
> Of Moral Truth, of Causes Infinite,
> Creating Power! or Uncreated Worlds
> Eternal and uncaus'd! or whatsoe'er,
> Of Metaphysic, or of Ethic lore,
> The mind, with curious subtilty, pursues—
> Agreeing, or dissenting—sweet alike,
> When wisdom, and not victory, the end.[105]

It would be a fitting tribute to Thelwall's materialist imagination if its commitment to bridging the chasm with alternative views and traditions in the name of collective wisdom were to be a vital stimulus to critical conversations about Romanticism today.

Appendices

1

Peter Crompton, Letter to John Thelwall, 11 Sept. 1800

Source: The Morgan Library, New York, MA 77 (19)
[Addressee: M[r] John Thelwall/Llyswen/near the Hay/Brecknockshire]

Eton, near Liverpool. Sep.[r] 11.th 1800.

My Dear Friend,

It is very long since I wrote to you which is to be imputed to my various occupations & cares & also to my being much engaged by company, as well as my having nothing of very great importance to communicate to you; & I write now more with a view of hearing from you than for any other object.

I hope you will be able to send me a good account [word almost illegible: both?] of yourself & Mrs Thelwall, & that your journey with Miss Hawes[1] was an agreeable one to you both. Shepherd[2] gave up visiting you in consequence of his suspicion of his mare being with foal, he seem'd very desirous of seeing you, but as he went in Coaches he could not have done it without great inconvenience. He continues pleased with your Poem,[3] some more of it we expect you will soon send us. Coleridge & Sara were with us on their way to the Lakes, where they are gone to reside; they are both much improved, our Ladies were much pleased with her, contrary to expectation; he was quite a favourite at Liverpool.[4] We had much conversation about you, in which he was very greatly interested. He seems tinctured deeply with the metaphysics of Germany, where he has been for the sake of obtaining the language: I wrote the former part of this letter yesterday morning, Shepherd supped with us last night. The conversation turned upon your Poem, he said he had left it at Roscoes,[5] but was very doubtful whether he would be able to read it in consequence of his numerous avocations &c. Shepherd admires your Poem, but he says he durst not advise you to publish it on your own account for fear you sh.[d] lose cash by it; if you can, it would be desirable for you to sell the copy; he says if it be published he will make honorable mention of it in the Review he writes for.[6] Shepherd spent the day at Dorchester very pleasantly, & seem'd much better for his journey, he imbibed D[r] Beddoes's air at Bristol which greatly affected him, a circumstance he did not in the least expect.[7] I have heard lately from Derby, Mrs Evans has a son born abt.[t] 8 weeks ago, she is but poorly, & is gone for the recovery of her health to Scarborough.[8] Old W.[m] Strutt I think I informed you is dead, the rest of the Strutts were well.[9] Mr Ward, who lent his Baptist Chapel for you to lecture in, & where I & many others were almost knock'd on the head, has likewise given up the Ghost.[10] There has been rioting in Derby, Nottingham & several other places, concerning which I have had no particular information. B[utter? Bread? is? paper damaged] a very scarce article in Liverpool, where there were symptoms of rioting, which I believe are removed, a few days ago. Do not copy me in my long neglecting to write to you, but be assured whenever you find yourself at liberty to write it will give the Mrs & Miss Crompton great pleasure to hear of you Mrs Thelwall & the Children, if you can but send good accounts of them.

Farewell   Yr.ˢ affect.ᵗˡʸ   Peter Crompton

2

Thelwall, 'To Dr. Peter Crompton', *Poems, Chiefly Written in Retirement* (1801)

Source: Cambridge University Library, Rare Books Y.19.43 (no. 1)

TO DR. PETER CROMPTON.
ETON-HOUSE NEAR LIVERPOOL.

My dear Friend!

DEDICATIONS have generally originated in the expectation of future Favours: They reflect, therefore, but little Honour, either upon the Writers, or the Patrons to whom they are addressed. In such Dedications I have never trafficked; and my mind is not yet subdued enough, either by its Wrongs, or its Afflictions, to stoop to the accustomed Barter.—If the Literature of my Country is not dishonoured by my want of talent, it shall not be degraded by my servility.

In the present Address, indeed, I have little temptation. Your Kindness needs not the auxiliary stimulus of Adulation; and your Domestic Habits, and Domestic Happiness, render you little solicitous of 'the Babbling of a Name'.[11] *And sure I am, that if, in this expression of an Ardent and Sincere Esteem, I had any view whatever upon your future liberality, I should prove myself unworthy of the Favours I have already received.*

Yet I freely confess that the mere disinterested acknowledgement of those Favours is not the sole motive for my Dedication. Tho on You it can bestow no Honour, some, perhaps, it may reflect on me. It is a consolation, and a credit I am unwilling to lose the opportunity of boasting, that (in the midst of that general defection and desertion, of which it has suited the timidity of some, and, perhaps, the interest of others, to render me the Victim) one Family, at least, there has been, of property and consideration in the country, who have known me too intimately to give ear to the Calumnies by which I have been proscribed—One generous and self-judging Friend, among that Class of the Community so successfully enflamed against me, who, when Ruin overwhelmed, stretched forth the ready arm to rescue me, as from unmerited evil; and who (still more generous) when the last of Human Miseries had fallen upon me—when Reason was prostrate, and the Heart was broken, poured into my Wounds the only Balm of which they were susceptible; and, with a solicitude, that neither distance of Space nor of Circumstances could chill, aroused me (as far as I was capable of being roused) from unavailing Remembrances to more Vital Duties; and restored me to my Family, and to my Muse.[12]

Yes,—One such there is: who has known how to heap me with Obligations without bending me before him—who has been at once 'My Benefactor and my Brother Man'[13]——*and whose open Hospitality, and the publicity of whose Attentions, have encouraged me to believe that He will not shrink from this public acknowledgment of the feelings with which he (and all that I have known of the name of Crompton) will ever be remembered,*

By
His obliged,
Protected,
Consoled,
And devoted Friend,
JOHN THELWALL.

Castle-Street, Hereford,
Sept. 16, 1801.

3

Thelwall, 'The Star that Shone When Other Stars Were Dim: A Night-Walk in the Vicinity of Whitehall', *Monthly Magazine* 59 Supplement (1825), 661–3

THE STAR THAT SHONE
WHEN OTHER STARS WERE DIM.

––––

[The ensuing Verses were written at a time when, though the disastrous crisis was fast approaching, the fate of Spain was not decided—when the armies of France (with the tacit, though dissembled, connivance of the English Court and Government) were advancing in their liberticide career—when defection after defection had thinned the ranks of patriotism, and Mina, alone, was conspicuously upholding, with dauntless valour and incorruptible independence, the standard of liberty around which the hopes of patriot humanity could rally.[14]

At such a point of eventful time, the idea of the poem was suggested, and some of the lines were mentally composed, while the author was walking along, at midnight, in the neighbourhood of Whitehall, towards his cottage in the rural vicinage of the metropolis.

The singular phenomenon (for he never remembers to have seen it so conspicuous on any other occasion), from the blaze of the gas-lights all around him—the complete apparent blackness of the sky, in which one solitary star alone had lustre sufficient to overpower the dazzling effect of the more approximate glare—struck (as is the tendency of all singular atmospheric or planetary phenomena) strongly on his imagination: and the similitude to the state of the political horizon, in a country towards which all eyes, at that time, were so anxiously turned, was so irresistible, that his mind could not resume a settled tranquillity, till it had vented the feelings which the comparison had excited.

The total overthrow which ensued, of every hope to which the wishes of humanity had struggled to cling, prevented any immediate use from being made of what the imagination had suggested. The poet (if the author may presume to arrogate that name) was proved, at least, to be no *prophet*; and the *local* interest (in a production which, perhaps, can aspire to *no other*) was of course abated. Circumstances, however, are every now and then occurring, which cannot but impel the mind occasionally to return to the feelings then awake. The utter impossibility of the permanent continuance of the present state of things in Spain (if state it may be called, that stability, or shape, hath none), cannot but be apparent to every one; and some symptoms have manifested themselves which may encourage at least the hope, that, at no very distant period, the cause of Constitutional Patriotism may yet revive, in a country the most miserably afflicted, the most wantonly and stupidly oppressed, and the most contemptibly degraded, of all the priest-ridden and tyrant-goaded nations, whose abject, or whose compelled submission, has scandalized the annals of modern Europe. If such event should occur, the memory (perhaps the re-manifestation) of the patriot valour and enterprize of Mina must be the loadstar to which the hopes and emulation of Spanish heroism will be directed. Those who can still cherish such hopes, may perhaps feel some interest in the subject of the ensuing lines; and to such, alone, they can be dedicated with any very sanguine hope of attention.][15]

———

I WALK'D at midnight in the cluster'd glare
Of the throng'd street—for, maugre the dull hour,
The sons of Belial and the sons of care,
From wine-cup or protracted toil, were there,
Even yet in throng: nor had the sleep-god's power
Clos'd half the city's eye.—And while around
(As 'twould the midnight and mid-noon confound)
The flaring gas, in implicative shower,
O'er the blanch'd pavement shed factitious day,
I gaz'd aloft:—for more I love to view,
At such an hour, the soft and pensive hue
Of heaven's blue concave, and the glimmering star,
That whispers of the myriad worlds afar,
Lit by the eternal splendours of such car—
To us though dimly seen,—than to survey
Whate'er the gorgeous city can display,
In street or hall, of banquet-revelry:
Even though the reeling carnival of joy
Make every window blaze, and every tower.
　　　　So to the azure-wonted canopy
I gaz'd aloft—in hopes I there might spy,
Above the dazzling of that glare terrene,
Which but my weaker vision did annoy,
The eternal lamps that o'er my pensive bower,
In distance from the city's fretful stour,
Had hung so glorious through the yestere'en.
　　　　Intent I gaz'd. But no accustom'd ray
Of night-consoling azure there was seen;
Though the soft air, with genial breath serene,
Signall'd nor cloud, nor mist, that should obscure
The wakeful eye of heav'n. All, all on high
Was Stygian gloom—as though from out the sky
The vanquish'd stars had fall'n, and lent their rays,
That should through ever-changing time endure,
Subservient to that earth-engender'd blaze
That warr'd on Nature's light:—all, but one pure—
One bright ethereal guide—one star of stars,
That (as with emanation more divine
His lamp were fed) continu'd still to shine,
And his essential splendour scorn'd to veil,—
Though round he saw the lesser suns turn pale,
And merge the lustre of their burnish'd cars
In adventitious beams.
　　　　　　　　Entranc'd I gaz'd.
Those earth-born stars around unnotic'd blaz'd,
Thought-dimm'd; and on the mental eye alone

That isolated beam of glory shone,
Keeping the pauseless tenour of its way,—
Vicegerent of an else-extinguish'd zone;
As only to the eternal font of day,
When HE should re-assert his glorious throne,
The tribute of its homage it could pay,—
Or mingle but with lustres like its own.
      I gaz'd, and gaz'd, till thought began to climb,
And with that solitary star to stray;
Communing with the attribute sublime,
Which its ethereal progress would not stay
For those false glares, that, in our mole-weak eyes,
Eclipse the lustrous virtues of the skies,
And make heaven's concave dark; when from that beam
A voice—or emanation that might seem,
To the tense-listening heart, an in-voic'd stream
Of more than mortal colloquy, there came:—
A music of the spheres!
                'And marvel'st thou—'
So spake that voice—'and strain'st thy vaulting brow,
As in the rapture of some waking dream,
To the crystalline arch, there to descry
My seeming lonely path?—as it were strange
To mortal sense, that the seraphic eye
Its uncontaminate lustre should not change,
Nor blench the life of heaven's eternal flame;
But the brief tapers of earth's pomp defy;
And, 'midst the semblant darkness, still the same
Fix'd course pursue, as when, distinct and clear,
A thousand ministering seraphim appear,
Thronging his path through the resplendent sphere,
And with the lustre of his progress vie!
      'Return to earth. Can that no proof supply
Of heaven-illumin'd worth, which, even now,
The high ethereal spirit scorns to bow,
Or, in a sphere of seeming darkness, quail?
      'What though a thousand vauntful weaklings fail
Before those earth-dissembled glories vain,
That dazzle with their glare the sordid train
And feeble!—or whose weak orbs cannot strain
Beyond the ignorant present, but think bright
Whate'er o'erpowers the frailty of their sight;—
Though to such narrow circumstance confin'd,
The half-fledg'd swallow, yet unimp'd for flight,
Shall leave it on unpractic'd wing behind!—
Or, stint it but an hour the wonted aid
Of servile ministry, and it shall fade,
And like the fen-fire sink: or, if the breath
Of heaven but stir it rudely, in the death
Of darkness 't shall expire,—leaving its blind

Adorers to unpitied scorn resign'd—
Credulity's meet wage! So—even so!—
Spite of the glare these mimic suns have made,
That o'er their tracks a semblant glory throw,
Casting the stellar virtues into shade,
Shall their benighting lustre fade: for know,
Though now Oppression urge its meteor car
Triumphant in a dazzled sphere below,
Earth hath its MINA still, and Heaven its Star:
And they shall shine, and spread their glorious light,
Victorious o'er the envious shades of night,—
When in primeval gloom extinct shall lie
Those earth-deluding lamps, that vauntful now
Appear to merge all lustre in their brow!
     'Nor think that, though to the deluded sight
One star alone of all the expanse seem bright,
That all beside is dim. Thy way pursue
As meditation leads—leaving behind
This sense-confounding glare; and thou shalt find
(The free horizon opening to thy view)
That not in isolated splendour I
Maintain the regency of this deep sky:
Nor solitary, though transcending, HE—
The earth-star of fair Freedom's galaxy.
A thousand and a thousand spirits still
(Though not the dazzled optic hence descry
Their watchful fires) hover o'er stream and hill
Of gloom'd Iberia; and their light shall fill
Even yet again the horizon, and re-shine
(When fade the baser fires—as fade they will!)—
In constellated glory round the shrine
Of Liberty, eternal and divine!
And MINA, with a patriot's joy, shall own—
Though hail'd her brightest star, he shines not all alone.'   Δ[16]

Notes

Introduction

1. 'Jack Bull', 'On Mister Surgeon Thelwall', *Tomahawk* 27 Oct. 1795, repr. in *British War Poetry in the Age of Romanticism 1793–1815*, comp. Betty T. Bennett, digital edn, ed. Orianne Smith, Romantic Circles, Sept. 2004, http://www.rc.umd.edu/editions/warpoetry/1795/1795_17.html (accessed 23 Oct. 2012).
2. Thelwall, 'A Sheep-Shearing Song', repr. in Mrs. Thelwall [Henrietta Cecil Thelwall], *The Life of John Thelwall* (London, 1837), pp. 261–3, 449.
3. Although the term 'scientist' was not coined until 1833, I use 'science' here interchangeably with 'natural philosophy', following recent scholarship and Thelwall's own practice. He defined elocution, for instance, as both a 'branch of Natural Philosophy' and a science 'founded on *ascertainable principles, and susceptible of palpable demonstrations'*. See *The Vestibule of Eloquence: Original Articles, Oratorical and Poetical, Intended as Exercises in Recitation, at the Institution, Bedford Place, Russell Square* (London, 1810), pp. 3, 12.
4. [Francis Jeffrey], *Observations on Mr. Thelwall's Letter to the Editor of the Edinburgh Review* (Edinburgh, 1804), p. 14. Chalk Farm, north of London, was the site of a large outdoor meeting of reformers in April 1794.
5. Britton, *The Auto-Biography of John Britton* (London, 1849), vol. I, p. 146. Thelwall's widow Henrietta Cecil, having devoted the first volume of her *Life of John Thelwall* to his achievements in politics, planned a second that would encompass his literary and scientific (specifically elocutionary) pursuits, but that second volume never appeared. Mrs. Thelwall, *Life*, p. xii.
6. Thompson, *The Making of the English Working Class* (London: Victor Gollancz, 1963; repr. London: Penguin, 1991). The earliest book about Thelwall was Charles Cestre's *John Thelwall: A Pioneer of Democracy and Social Reform in England during the French Revolution* (London: Swan Sonnenschein, 1906), which was based partly on six volumes of Thelwall's letters, notes and outlines of intended books and lectures that Cestre purchased at Sotheby's in June 1904 and are now lost. Nicholas Roe reconstructs the volumes' likely contents in 'The Lives of John Thelwall: Another View of the "Jacobin Fox"', in *John Thelwall: Radical Romantic and Acquitted Felon*, ed. Steve Poole, The Enlightenment World 11 (London: Pickering and Chatto, 2009), pp. 17–19. Another loss to the Thelwall archive was the seizure, on his arrest in 1794, of many of his early manuscripts – 'all the unpublished material of ten years' – including poems, plays, novels and essays. Mrs. Thelwall, *Life*, p. 163.
7. E. P. Thompson, 'Hunting the Jacobin Fox', *Past and Present* 142 (1994), 94–140; Claeys (ed.), *The Politics of English Jacobinism: Writings of John Thelwall* (University Park: Pennsylvania State University Press, 1995); Claeys, 'The Origins of the Rights of Labour: Republicanism, Commerce, and the Construction of Modern Social Theory in Britain, 1796–1805', *Journal of Modern History* 66 (1994), 249–90; Barrell, *Imagining the King's*

Death: Figurative Treason, Fantasies of Regicide, 1793–1796 (Oxford: Oxford University Press, 2000), pp. 104–8, 391–401.

8. Scrivener, *Seditious Allegories: John Thelwall and Jacobin Writing* (University Park: Pennsylvania State University Press, 2001); Thompson, *John Thelwall in the Wordsworth Circle: The Silenced Partner*, Nineteenth-Century Major Lives and Letters (New York: Palgrave Macmillan, 2012). A catalyst of Thelwall's literary recovery was Nicholas Roe's discussion of his relationship with the canonical poets in *Wordsworth and Coleridge: The Radical Years* (Oxford: Clarendon Press, 1988).

9. See, for instance, Alan Richardson, *British Romanticism and the Science of the Mind*, Cambridge Studies in Romanticism 47 (Cambridge: Cambridge University Press, 2001); Nicholas Roe (ed.), *Samuel Taylor Coleridge and the Sciences of Life* (Oxford: Oxford University Press, 2001); Tim Fulford, Debbie Lee and Peter J. Kitson, *Literature, Science and Exploration in the Romantic Era: Bodies of Knowledge*, Cambridge Studies in Romanticism 60 (Cambridge: Cambridge University Press, 2004); Christa Knellwolf and Jane Goodall (eds), *Frankenstein's Science: Experimentation and Discovery in Romantic Culture, 1780–1830* (Aldershot: Ashgate, 2008); and Noel Jackson, *Science and Sensation in Romantic Poetry*, Cambridge Studies in Romanticism 73 (Cambridge: Cambridge University Press, 2008).

10. Thelwall, *An Essay, Towards a Definition of Animal Vitality* (London, 1793), repr. in *Selected Political Writings of John Thelwall*, ed. Robert Lamb and Corinna Wagner, 4 vols (London: Pickering and Chatto, 2009), vol. I, pp. 17, 29.

11. Thelwall, *Poems, Chiefly Written in Retirement* (Hereford, 1801; repr. Oxford: Woodstock, 1989), pp. xxii–xxiii.

12. Thelwall, *A Letter to Henry Cline, Esq., on Imperfect Developments of the Faculties, Mental and Moral, as well as Constitutional and Organic; and on the Treatment of Impediments of Speech* (London, 1810), repr. in *Selected Political Writings of John Thelwall*, ed. Robert Lamb and Corinna Wagner, 4 vols (London: Pickering and Chatto, 2009), vol. IV, p. 7.

13. Shelley, *A Defence of Poetry*, in *Percy Bysshe Shelley: The Major Works*, ed. Zachary Leader and Michael O'Neill (Oxford: Oxford University Press, 2003; repr. 2009), p. 701.

14. Donald Reiman (ed.), *Ode to Science, John Gilpin's Ghost, Poems, The Trident of Albion*, by John Thelwall (New York: Garland, 1978), p. x.

15. I allude to the original title of William Godwin's 1794 novel *Things As They Are; or, The Adventures of Caleb Williams* and to Jerome McGann's *The Romantic Ideology: A Critical Investigation* (Chicago: University of Chicago Press, 1983) and the scholarship inspired by it.

16. Michel Foucault, *The Birth of the Clinic: An Archaeology of Medical Perception*, trans. A. M. Sheridan Smith (London: Tavistock, 1973; repr. New York: Vintage, 1994), p. 145. Simon Blackburn offers a comparable definition in *The Oxford Dictionary of Philosophy* (Oxford: Oxford University Press, 1994), s.v. 'vitalism'. Cf. also George Rousseau's definition of vitalism as the belief in the existence of 'a mysterious force running through *all matter* in the universe', in 'The Perpetual Crises of Modernism and the Traditions of Enlightenment Vitalism: with a Note on Mikhail Bakhtin', in *The Crisis of Modernism: Bergson and the Vitalist Controversy*, ed. Frederick Burwick and Paul Douglass (Cambridge: Cambridge University Press, 1992), p. 24.

17. Vickers, *Coleridge and the Doctors, 1795–1806* (Oxford: Clarendon Press, 2004); Gigante, *Life: Organic Form and Romanticism* (New Haven, CT: Yale University Press, 2009). A landmark study of the organic and vitalistic qualities of the Romantic imagination remains M. H. Abrams's *The Mirror and the Lamp: Romantic Theory and the Critical Tradition* (Oxford: Oxford University Press, 1953; repr. New York: Norton, 1958).

18. McGann, *Romantic Ideology*; Richardson, *Science of the Mind*, p. 36. See also Richardson, *The Neural Sublime: Cognitive Theories and Romantic Texts* (Baltimore, MD: Johns Hopkins University Press, 2010); Sha, 'Romantic Physiology and the Work of Romantic Imagination: Hypothesis and Speculation in Science and Coleridge', *European Romantic Review* 24, no. 4 (2013), 403–19; Sha, 'Toward a Physiology of the Romantic Imagination', *Configurations* 17 (2009), 206–9; Sha, 'Imagination as Inter-Science', *European Romantic Review* 20, no. 5 (Dec. 2009), 661–9; Levinson, 'A Motion and a Spirit: Romancing Spinoza', *Studies in Romanticism* 46 (Winter 2007), 367–408; and Ruston, *Shelley and Vitality* (Houndmills: Palgrave Macmillan, 2005; repr. 2012).

19. Richardson, 'Reimagining the Romantic Imagination', *European Romantic Review* 24, no. 4 (2013), 385.

20. Hartman, 'Wordsworth and Metapsychology', in *Wordsworth's Poetic Theory: Knowledge, Language, Experience*, ed. Alexander Regier and Stefan H. Uhlig (Houndmills: Palgrave Macmillan, 2010), p. 195.

21. Ruston, *Shelley and Vitality*; Levinson, 'A Motion and a Spirit'; Jackson, *Science and Sensation*; Gilmore, *Aesthetic Materialism: Electricity and American Romanticism* (Stanford: Stanford University Press, 2009).

22. Roe, *The Politics of Nature: Wordsworth and Some Contemporaries*, 2nd edn (Houndmills: Palgrave, 2002), especially pp. 87–119, where Roe reprints the *Animal Vitality* essay and provides illuminating commentary.

23. Rousseau, 'Perpetual Crises', 66.

24. Packham, *Eighteenth-Century Vitalism: Bodies, Culture, Politics*, Palgrave Studies in the Enlightenment, Romanticism and the Cultures of Print (Houndmills: Palgrave Macmillan, 2012), pp. 122–43. Thelwall's materialist speculations about 'animal vitality' are also discussed in James Robert Allard, *Romanticism, Medicine, and the Poet's Body*, The Nineteenth Century (Aldershot: Ashgate, 2007), pp. 66–70; and Mary Fairclough, *The Romantic Crowd: Sympathy, Controversy and Print Culture*, Cambridge Studies in Romanticism 97 (Cambridge: Cambridge University Press, 2013), pp. 107–21. I engage their readings in the ensuing chapters.

25. Alan Richardson similarly notes that a rigid retrospective distinction between materialists and vitalists can be misleading, but he concurs in aligning Thelwall with 'the new, biological materialism', in *Science of the Mind*, pp. 29–30, 68. On electricity's vexed ontological status, see Gilmore, *Aesthetic Materialism*, pp. 22–6.

26. Macherey, 'In a Materialist Way', in *Philosophy in France Today*, ed. Alan Montefiore (Cambridge: Cambridge University Press, 1983), p. 142.

27. See, for instance, the essays collected in *New Materialisms: Ontology, Agency, and Politics*, ed. Diana Coole and Samantha Frost (Durham: Duke University Press, 2010).

28. Williams, *Keywords: A Vocabulary of Culture and Society*, rev. edn (New York: Oxford University Press, 1983), p. 197, where he notes that the use of

'materialism' to designate 'an overriding or primary concern with the production and acquisition of things and money' has 'no necessary philosophical and scientific connection' to the first two definitions.

29. Gilmore, *Aesthetic Materialism*, pp. 9–10.
30. The volumes were first located by Judith Thompson in the summer of 2004 in the Derby Local Studies Library, where I consulted them in February 2005. So far they have received sustained attention only in Thompson's *Silenced Partner*.
31. [Jeffrey], *Observations*, p. 14.
32. Coleridge, 'Irregular Sonnet: To John Thelwall', in *Poetical Works*, ed. J. C. C. Mays, 3 vols, Bollingen Series 75 (London: Routledge and Kegan Paul, 2001), vol. I, pp. 264–5; and *The Collected Letters of Samuel Taylor Coleridge*, ed. Earl Leslie Griggs, 6 vols (Oxford: Clarendon, 1956–71), vol. I, p. 137.
33. *Oxford English Dictionary (OED) Online*, s.v. 'vigour, *n.*' and 'vigorous, *adj.*' Samuel Johnson defines 'vigour' primarily as force or strength, secondarily as mental force or intellectual ability, and thirdly as energy or efficacy, in *A Dictionary of the English Language*, 2 vols (London, 1786), vol. II, n. pag., Eighteenth Century Collections Online, http://find.galegroup.com.proxy. library.nd.edu/ecco (accessed 22 Oct. 2012).
34. Thelwall, Marginalia on Coleridge's *Biographia Literaria*, repr. in Burton R. Pollin and Redmond Burke, 'John Thelwall's Marginalia in a Copy of Coleridge's *Biographia Literaria*', *Bulletin of the New York Public Library* 74 (1970), 82.
35. *OED Online*, s.v. 'nervous, *adj.*' George Rousseau notes that the eighteenth-century rise of a 'nervous style' was tied to an empiricist-sensationalist aesthetics of perception based on the functions of the brain and nervous system, in *Nervous Acts: Essays on Literature, Culture and Sensibility* (Houndmills: Palgrave Macmillan, 2004), pp. 40–6.
36. Coleridge, *Collected Letters*, vol. I, p. 307.
37. On the political contests over language use and theory in the period, see, notably, James T. Boulton, *The Language of Politics in the Age of Wilkes and Burke* (London: Routledge and Kegan Paul, 1963; repr. Westport: Greenwood, 1975); and Olivia Smith, *The Politics of Language 1791–1819* (Oxford: Clarendon Press, 1984).
38. Thelwall, *Musalogia: or The Paths of Poesy*, in *Poems, Chiefly Suggested by the Scenery of Nature; to Which are Added Odes &c. Amatory and Congratulatory, Translations, and Attempts at Humour* ('Derby manuscript'), 3 vols, Derby Local Studies Library, Derby, England, 5868–5870, vol. III, p. 746v.
39. Thelwall had by this time published *Poems on Various Subjects*, 2 vols (London, 1787) and *Poems Written in Close Confinement* (London, 1795). Coleridge may be referring to either collection when he remarks in a letter of November 1796 that he now owns all of Thelwall's works 'except your essay on animal vitality which I never had, & your *poems* which I bought on their first publication, & lost them'. *Collected Letters*, vol. I, p. 258.
40. See Nicholas Roe's remarks about this 'positive' mode of historical reading in *Politics of Nature*, p. 9, and Damian Walford Davies's comparable remarks about his attention to 'the modalities of presence' in *Presences that Disturb: Models of Romantic Identity in the Literature and Culture of the 1790s* (Cardiff: University of Wales Press, 2002), p. 3.

41. Magnuson, *Reading Public Romanticism* (Princeton: Princeton University Press, 1998).
42. Thompson, *Making of the English Working Class*, p. 172.
43. The phrase 'literal archaeology' is borrowed from Nicholas Roe, *John Keats and the Culture of Dissent* (Oxford: Clarendon Press, 1997), p. ix.
44. Thelwall, *Animal Vitality*, repr. in *SPW*, vol. I, p. 30.
45. Richardson, *Science of the Mind*, p. 122.
46. Raymond Williams notes in *Keywords*, pp. 201–2, that although 'mechanism' has been used synonymously with 'materialism' since the seventeenth century, especially by materialism's critics, the former term has specific associations with mechanical arts and crafts, and by extension with the actions of machines. The materialist Thelwall was strongly opposed to the view that man might be merely a machine, as the following chapters explain.
47. On this effect in Keats's poetry, see Richardson, *Science of the Mind*, p. 122.
48. See, notably, E. P. Thompson, 'Disenchantment or Default? A Lay Sermon', in *The Romantics: England in a Revolutionary Age* (New York: New Press, 1997), pp. 33–74.
49. Philp, 'The Fragmented Ideology of Reform', in *The French Revolution and British Popular Politics*, ed. Mark Philp (Cambridge: Cambridge University Press, 1991), pp. 72–3.
50. Thelwall, *The Speech of John Thelwall, at the Second Meeting of the London Corresponding Society, and Other Friends of Reform, Held at Copenhagen-House, on Thursday, November 12, 1795* (London, 1795), p. i.
51. Thelwall, *Poems Written in Close Confinement in the Tower and Newgate, under a Charge of High Treason* (London, 1795; repr. Otley: Woodstock, 2000), p. 22.
52. Klancher, 'Godwin and the Republican Romance: Genre, Politics, and Contingency in Cultural History', *Modern Language Quarterly* 56, no. 2 (June 1995), 145–65.
53. Coleridge, *Collected Letters*, vol. II, p. 723.

1 Vital Principles

1. Thelwall, *Animal Vitality*, repr. in *SPW*, vol. I, p. 29.
2. Mrs. Thelwall, *Life*, p. 80.
3. 'Mr. Thelwall', *Gentleman's Magazine* ns 2 (1834), 550.
4. Foucault, *Birth of the Clinic*, p. 197; Porter, *Flesh in the Age of Reason: How the Enlightenment Transformed the Way We See Our Bodies and Souls* (London: Allen Lane, 2003; repr. London: Penguin, 2004); Porter, 'Medical Science and Human Science in the Enlightenment', in *Inventing Human Science: Eighteenth-Century Domains*, ed. Christopher Fox, Roy Porter and Robert Wokler (Berkeley: University of California Press, 1995), pp. 53–87; Rousseau, *Nervous Acts*; and Rousseau, 'Science and the Discovery of the Imagination in Enlightened England', *Eighteenth-Century Studies* 3, no. 1 (Autumn 1969), 108–35.
5. Richardson, *Science of the Mind*, p. 67. Thelwall's 1793 paper on 'animal vitality' receives attention chiefly as a source for his radical politics in Roe, *Politics of Nature*, pp. 87–95; Allard, *Poet's Body*, pp. 66–70; Packham, *Eighteenth-Century Vitalism*, pp. 116–43; and Fairclough, *Romantic Crowd*, pp. 108–10.

6. Thelwall, 'Mr. Thelwall's Lecture. On the Harmonic Qualities of the Literal Elements, and Their Classification, According to Their Musical and Other Inherent Properties', *Panoramic Miscellany* 1 (1826), 193–4; repr. in *Selected Political Writings of John Thelwall*, ed. Robert Lamb and Corinna Wagner, 4 vols (London: Pickering and Chatto, 2009), vol. IV, p. 208.

7. Thelwall, *Retirement*, p. vii. The 'Prefatory Memoir' in the *Retirement* collection and the posthumous *Life of John Thelwall* by Henrietta Cecil Thelwall are the two chief sources of information about his life. See also Nicholas Roe, 'Thelwall, John (1764–1834)', in *Oxford Dictionary of National Biography*, ed. H. C. G. Matthew and Brian Harrison, Oxford: Oxford University Press, 2004, online edn, ed. Lawrence Goldman, Sept. 2012, http://www.oxforddnb.com/view/article/27167 (accessed 16 Nov. 2012); and Judith Thompson (ed.), 'John Thelwall in Time and Text', Romantic Circles, Aug. 2012, http://www.rc.umd.edu/reference/thelwall_chronology/index.html (accessed 27 Oct. 2012).

8. Thelwall, *Retirement*, p. ix.

9. Thelwall, *Retirement*, pp. xvii, xv.

10. Thelwall, *Retirement*, p. xviii. Thelwall's decision to quit his legal apprenticeship was also spurred by 'an attack made upon his innocence' by a partner of his employer John Impey. The aggressor committed suicide when his transgressions came to light.

11. *Poems on Various Subjects* was modestly received: the *Critical Review* judged it to contain 'indications of an *original* and bold imagination'. Quoted in Mrs. Thelwall, *Life*, p. 36.

12. Thelwall used the interval of their long-distance courtship to educate his future wife, as recounted in Mrs. Thelwall, *Life*, pp. 37–8.

13. Mrs. Thelwall, *Life*, pp. 1–2.

14. Druin Burch, *Digging up the Dead: The Life and Times of Astley Cooper, an Extraordinary Surgeon* (London: Vintage, 2008), pp. 98–9.

15. Parkinson, a member of the Society for Constitutional Information and London Corresponding Society, published several radical pamphlets. Walker went to Paris, became acquainted with many radicals and translated the manifesto of the Theophilanthropists, an atheistic society. See Michael Bevan, 'Parkinson, James (1755–1824)' and Deborah Brunton, 'Walker, John (1759–1830)', both in *Oxford Dictionary of National Biography*, online edn, ed. Lawrence Goldman, Oct. 2009, http://www.oxforddnb.com (accessed 16 Oct. 2012 and 22 June 2011).

16. Mrs. Thelwall, *Life*, pp. 79–80.

17. Burch, *Digging*, p. 41.

18. Mrs. Thelwall, *Life*, p. 104.

19. I have so far been able to consult only the second volume of the *Biographical and Imperial Magazine* for 1789 (July–Dec.) and the first volume for 1790 (Jan.–June). 'Phlogiston' referred to a substance supposed to exist in all combustible bodies.

20. Carolyn D. Williams, 'Hawes, William (1736–1808)', in *Oxford Dictionary of National Biography*, online edn, ed. Lawrence Goldman, Oct. 2009, http://www.oxforddnb.com/view/article/12648 (accessed 11 June 2012).

21. 'Description of a Machine Invented by M. Roulaud, Professor of Natural Philosophy at the University of Paris, for Restoring Respiration to Persons

Drowned, or Otherwise Suffocated', *Biographical and Imperial Magazine* (June 1790), 339–40; and 'The Electric Shock, a Test of Remaining Life', in *Biographical and Imperial Magazine* (June 1790), 340. Both items are taken from the 'Reports of the Humane Society'.

22. Thelwall, *Animal Vitality*, repr. in *SPW*, vol. I, p. 20.
23. Thelwall, *Animal Vitality*, repr. in *SPW*, vol. I, p. 17.
24. As noted in Roe, *Politics of Nature*, p. 215n.
25. Thelwall, *Animal Vitality*, repr. in *SPW*, vol. I, p. 13.
26. Thelwall, *Animal Vitality*, repr. in *SPW*, vol. I, p. 15.
27. Rousseau, 'Perpetual Crises', p. 24.
28. L. S. Jacyna, 'Immanence or Transcendence: Theories of Life and Organization in Britain, 1790–1835', *Isis* 74, no. 3 (1983), 311–29; and George S. Erving, 'The Politics of Matter: Newtonian Science and Priestleyan Metaphysics in Coleridge's "Preternatural Agency"', *European Romantic Review* 19, no. 3 (2008), 221.
29. Thelwall, *Animal Vitality*, repr. in *SPW*, vol. I, pp. 15–18.
30. Mrs. Thelwall, *Life*, p. 80; Hunter, *A Treatise on the Blood, Inflammation, and Gun-Shot Wounds* (London, 1794), pp. 76–93, Eighteenth Century Collections Online, http://find.galegroup.com.proxy.library.nd.edu/ecco (accessed 15 Feb. 2014).
31. Thelwall, *Animal Vitality*, repr. in *SPW*, vol. I, pp. 24–5, 18.
32. On late eighteenth-century brain science, see Richardson, *Science of the Mind*, pp. 12–23.
33. Thelwall, *Animal Vitality*, repr. in *SPW*, vol. I, p. 25.
34. Pantheism can be defined simply as the doctrine that identifies God with the universe, while hylozoism is the ancient doctrine that all matter has life. Simon Blackburn, *The Oxford Dictionary of Philosophy*, s.v. 'pantheism' and 'hylozoism'. For fuller treatments of Romantic-era pantheism, see Ian Wylie, *Young Coleridge and the Philosophers of Nature* (Oxford: Clarendon Press, 1989), pp. 122–42; and Thomas McFarland, *Coleridge and the Pantheist Tradition* (Oxford: Clarendon Press, 1969).
35. Thelwall, *Animal Vitality*, repr. in *SPW*, vol. I, p. 27.
36. Priestley, *Disquisitions Relating to Matter and Spirit*, 2nd edn (Birmingham, 1782), Eighteenth Century Collections Online, http://find.galegroup.com. proxy.library.nd.edu/ecco (accessed 12 June 2012). I also draw here on Robert R. Schofield, *The Enlightened Joseph Priestley: A Study of His Life and Work from 1773 to 1804* (University Park: Pennsylvania State University Press, 2004), pp. 59–76; Schofield, *Mechanism and Materialism: British Natural Philosophy in an Age of Reason* (Princeton: Princeton University Press, 1970), especially pp. 263–7; and John W. Yolton, *Thinking Matter: Materialism in Eighteenth-Century Britain* (Minneapolis: University of Minnesota Press, 1983), pp. 107–26. Thelwall's substitution of 'vacuum' for 'spirit' in the *Animal Vitality* essay recalls Priestley's famous experiments with air pumps and other kinds of apparatus to manipulate gases.
37. Erving, 'Politics of Matter', 223–28.
38. Priestley, *Disquisitions*, pp. 45–6.
39. On the immanentism of Bichat and Lawrence, both targets for charges of atheism, see Jacyna, 'Immanence or Transcendence', 313. The atheistic implications of materialism are also latent in Thelwall's essay: he does not

deny the existence of God but refrains from speculating about matters beyond the 'gross conception of [his] material organs'. *Animal Vitality*, repr. in *SPW*, vol. I, p. 27. Sharon Ruston notes in *Shelley and Vitality*, p. 49, that for contemporary readers an epigraph from Lucretius would have been tantamount to a profession of materialist atheism.

40. Thelwall, *Animal Vitality*, repr. in *SPW*, vol. I, pp. 26, 29.

41. Thelwall, *Animal Vitality*, repr. in *SPW*, vol. I, p. 17.

42. Thelwall, *Animal Vitality*, repr. in *SPW*, vol. I, p. 26, the whole passage originally in italics.

43. Thelwall, *Animal Vitality*, repr. in *SPW*, vol. I, pp. 29–30.

44. Roe, *Politics of Nature*, pp. 92, 218n.

45. Patricia Fara, *An Entertainment for Angels: Electricity in the Enlightenment*, Revolutions in Science (New York: Columbia University Press, 2002), pp. 51–61; and Jenny Uglow, *The Lunar Men: The Friends Who Made the Future, 1730–1810* (London: Faber and Faber, 2002), pp. 12–14.

46. Fara, *Entertainment for Angels*, pp. 145–64. Thelwall later published a report on the 'Galvanic Battery' in his periodical the *Panoramic Miscellany* 1 (1826), 103.

47. See, for instance, Paola Bertucci, 'Therapeutic Attractions: Early Applications of Electricity to the Art of Healing', in *Brain, Mind and Medicine: Essays in Eighteenth-Century Neuroscience*, ed. Harry Whitaker, C. U. M. Smith and Stanley Finger (New York: Springer, 2007), pp. 271–83.

48. Richardson, *Science of the Mind*, p. 6.

49. Darwin, *The Botanic Garden: A Poem, in Two Parts* (London, 1791), p. 39, Eighteenth Century Collections Online, http://find.galegroup.com.proxy.library.nd.edu/ecco (accessed 16 Oct. 2012).

50. See, for instance, Ruston, *Shelley and Vitality*; Richard Holmes, *The Age of Wonder: How the Romantic Generation Discovered the Beauty and Terror of Science* (London: Harper, 2008), pp. 305–36; and Miranda Seymour, *Mary Shelley* (New York: Grove, 2000), pp. 3–20.

51. Abernethy, *An Enquiry into the Probability and Rationality of Mr. Hunter's Theory of Life; Being the Subject of the First Two Anatomical Lectures Delivered before the Royal College of Surgeons, of London* (London, 1814), p. 39, Eighteenth Century Collections Online, http://find.galegroup.com.proxy.library.nd.edu/ecco (accessed 16 Oct. 2012). Abernethy concluded the lecture by remarking that once natural philosophers came to understand that life was 'something of an invisible and active nature superadded to organization', they would also understand that 'mind might be superadded to life, as life is to structure', pp. 94–5.

52. Abernethy, *Mr. Hunter's Theory*, pp. 42–52.

53. Ruston, *Shelley and Vitality*, p. 43.

54. Ruston, *Shelley and Vitality*, pp. 46–7; Jacyna, 'Immanence or Transcendence', 312.

55. [Jeffrey], *Observations*, p. 14.

56. Rogers, *The Matter of Revolution: Science, Poetry, and Politics in the Age of Milton* (Ithaca, NY: Cornell University Press, 1996), p. 9.

57. Stephen M. Fallon, *Milton among the Philosophers: Poetry and Materialism in Seventeenth-Century England* (Ithaca, NY: Cornell University Press, 1991), pp. 81, 102, referring to Milton's views from the late 1650s onwards.

58. Fallon, *Milton*, pp. 109, 110.

59. Rogers, *Matter of Revolution*, pp. 212–27.
60. Rogers, *Matter of Revolution*, p. 225.
61. Erving, 'Politics of Matter', 221–2.
62. Thelwall, *Letter to Cline*, repr. in *SPW*, vol. IV, p. 7.
63. Mrs. Thelwall, *Life*, pp. 40, 42.
64. Thelwall, *Retirement*, p. xxiv.
65. Thelwall, *Retirement*, p. xxiii.
66. Mrs. Thelwall, *Life*, pp. 44, 58–9, which also notes that Thelwall's 'first political publication' was his 'Ode on the Destruction of the Bastille', which appeared in *Biographical and Imperial Magazine* 2 (1790), 312–15. See also Christopher Hill, 'The Norman Yoke', in *Democracy and the Labour Movement: Essays in Honour of Dona Torr*, ed. John Saville (London: Lawrence and Wishart, 1954), pp. 11–66.
67. Mrs. Thelwall, *Life*, p. 76.
68. The Cambridge University Library holds a copy of the *Tribune* inscribed by Thelwall 'To Citizen Thomas Paine, [a]s a small tribute of respect & admiration for that most entrepid [sic] & truely [sic] enlightened of all the known advocates for human liberty & universal benevolence'. The inscription is dated 26 Oct. 1796 and indicates that the volumes were to be delivered 'through the friendly hand of Citizen De Luzot'. It is unclear whether Paine ever received them. *The Tribune, a Periodical Publication, Consisting Chiefly of the Political Lectures of J. Thelwall*, 3 vols (London, 1795–96), Cambridge University Library, Rare Books, Acton.c.25.418.
69. Thelwall, *Rights of Nature, against the Usurpations of Establishments: A Series of Letters to the People of Britain, on the State of Public Affairs, and the Recent Effusions of the Right Honourable Edmund Burke* (London, 1796), repr. in *The Politics of English Jacobinism: Writings of John Thelwall*, ed. Gregory Claeys (University Park: Pennsylvania State University Press, 1995), pp. 487, 309. Thelwall's widow claims in *Life*, p. 115, that only in prison did he come fully to endorse the London Corresponding Society's demands for annual parliaments and universal male suffrage.
70. In 1792 the Society for Free Debate was barred from several venues for addressing political topics, prompting Thelwall to organize a debate on 'the right of magisterial interference with the freedom of popular discussion'. He kept the peace until someone extinguished the lights and threw over his table, starting a scuffle. Thelwall was escorted home for his safety and the Society dissolved soon afterwards. Mrs. Thelwall, *Life*, pp. 93–103.
71. Albert Goodwin, *The Friends of Liberty: The English Democratic Movement in the Age of the French Revolution* (Cambridge, MA: Harvard University Press, 1979), p. 318; and Claeys (ed.), *PEJ*, p. xix.
72. Thelwall, *Political Lectures. Volume the First – Part the First: Containing the Lecture on Spies and Informers, and the First Lecture on Prosecutions for Political Opinion* (London, 1795), pp. v–xv.
73. Thelwall, *The Tribune*, 3 vols (London, 1795–96), repr. in *The Politics of English Jacobinism: Writings of John Thelwall*, ed. Gregory Claeys (University Park: Pennsylvania State University Press, 1995), p. 313. Recognizing that the ancient model of a 'pure' republic was impracticable in so large a territory as Britain, Thelwall was willing to endorse the alternative of a representative democracy checked by a hereditary aristocracy and vesting executive

power in a king. But 'king', according to Thelwall, did not mean hereditary monarch; rather, he claimed that the word's derivation from a Saxon word meaning 'cunning man' reflected the Saxon practice of choosing the wisest member of a given family as ruler. Thelwall, *Tribune*, repr. in *PEJ*, pp. 210, 217, 214. In 1796 Thelwall published an edition of the seventeenth-century Whig 'Commonwealthman' Walter Moyle's treatise *An Essay on the Constitution of the Roman Government* (c. 1699), taking the liberty of giving it the new title *Democracy Vindicated: An Essay on the Constitution and Government of the Roman State* (Norwich, 1796). On 'Commonwealthman' republicanism see Caroline Robbins, *The Eighteenth-Century Commonwealthman* (Cambridge, MA: Harvard University Press, 1959), pp. 3–21.

74. Thelwall, *The Natural and Constitutional Right of Britons to Annual Parliaments, Universal Suffrage, and the Freedom of Popular Association* (London, 1795), repr. in *The Politics of English Jacobinism: Writings of John Thelwall*, ed. Gregory Claeys (University Park: Pennsylvania State University Press, 1995), p. 46.

75. Burke, *Reflections on the Revolution in France*, in *The French Revolution, 1790–1794*, ed. L. G. Mitchell, The Writings and Speeches of Edmund Burke (Oxford: Clarendon Press, 1989), p. 111.

76. Burke, *Reflections*, p. 86.

77. Thelwall, *Rights of Nature*, repr. in *PEJ*, p. 404.

78. Thelwall, *Political Lectures*, p. 52.

79. Thelwall, *Tribune*, repr. in *PEJ*, p. 309.

80. Thelwall, *Tribune*, repr. in *PEJ*, pp. 302–3, 308.

81. Godwin, *An Enquiry Concerning Political Justice*, ed. Mark Philp, The Pickering Masters (London: Pickering and Chatto, 1993), p. 15.

82. Thelwall, *Tribune* 1 (1795), 163. I cite the original here rather than the version in *PEJ*, p. 102, because the latter substitutes 'palpillary' for the original 'palpilliary', which does not appear in the *OED*. Thelwall probably meant 'palpatory', i.e., relating to touch.

83. Thelwall, *The Vestibule of Eloquence: Original Articles, Oratorical and Poetical, Intended as Exercises in Recitation, at the Institution, Bedford Place, Russell Square* (London, 1810), p. 42. Many Scottish philosophers of the mid- to late eighteenth century likewise discussed economic and social life in physiological terms, as Christopher Lawrence has shown in 'The Nervous System and Society in the Scottish Enlightenment', in *Natural Order: Historical Studies of Scientific Culture*, ed. Barry Barnes and Steven Shapin, Sage Focus Editions 6 (Beverly Hills, CA: Sage, 1979), pp. 19–40.

84. Roe, *Politics of Nature*, p. 92. John Barrell highlights the organic structure of the LCS, which was divided into many independently organized units spread throughout London and thus resembled the polype (or polypus), a group of worm-like organisms described by Linnaeus. Barrell notes that critics of the LCS thought of it instead as a cancerous tumour capable of relentless growth; *The Spirit of Despotism: Invasions of Privacy in the 1790s* (Oxford: Oxford University Press, 2006), pp. 66–7.

85. Eyre's charge is reprinted in Godwin, *Political Writings II*, ed. Mark Philp, The Pickering Masters (London: Pickering and Chatto, 1993), p. 73.

86. Godwin, *Political Writings II*, pp. 130–3, writing in the anonymous pamphlet *Considerations on Lord Grenville's and Mr. Pitt's Bills, Concerning Treasonable and Seditious Practices, and Unlawful Assemblies* (London, 1795).

87. Burke, *Letters on a Regicide Peace*, in *The Revolutionary War, 1794–1797, and Ireland*, ed. R. B. McDowell, The Writings and Speeches of Edmund Burke (Oxford: Clarendon Press, 1996), p. 224; and Thelwall quoting Burke in *Rights of Nature*, repr. in *PEJ*, p. 409.

88. Thelwall, *Rights of Nature*, repr. in *PEJ*, pp. 400–1.

89. 'Description of a Machine', 340.

90. Thelwall, *Tribune*, repr. in *PEJ*, p. 309.

91. Mrs. Thelwall, *Life*, p. 367.

92. On these speculations see Richardson, *Science of the Mind*, p. 122.

93. Burke, *Regicide Peace*, p. 292. For further discussion of Thelwall's 'deploy-ment of a language of political animation' in his political writings of the 1790s, especially in response to Burke, see Packham, *Eighteenth-Century Vitalism*, pp. 132–43, 133.

94. Thelwall, *Retirement*, pp. xxii–xxiii. According to Diana Manipud, Information Assistant at the King's College London Library, which man-ages the Guy's Hospital archive, the 'private minutes' of the Physical Society mention only that on 14 Dec. 1793 'Mr Thelwall delivered in his Paper on the origin of mental action, explained on the system of materi-alism', while the 'public minutes' record only that 'Mr Thelwall read his Paper'. Manipud, email to the author, 12 Nov. 2012.

95. Bransby Blake Cooper, *The Life of Sir Astley Cooper*, 2 vols (London, 1843), vol. I, p. 237; and [Jeffrey], *Observations*, pp. 249–50.

96. Cooper, *Life of Sir Astley Cooper*, vol. I, p. 243; see also p. 237, where Bransby Blake Cooper objects to the influence on his uncle of Thelwall's 'peculiar tenets of materialism'.

97. Topics of discussion at the Philomathian Society included religion, poli-tics, the law, the theatres, property, free will and marriage, according to William St. Clair in *The Godwins and the Shelleys: The Biography of a Family* (New York: Norton, 1989; repr. Baltimore, MD: Johns Hopkins University Press, 1991), pp. 92–3. Thelwall was a member of the Philomathians by 1791, when he delivered his 'Ode to Science' to mark its anniversary. Godwin joined the Philomathians in 1793, as did Thomas Holcroft (St. Clair, *Godwins and Shelleys*, p. 93). However, Godwin's diary records that he first met Thelwall at John Horne Tooke's house on 18 Aug. 1793, as noted by Pamela Clemit (ed.), *The Letters of William Godwin*, vol. I: *1778–1797* (Oxford: Oxford University Press, 2011), p. 104. Godwin's *Political Justice* was among the books seized from Thelwall's home on his arrest (Mrs. Thelwall, *Life*, p. 164).

98. Godwin, *Political Justice*, p. 11.

99. Godwin, *An Enquiry Concerning Political Justice: Variants*, ed. Mark Philp, The Pickering Masters (London: Pickering and Chatto, 1993), p. 45.

100. Hartley, *Observations on Man, His Frame, His Duty, and His Expectations*, vol. I (London, 1749; repr. [1791]), pp. 5–84, Eighteenth Century Collections Online, <http://find.galegroup.com.proxy.library.nd.edu/ecco> (accessed 24 Oct. 2012); Richardson, *Science of the Mind*, pp. 9–10. My discussion of eighteenth-century associationism is also informed by Cairns Craig, *Associationism and the Literary Imagination: From the Phantasmal Chaos* (Edinburgh: Edinburgh University Press, 2007); Walter Jackson Bate, *From Classic to Romantic: Premises of Taste in Eighteenth-Century England*

(New York: Harper Torchbooks, 1961), pp. 93–128; Martin Kallich, *The Association of Ideas and Critical Theory in Eighteenth-Century England* (The Hague: Mouton, 1970); and Graham Richards, *Mental Machinery: The Origins and Consequences of Psychological Ideas. Part I: 1600–1850* (London: Athlone, 1992). Wayne A. Davis notes in *Meaning, Expression, and Thought* (Cambridge: Cambridge University Press, 2003), pp. 461–80, that although most of association's theoretical claims are false, it remains an important psychological phenomenon and a necessary complement to the focus on belief and desire in contemporary cognitive science.

101. Godwin, *Political Justice*, p. 176. As Godwin maintains in the second edition of *Political Justice* (1796), 'the great stream of our voluntary actions essentially depends, not upon the direct and immediate impulses of sense, but upon the decisions of the understanding'. *Political Justice Variants*, p. 17.

102. Godwin, *Political Justice*, p. 178. On Godwin's reconciliation of necessity and individual rationality, see Philp, *Godwin's Political Justice* (Ithaca, NY: Cornell University Press, 1986), pp. 92–3.

103. Kramnick, 'Eighteenth-Century Science and Radical Social Theory: The Case of Joseph Priestley's Scientific Liberalism', *Journal of British Studies* 25, no. 1 (Jan. 1986), 15.

104. As per chapter titles in the first and second editions of *Political Justice*.

105. Kramnick, 'Eighteenth-Century Science', 17.

106. Godwin, *Political Justice*, p. 15.

107. Godwin, *Political Justice*, pp. 170–1.

108. Thelwall, 'On the Influence of the Scenery of Nature on the Intellectual and Moral Character, as well as on the Taste and Imagination', *Champion* 9 Sept. 1820, repr. in *The Poetical Recreations of* The Champion, *and His Literary Correspondents; with a Selection of Essays, Literary and Critical, Which Have Appeared in* The Champion *Newspaper* (London, 1822), p. 74.

109. Thelwall, 'Scenery of Nature', repr. in *Poetical Recreations*, p. 74. A relationship between the tea-caddy metaphor and Thelwall's belief that 'lived conditions and intercourse with others influenced how citizens experienced their world' is noted by Molly Desjardins in 'John Thelwall and Association', in *John Thelwall: Critical Reassessments*, ed. Yasmin Solomonescu, Romantic Circles, Sept. 2011, http://romantic.arhu.umd.edu/praxis/thelwall/HTML/praxis.2011.desjardins.html (accessed 12 June 2012), para. 4.

110. [Thelwall], 'The Sceptic. (No. IV.)', *Biographical and Imperial Magazine* (Feb. 1790), 103. Although not signed by Thelwall, the essay so closely resembles portions of his *Peripatetic* that the attribution seems certain.

111. Thelwall, 'King Chaunticlere; or, the Fate of Tyranny', *Politics for the People: Or a Salmagundy for Swine* 1 (1794), 102–7, repr. in *Selected Political Writings of John Thelwall*, ed. Robert Lamb and Corinna Wagner, 4 vols (London: Pickering and Chatto, 2009), vol. I, pp. 33–4.

112. Thelwall, 'King Chaunticlere', repr. in *SPW*, vol. I, pp. 34–5.

113. Thelwall, *Sober Reflections on the Seditious and Inflammatory Letter of the Right Hon. Edmund Burke, to a Noble Lord* (London, 1796), repr. in *The Politics of English Jacobinism: Writings of John Thelwall*, ed. Gregory Claeys (University Park: Pennsylvania State University Press, 1995), p. 386; 'King Chaunticlere', repr. in *SPW*, vol. I, p. 34.

114. Thelwall, *The Peripatetic*, ed. Judith Thompson (Detroit, MI: Wayne State University Press, 2001), p. 339.
115. Thelwall, *Political Lectures*, pp. 8–9.
116. On the 'allusive and elusive' character of radical writing, see Jon Mee, '"Examples of Safe Printing": Censorship and Popular Radical Literature in the 1790s', in *Literature and Censorship*, ed. Nigel Smith, Essays and Studies ns 46 (Cambridge: Brewer, 1993), p. 86.
117. Chris Jones, *Radical Sensibility: Literature and Ideas in the 1790s* (London: Routledge, 1993).
118. According to Mrs. Thelwall, *Life*, p. 110, Daniel Isaac Eaton published 'King Chaunticlere' in his newspaper *Politics for the People* 'after dressing it up in certainly very strong terms, which Thelwall would never have used', and was charged with libel as a result. The anecdote has been variously interpreted as an allegory of regicide, a parody of Burkean alarmism and a narrative of the death of Thelwall's early church-and-king conservatism. For the first perspective, see Philp, 'Fragmented Ideology', 70–2; Barrell, *Imagining*, pp. 106–7; and Michael Scrivener, 'John Thelwall and Popular Jacobin Allegory, 1793–95', *ELH* 67 (2000), 956. For the second perspective, see Marcus Wood, 'William Cobbett, John Thelwall, Radicalism, Racism and Slavery: A Study in Burkean Parodics', *Romanticism on the Net* 15 (Aug. 1999), http://www.erudit.org/revue/ron/1999/v/n15/005873ar.html (accessed 23 May 2007); and for the third, Damian Walford Davies, 'Capital Crimes: John Thelwall, "Gallucide" and Psychobiography', *Romanticism* 18, no. 1 (2012), 62.
119. Packham, *Eighteenth-Century Vitalism*, p. 131.
120. Thelwall, *Rights of Nature*, repr. in *PEJ*, p. 430.
121. Introducing excerpts from Thelwall's political writings of the 1790s, Marilyn Butler claims that he 'made little use of Tooke's hostile analysis of upper-class language, or implied preference for a plain Anglo-Saxon discourse as a vehicle for ideas'; *Burke, Paine, Godwin, and the Revolution Controversy* (Cambridge: Cambridge University Press, 1984), p. 207. Similarly, Olivia Smith observes of *The Peripatetic* that, '[t]he emotive heart and the political mind which Thelwall hoped to unite in his writings are kept apart by two styles of language, one for sentiment and another for thought'; *Politics of Language*, p. 87.
122. Tooke, *Epea Pteroenta: or, The Diversions of Purley, Part I*, 2nd edn, (London, 1798), pp. 51, 10, Eighteenth Century Collections Online, http://find.galegroup.com.proxy.library.nd.edu/ecco (accessed 27 Oct. 2012).
123. Thelwall, 'Mr. Thelwall's Lecture. On the Harmonic Qualities', repr. in *SPW*, vol. IV, pp. 207–8.

2   Errant Sympathies

1. Thelwall, *Peripatetic*, p. 339.
2. Thelwall, *Peripatetic*, p. 72.
3. Holcroft, preface, *Alwyn, or the Gentleman Comedian* (London, 1780), vol. I, p. vi, Eighteenth Century Collections Online, http://find.galegroup.com.proxy.library.nd.edu/ecco (accessed 2 Nov. 2012); Thelwall, *Peripatetic*, p. 72.

4. Thelwall, *Peripatetic*, p. 224.

5. By contrast with *The Peripatetic*, Thelwall's early poems and plays contain few references to contemporaneous medical science. A notable exception is his 'Dramatic Poem, Founded on Facts, Recorded in the Reports of the Humane Society', which celebrates the Society's mission to advance resuscitative techniques and anticipates the conclusion of *The Peripatetic* by recounting the rescue of a suicide named Sophia. See *Poems on Various Subjects*, 2 vols (London, 1787), vol. II, pp. 1–87, repr. in *Literature Online* (Cambridge: Chadwyck-Healey, 1992), http://lion.chadwyck.com.proxy.library.nd.edu/ (accessed 13 Aug. 2013).

6. Several scholars have noted affinities between the physiological ideas of Thelwall's *Animal Vitality* essay and those of *The Peripatetic*. James Robert Allard calls attention to the latter's narrator as an exemplary 'anatomical philosopher', in *Poet's Body*, pp. 75–83, while Mary Fairclough emphasizes the radical optimism of *The Peripatetic*'s attention to sympathy as an agent of reform, in *Romantic Crowd*, pp. 110–14. I respond to both positions hereafter.

7. Thelwall, *Peripatetic*, p. 255. Judith Thompson draws attention to *The Peripatetic*'s attempt to 'dismantle discursive structures and replace them with an ideal of intergeneric conversation', in 'John Thelwall and the Politics of Genre 1793/1993', *Wordsworth Circle* 25, no. 1 (1994), 22; and Thompson (ed.), *The Peripatetic*, by John Thelwall (Detroit, MI: Wayne State University Press, 2001), pp. 40–1; and she has more recently highlighted the work's contribution to the 'autobiographical conversation' of Thelwall and Wordsworth, in *Silenced Partner*, pp. 189–201, 189. Michael Scrivener discusses *The Peripatetic*'s literal and figurative performance of 'eccentricity', or divergence from a centre, in relation chiefly to Wordsworth, in *Seditious Allegories*, pp. 210–19. Gary Kelly sees *The Peripatetic* as an example of the Romantic 'quasi-novel', which appropriated the factual discourses of history, travel writing, antiquarianism and autobiography to redeem the novel from its status as an effeminate, commercialized and sub-literary genre; see 'The Limits of Genre and the Institution of Literature: Romanticism between Fact and Fiction', in *Romantic Revolutions: Criticism and Theory*, ed. Kenneth R. Johnston et al. (Bloomington: Indiana University Press, 1990), p. 167. According to Henry Crabb Robinson, Wordsworth borrowed from Thelwall 'without acknowledgment'. *Diary, Reminiscences, and Correspondence of Henry Crabb Robinson*, ed. Thomas Sadler, 2nd edn, 3 vols (London: Macmillan, 1869), vol. I, p. 473. On this influence see also Thompson, *Silenced Partner*, pp. 187–218; Kenneth R. Johnston, *Wordsworth and* The Recluse (New Haven, CT: Yale University Press, 1984), pp. 11–14; and Judson Stanley Lyon, The Excursion: *A Study* (New Haven, CT: Yale University Press, 1950), pp. 35–7.

8. Thelwall, *Peripatetic*, p. 77.

9. Mrs. Thelwall, *Life*, pp. 14–16.

10. Thelwall, *Animal Vitality*, repr. in *SPW*, vol. I, p. 26, the whole passage originally in italics.

11. Thelwall, *Peripatetic*, pp. 146–8.

12. Thelwall, *Peripatetic*, pp. 147–8.

13. Thelwall, *Peripatetic*, p. 153; the rebuttal of Smith is noted by Thompson (ed.), *Peripatetic*, p. 31.

14. Phyllis Deane, *The First Industrial Revolution*, 2nd edn (Cambridge: Cambridge University Press, 1998), p. 266.
15. Thelwall, *Tribune*, repr. in *PEJ*, pp. 165–6.
16. Such theories are discussed in J. R. Poynter, *Society and Pauperism: English Ideas on Poor Relief, 1795–1834* (London: Routledge and Kegan Paul, 1969), pp. 1–44.
17. Thelwall, *Rights of Nature*, in *PEJ*, p. 477–8. Thelwall postulates, p. 452, that '*Man has naturally an equal claim to the elements of nature*; and although earth has been appropriated, by expediency and compact [...] light, air, and water (with some exceptions) still continue to be claimed in common'.
18. Claeys (ed.), *PEJ*, p. lii. Claeys discusses Thelwall's 'new vision of egalitarian commercial republicanism' as it laid a foundation for the development of both socialist and liberal thought in the nineteenth century in 'Rights of Labour', 263–74. Other insightful accounts of Thelwall's economic and political theory include Geoffrey Gallop, 'Ideology and the English Jacobins: The Case of John Thelwall', *Enlightenment and Dissent* 5 (1986), 3–20; Iain Hampsher-Monk, 'John Thelwall and the Eighteenth-Century Radical Response to Political Economy', *Historical Journal* 34 (1991), 1–20; Robert Lamb, 'Labour, Contingency, Utility: Thelwall's Theory of Property', in *John Thelwall: Radical Romantic and Acquitted Felon*, ed. Steve Poole, The Enlightenment World 11 (London: Pickering and Chatto, 2009), pp. 51–60; and Richard Sheldon '"A Loud, a Fervid, and Resolute Remonstrance with our Rulers": John Thelwall, the People and Political Economy', in *John Thelwall: Radical Romantic and Acquitted Felon*, ed. Steve Poole, The Enlightenment World 11 (London: Pickering and Chatto, 2009), pp. 61–70.
19. Thelwall, *Peripatetic*, pp. 136, 200, 91–92.
20. Thelwall, *Peripatetic*, pp. 102–4.
21. Thelwall, *Peripatetic*, pp. 236–9.
22. Thelwall, marginalia on Coleridge, 79, where he distinguishes 'mania' from 'delirium', which 'displays itself in *distempered fancy*, or incoherency of mind'. Thelwall's marginalia on Coleridge's *Biographia Literaria* are discussed more fully in Chapter 6.
23. Thelwall, *Peripatetic*, p. 185.
24. Thelwall, *Peripatetic*, p. 118.
25. John Armstrong, *The Art of Preserving Health*, Book IV, lines 40–6 and 84–5, repr. in Thelwall, *Selections for the Illustration of a Course of Instructions on the Rhythmus and Utterance of the English Language* (London, 1812), pp. 117–20.
26. Thelwall, *Peripatetic*, pp. 78, 115.
27. Thelwall, *Peripatetic*, p. 89.
28. Thompson (ed.), *Peripatetic*, p. 34.
29. Jarvis, *Romantic Writing and Pedestrian Travel* (Houndmills: Macmillan, 1997), pp. 33–4.
30. Thelwall, *Peripatetic*, p. 132.
31. Wordsworth, 'Lines Written a Few Miles above Tintern Abbey', l. 50, in *Lyrical Ballads, and Other Poems, 1797–1800*, ed. James Butler and Karen Green, The Cornell Wordsworth (Ithaca, NY: Cornell University Press, 1992), p. 117. I have in mind also Marjorie Levinson's critique of Wordsworth's 'transcendentalizing impulse' in this poem, which leads him to 'exclude from his field [of vision] certain conflictual sights and meanings – roughly,

the *life* of things', as noted in *Wordsworth's Great Period Poems: Four Essays* (Cambridge: Cambridge University Press, 1986), p. 25.

32. Robinson, *The Walk: Notes on a Romantic Image* (Norman: University of Oklahoma Press, 1989), p. 52.

33. Thelwall, *Peripatetic*, pp. 73, 257. 'Observe' and its cognates are used more than 60 times in *The Peripatetic*, not counting synonyms such as glance, survey and view. The number is the result of a search for 'observ*' in the electronic edition of *The Peripatetic* in Eighteenth Century Collections Online, http://find.galegroup.com.proxy.library.nd.edu/ecco (accessed 21 Nov. 2012).

34. Thelwall, *Peripatetic*, p. 251; Jones, *Radical Sensibility*, p. 7.

35. Thelwall, *Peripatetic*, pp. 82–3.

36. Thelwall, *Peripatetic*, p. 121; Thelwall, *Tribune*, repr. in *PEJ*, p. 90.

37. Thelwall, *Peripatetic*, pp. 312, 319.

38. Thelwall, *Peripatetic*, p. 321.

39. Thelwall, *Peripatetic*, p. 255.

40. Roe, *Politics of Nature*, pp. 93–5.

41. Wordsworth, 'Tintern Abbey', ll. 28–31, 46–7, in *Lyrical Ballads*, p. 117.

42. Thelwall, *Peripatetic*, p. 236–7.

43. Smith, *The Theory of Moral Sentiments* (London, 1759), ed. D. D. Raphael and A. L. Macfie (Oxford: Clarendon Press, 1976), pp. 82–3.

44. Johann Wolfgang von Goethe, *Elective Affinities: A Novel*, trans. of *Die Wahlverwandtschaften*, 1809, ed. David Constantine (Oxford: Oxford University Press, 1994; repr. 1999), especially pp. 26–35; Thelwall, *Peripatetic*, 112.

45. Thelwall, *Peripatetic*, pp. 85–6.

46. Thelwall, *Peripatetic*, pp. 87–8.

47. Thelwall, *Peripatetic*, p. 71; Sterne, *A Sentimental Journey and Other Writings*, ed. Ian Jack and Tim Parnell (Oxford: Oxford University Press, 2003; repr. 2008), p. 4.

48. Chandler, *An Archaeology of Sympathy: The Sentimental Mode in Literature and Cinema* (Chicago: University of Chicago Press, 2013), pp. 5–12.

49. On these speculations see Richardson, *Science of the Mind*, p. 122.

50. For the contrary view that sympathy is instinctive and infallible in *The Peripatetic*, see Fairclough, *Romantic Crowd*, pp. 110–14.

51. Allard, *Poet's Body*, pp. 77–8.

52. Thelwall, *Peripatetic*, p. 111.

53. Thelwall, *Peripatetic*, p. 360.

54. Thelwall, *Peripatetic*, p. 318.

55. J. W. Smeed, *The Theophrastan 'Character': The History of a Literary Genre* (Oxford: Clarendon Press, 1985), pp. 64–5.

56. Thelwall, *Peripatetic*, pp. 104, 318–19.

57. Thelwall, *Peripatetic*, pp. 77, 285.

58. *Ambulator: Or, a Pocket Companion in a Tour Round London, within the Circuit of Twenty-Five Miles, Describing Whatever is Most Remarkable for Antiquity, Grandeur, Elegance, or Rural Beauty*, 4th edn (London, 1792).

59. Aristotle, *Nicomachean Ethics*, trans. Terence Irwin (Indianapolis, IN: Hackett, 1985), p. 88.

60. Thelwall, *Peripatetic*, pp. 195–6.

61. Godwin, *Political Justice*, p. 121.
62. Thelwall, *Peripatetic*, p. 353.
63. Thelwall, *Peripatetic*, pp. 90, 209; 'Scenery of Nature', repr. in *Poetical Recreations*, pp. 76, 75. The essay appeared alongside the poem 'Sylvanus; or, the Pupil of the Groves', as discussed in Chapter 5.
64. Anne D. Wallace, *Walking, Literature, and English Culture: The Origin and Uses of Peripatetic in the Nineteenth Century* (Oxford: Oxford University Press, 1993), pp. 93–4.
65. Thelwall, *Peripatetic*, p. 71.
66. Thelwall, *Peripatetic*, pp. 194–6.
67. Thelwall, *Peripatetic*, pp. 196–7, 208–9, 214–16, 234–6.
68. Lamb, 'Language and Hartleian Associationism in *A Sentimental Journey*', *Eighteenth-Century Studies* 13, no. 3 (Spring 1980), 304. The gypsies cluster, like the haymaker episode, also instantiates what Alan Richardson describes as the 'shuttling among memory, imagination, mind reading, reverie, and even navigation' that occurs in a wide range of Romantic-era fiction and poetry, and which he compares with the age-old practice of 'wayfinding', finding one's way by repeatedly taking stock of one's past, present and future locations. 'Reimagining', 393–4. For Michael Scrivener's reading of the gypsies cluster as it educates the reader in 'the art of making analogies', see *Seditious Allegories*, p. 212.
69. Gary Kelly, *The English Jacobin Novel, 1780–1805* (Oxford: Clarendon Press, 1976), pp. 15–16, which does not discuss *The Peripatetic*; Miriam L. Wallace, *Revolutionary Subjects in the English 'Jacobin' Novel, 1790–1805*, Bucknell Studies in Eighteenth-Century Literature and Culture (Lewisburg, PA: Bucknell University Press, 2009), p. 31.
70. Thelwall, *Peripatetic*, subtitle.
71. Thelwall, *Peripatetic*, pp. 106, 350. *The Peripatetic* thus contributes to what Tilottama Rajan describes as the development of a Romantic hermeneutic tradition that encouraged reading beyond the ends of novels; 'Wollstonecraft and Godwin: Reading the Secrets of the Political Novel', *Studies in Romanticism* 27 (1988), 221–51.
72. Rothstein, '"Ideal Presence" and the "Non Finito" in Eighteenth-Century Aesthetics', *Eighteenth-Century Studies* 9, no. 3 (1976), 323.
73. Rothstein, 'Non Finito', 310, 312.
74. Rothstein, 'Non Finito', 321–2.
75. Kames, *Elements of Criticism*, vol. I (Edinburgh, 1762), pp. 108, 112, The Online Library of Liberty, http://oll.libertyfund.org/title/1430 (accessed 28 June 2012). Thelwall might have become acquainted with the concept of the 'non finito' through his early ambition to become a painter and his interest in aesthetic theory, and with the concept of 'ideal presence' from his reading of Darwin's *Botanic Garden*, p. 55, where it is a subject of discussion between the poet and his bookseller.
76. Thelwall, *Peripatetic*, p. 339.
77. Thelwall, *Peripatetic*, p. 255. The work also directly enjoins the reader to show that '*he has a heart*' by 'feel[ing] the same interest' as the peripatetic company in their 'little adventures' on the road, pp. 380, 115.
78. Thelwall, *Peripatetic*, pp. 348–9.
79. Thelwall, *Peripatetic*, pp. 183–4.

80. Thelwall, *Peripatetic*, p. 255.
81. Thelwall, *Peripatetic*, pp. 223–4.
82. Thelwall, *Peripatetic*, p. 224.
83. Burke, *Reflections*, p. 58.
84. Thelwall, *Peripatetic*, p. 225.
85. Smith, *Moral Sentiments*, p. 21. Godwin likewise asserts in the 1796 edition of *Political Justice* that truth, when 'brought home to the conviction of the individual', is all-powerful. *Political Justice: Variants*, p. 42.
86. Thelwall, *Peripatetic*, p. 113.
87. Thelwall, *Peripatetic*, p. 111.
88. Mee, *Romanticism, Enthusiasm, and Regulation: Poetics and the Policing of Culture in the Romantic Period* (Oxford: Oxford University Press, 2003; repr. 2005), p. 121.
89. Thelwall, *Peripatetic*, p. 225.
90. McCann, *Cultural Politics in the 1790s: Literature, Radicalism and the Public Sphere* (Houndmills: Macmillan, 1999), pp. 87–9.
91. See, in addition, *Political Lectures*, p. 3, where Thelwall notes 'this is no season for the idle sallies of imagination: the womb of Time is labouring with great events [...]. In short, this is a season for enquiry and instruction, not for pastime and jocularity'.
92. Thelwall, *Peripatetic*, pp. 380–1. The recent discovery of three manuscript volumes of Thelwall's poetry in Derby provides us with another possible explanation of *The Peripatetic*'s renunciation of the '*Sportive* lyre'. Alongside the fragments of an unfinished mock-epic poem on late eighteenth-century visual and print culture (a version of which Sylvanus recites to his companions), Thelwall observes that the poem was originally designed as 'a vehicle for political Satyr [*sic*]', adding,

> P.S. What I had written was at first very highly commended by J. Horne Tooke, with whom I had recently becomes acquainted; but he afterwards discouraged me from proceeding; being very desirous of drawing me to some subject more exclusively political. He proposed a Satire on the Coalition of Kings: but tho I dropt (unwisely I think) my own [illegible word crossed out] project, I could never see his in that point of view which would furnish materials for a mock heroic poem. Had I then written upon such a subject I should have written with a bitterness which might have been amusing to him; but would have been dangerous to me.

Tooke's interest in seeing his protégé apply his talents to 'some subject more exclusively political' might explain not only Thelwall's abandonment of the poem (which he later recopied into the Derby volumes under the title *Typopictoromania*, possibly intending to revise and complete it), but also his renunciation of the 'playful lyre' that produced *The Peripatetic*. Thelwall, Derby manuscript, vol. II, p. 703v.
93. Thelwall, *Peripatetic*, p. 361.
94. The phrase is John W. Yolton's in *Thinking Matter*, p. 125.
95. Thelwall, *Peripatetic*, pp. 366–7.
96. Thelwall, *Peripatetic*, p. 140.

97. Thelwall, *Peripatetic*, p. 73. Thelwall sold the first volume of *The Peripatetic* himself before contracting with Daniel Isaac Eaton and a 'Mr. Reece'. He describes Reeves's unsuccessful attempts in 1793–94 to shut down his political lectures on grounds of libel and nuisance in *Political Lectures*, pp. 17–19.
98. Thelwall, *Peripatetic*, p. 73.

3 From Self to Sentient Nature

1. Thelwall, *Retirement*, p. xxxiv.
2. Thelwall, *Animal Vitality*, repr. in *SPW*, vol. I, p. 23.
3. Thelwall, *Retirement*, p. 147.
4. Thompson, *Making of the English Working Class*, p. 172. Anne Janowitz discusses Thelwall's *Confinement* poems as they define an 'identity of inwardness' and his *Retirement* poems in terms of the 'lyricism of individualism', in *Lyric and Labour in the Romantic Tradition*, Cambridge Studies in Romanticism 30 (Cambridge: Cambridge University Press, 1998), pp. 70, 89. Thelwall's intertextual connections with Wordsworth and Coleridge are explored in the range of criticism cited hereafter, as well as in Damian Walford Davies's *Presences that Disturb*, pp. 193–240, which examines Thelwall's 'dialectical construction of himself as a harassed and exiled second self' of Wordsworth and Coleridge in the 'Paternal Tears' elegies, p. 211; David Simpson's, 'Public Virtues, Private Vices: Reading between the Lines of Wordsworth's "Anecdote for Fathers"', in *Subject to History: Ideology, Class, Gender*, ed. David Simpson (Ithaca, NY: Cornell University Press, 1991), pp. 163–90, which discusses Wordsworth's personal and political anxieties in that poem as modulated by allusions to Thelwall; and David Collings, 'The Harsh Delights of Political Duty: Thelwall, Coleridge, Wordsworth, 1795–99', in *Romantic Wars: Studies in Culture and Conflict, 1793–1822*, ed. Philip Shaw (Aldershot: Ashgate, 2000), pp. 57–79, which considers the canonical poets' responses to Thelwall's discourse of political trauma.
5. Thompson, *Silenced Partner*, p. 6.
6. Abrams, 'Structure and Style in the Greater Romantic Lyric', in *From Sensibility to Romanticism: Essays Presented to Frederick A. Pottle*, ed. Frederick W. Hilles and Harold Bloom (New York: Oxford University Press, 1965), pp. 527–60.
7. Thelwall, *Confinement*, p. 22.
8. Thelwall, *Confinement*, p. ii.
9 Thelwall, *Peripatetic*, pp. 380–1.
10. For a detailed account of Thelwall's arrest, see Mrs. Thelwall, *Life*, pp. 150–70; and Thelwall, *Tribune* 1 (1795), 85–95, 301–26.
11. Mrs. Thelwall, *Life*, p. 229, notes that Thelwall contracted a 'complaint in [… his] bowels of the most malignant complexion' from which he never fully recovered. Ironically, his early verse includes an ode to the prison reformer John Howard: 'The Shrine of Howard', in *Poems on Various Subjects*, 2 vols (London, 1787), vol. II, pp. 180–8.
12. According to the letter of the law, the defendants would in fact have been sentenced to hanging, drawing and quartering, a procedure that Godwin describes in graphic detail in *Cursory Strictures on the Charge Delivered by*

Lord Chief Justice Eyre to the Grand Jury, October 2, 1794, repr. in *Political Writings II*, p. 100.

13. My main source for this overview of treason law as it applied in 1794 is John Barrell and Jon Mee (eds), *Trials for Treason and Sedition, 1792–1794*, 8 vols (London: Pickering and Chatto, 2006), vol. I, pp. xxviii–xxxvi. See also Barrell, *Imagining*, pp. 29–36, 285–441; Barrell, 'Imaginary Treason, Imaginary Law: The State Trials of 1794', in *The Birth of Pandora and the Division of Knowledge* (Basingstoke: Macmillan, 1992), pp. 119–43; and Alan Wharam, *The Treason Trials, 1794* (Leicester: Leicester University Press, 1992).

14. Barrell and Mee (eds), *Trials*, vol. I, pp. xxix–xxx.

15. Mrs. Thelwall, *Life*, pp. 267–8. Spy reports contained further anecdotal evidence of Thelwall's treasonous intentions. At a dinner following the Chalk Farm meeting, he had reportedly blown the head off a pot of porter and declared, 'This is the way I would serve kings'. LCS members contended that he had actually said, 'This is the way I would serve all tyrants'. Thelwall was also reported to have given a toast to 'The Lamp Iron at the End of Parliament Street', on which the heads of Pitt and his ministers would be stuck once a revolution began. See Barrell, *Imagining*, p. 213; Mary Thale (ed.), *Selections from the Papers of the London Corresponding Society, 1792–1799* (Cambridge: Cambridge University Press, 1983), p. 140; and Goodwin, *Friends of Liberty*, p. 329.

16. Coleridge, *Collected Letters*, vol. I, p. 307.

17. Coleridge, 'To John Thelwall', in *Poetical Works*, vol. I, pp. 264–5; and Thelwall, marginalia on Coleridge, 82.

18. Thelwall, *Confinement*, pp. 2–3, 6–7, 5.

19. Thelwall, *Confinement*, pp. 21–2.

20. James A. Epstein, *Radical Expression: Political Language, Ritual, and Symbol in England, 1790–1850* (New York: Oxford University Press, 1994); Linda Colley, 'Radical Patriotism in Eighteenth-Century England', in *Patriotism: The Making and Unmaking of British National Identity*, ed. Raphael Samuel (London: Routledge, 1989), vol. I, pp. 169–87; and Hugh Cunningham, 'The Language of Patriotism', in *Patriotism*, vol. I, pp. 57–89.

21. Thelwall, *Confinement*, p. 1.

22. Thelwall, *Tribune*, repr. in *PEJ*, pp. 90, 101.

23. Thelwall, *Tribune*, repr. in *PEJ*, p. 106.

24. Burke, *Reflections*, p. 147.

25. Thelwall, *Tribune*, repr. in *PEJ*, p. 105.

26. 'Phocion', 'To the Right Hon. William Pitt', *Morning Chronicle* 13 Nov. 1794, p. 2; Thelwall, *Confinement*, p. 11.

27. Francesco Cordasco, 'Junius (*fl.* 1768–1773)', in *Oxford Dictionary of National Biography*, eds. H. C. G. Matthew and Brian Harrison (Oxford: Oxford University Press, 2004), online edn, ed. Lawrence Goldman, Jan. 2008, http://www.oxforddnb.com/view/article/45912 (accessed 27 Oct. 2012).

28. Milton, *Samson Agonistes*, ll. 1697, 1699, 1704–7, in *John Milton: The Major Works*, ed. Stephen Orgel and Jonathan Goldberg (Oxford: Oxford University Press, 1991), p. 714.

29. Thelwall, *Confinement*, p. 28.

30. Thelwall, *Confinement*, p. i. Similar invocations of Russell, Hampden and Sidney occur, for instance, in John Augustus Bonney's *Ode to Liberty*, ll. 1–6,

repr. in Roe, *Politics of Nature*, p. 123; Charlotte Smith's Sonnet LXXVI, 'To a Young Man Entering the World', ll. 14–16, repr. in *The Poems of Charlotte Smith*, ed. Stuart Curran (New York: Oxford University Press, 1993), p. 65; and George Dyer's *Ode to Liberty*, repr. in Thelwall, *Tribune* 2 (1796), 147.

31. Burke, *Regicide Peace*, p. 224.
32. Thelwall, *Confinement*, p. i.
33. In 1789–90 as editor of the *Biographical and Imperial Magazine*, Thelwall published numerous excerpts from the English translation of the Swiss writer Johann Kaspar Lavater's *Essays on Physiognomy* (1789–98). A quasi-physiognomical conviction that language can serve as an index of the mind is also manifest in Thelwall's intended self-defence at trial, in which he argues that the papers and letters confiscated on his arrest are evidence of nothing more than 'a heart bleeding for the miseries of the lower orders of the community, and burning with indignation against the oppressive corruption from which those miseries proceed'. Thelwall, *Right of Britons*, repr. in *PEJ*, p. 37.
34. Thelwall, *Confinement*, p. 12.
35. Thompson, *Silenced Partner*, pp. 232–3.
36. Thelwall, *Confinement*, pp. ii–iii. The poem's allusion to the shaking palsy is especially striking when we consider that one of the character-witnesses at Thelwall's trial was the surgeon and fellow LCS member James Parkinson, who in 1817 would publish *An Essay on the Shaking Palsy*, the disease that now bears his name. Bevan, 'Parkinson, James (1755–1824)'.
37. Cf. Victor Brombert's observation that the late eighteenth-century prisoner discovers in writing 'not only his own self, but the universal status of man', in 'The Bastille and the Poetry of Prison Literature', *American Society of the Legion of Honor Magazine* 39 (1968), 84.
38. Thelwall, *Tribune* 1 (1795), 312–13.
39. Milton, *A Masque Presented at Ludlow Castle [Comus]*, ll. 662–5, in *John Milton*, p. 62. Thelwall adapts the original passage slightly, omitting the phrase 'With all thy charms' at the beginning of the third line and a reference to the will of heaven in the second half of the last line.
40. Thelwall, *Confinement*, p. 9.
41. For the argument that the prison poems inspired the 'out-in-out' movement of the speaker's mind that is characteristic of the 'Greater Romantic Lyric', see John Bugg, 'Close Confinement: John Thelwall and the Romantic Prison', *European Romantic Review* 20, no. 1 (2009), 37–56. Jon Mee discusses Coleridge's disavowal in 'This Lime-Tree Bower My Prison' of the prison poems' materialist vision in 'The Dungeon and the Cell: The Prison Verse of Coleridge and Thelwall', in *John Thelwall: Radical Romantic and Acquitted Felon*, ed. Steve Poole, The Enlightenment World 11 (London: Pickering and Chatto, 2009), pp. 107–16.
42. Milton, *Samson Agonistes*, l. 355, in *John Milton*, p. 681.
43. Thelwall, *Confinement*, p. 22.
44. Thelwall, *Political Lectures*, p. 9.
45. Thelwall, *Retirement*, p. xxix; Thelwall, 'Poems Written in the Tower', *Champion and Sunday Review of Weekly News, Literature, and the Arts* 12 May–14 July and 4 Aug.–8 Sept. 1821; Michael Scrivener, 'John Thelwall and The Press', in *Romanticism, Radicalism and the Press*, ed. Stephen C. Behrendt (Detroit, MI: Wayne State University Press, 1997), p 131. Although

the charge was eventually dropped, the *Champion* ceased publication the following year.

46. Thelwall, 'An Essay on the English Sonnet', *Universal Magazine* (Dec. 1792), 408–14, repr. in *The Peripatetic*, ed. Judith Thompson (Detroit, MI: Wayne State University Press, 2001), pp. 409, 414, 418. The essay's principles are echoed in *The Peripatetic* when the narrator and a companion defend Charlotte Smith's elegiac sonnets against charges of formal 'illegitimacy' and attribute their beauty to the 'glorious crime' of 'burst[ing] the unnatural fetters of arbitrary authority, and exert[ing] the free-born energies of the soul'; *Peripatetic*, pp. 130–1.

47. Curran, *Poetic Form and British Romanticism* (Oxford: Oxford University Press, 1986), p. 21; Wordsworth, 'Nuns fret not at their Convent's narrow room', 1802, in *William Wordsworth: Selected Poetry*, ed. Stephen Gill and Duncan Wu (Oxford: Oxford University Press, 1998), p. 137.

48. Thelwall, *Confinement*, p. 1.

49. Thelwall, *The Poetical Recreations of* The Champion, *and His Literary Correspondents; with a Selection of Essays, Literary and Critical, Which Have Appeared in* The Champion *Newspaper* (London, 1822), p. 150.

50. Thelwall, *Confinement*, p. 4.

51. Fairer, *Organising Poetry: The Coleridge Circle, 1790–1798* (Oxford: Oxford University Press, 2009), p. 254.

52. Of the three defendants to be tried, Thelwall was acquitted last, after a five-day trial in which he was defended by the celebrated barrister Thomas Erskine. The charges against the other defendants were dropped.

53. Under the provisions of the second bill, public lectures such as those delivered by Thelwall would be deemed disorderly unless authorized by two magistrates. See Michael T. Davis et al. (eds), *London Corresponding Society, 1792–1799*, 6 vols (London: Pickering and Chatto, 2002), vol. XI, p. 129. Thelwall publicized his strategy in *Prospectus of a Course of Lectures, to Be Delivered Every Monday, Wednesday, and Friday, during the Ensuing Lent. In Strict Conformity with the Restrictions of Mr. Pitt's Convention Act* (London, 1796).

54. Thompson, 'Disenchantment or Default?' pp. 44–5.

55. For the reference to the defendants of 1794 as 'acquitted felons', see the remarks of the Secretary of State for War, William Windham, in *The Parliamentary History of England, from the Earliest Period to the Year 1803*, ed. William Cobbett, T. C. Hansard and J. Wright, vol. XXXI (London, 1818), p. 1029. Thelwall's satirical counterparts appear in Isaac D'Israeli's *Vaurien; or, Sketches of the Times* (1797), George Walker's *The Vagabond* (1799), and Robert Bisset, *Douglas; or, The Highlander* (1800) respectively. In James Gillray's print 'Copenhagen House' Thelwall hectors the crowd that gathered at the open-air mass meetings of reformers in autumn 1795; in the same artist's 'The New Morality' he leads a procession of liberty-capped writers and politicians from astride the Leviathan figure of the reformist Duke of Bedford.

56. Thelwall, letter to Thomas Hardy, 19 May 1797, Hesburgh Library, University of Notre Dame, MSE/MD 3811-3.

57. Thelwall, *An Appeal to Popular Opinion, against Kidnapping and Murder; Including a Narrative of the Late Atrocious Proceedings, at Yarmouth* (London, 1796), p. 24.

58. For fuller accounts of the attacks on Thelwall in the provinces, see his *Address to the Inhabitants of Yarmouth* and *A Particular Account of the Late Outrages at*

Lynn and Wisbeach (London, 1796); and E. P. Thompson, 'Hunting'. Thelwall describes his precautionary measures in *Political Lectures*, p. 16.

59. Thelwall, *Retirement*, pp. 126, xxxvi.

60. Goodwin, *Friends of Liberty*, p. 414.

61. Thompson, 'Hunting', 95, 123.

62. Thelwall, *Retirement*, p. i.

63. Richard Cronin, *The Politics of Romantic Poetry: In Search of the Pure Commonwealth* (London: Macmillan, 2000), p. 73.

64. The 'retirement' poems properly speaking, those composed between 1796 and 1800, are preceded in the volume by selections from Thelwall's juvenilia spanning the years 1785 to 1793, which elegize lost friends and family members and celebrate a small community of the living knit together by symbolic exchange (gifts given and received include a crutch-stick, a rose and a candlestick). The juxtaposition of these sentimental early verses with the central sequence of poems composed 'in quest of a peaceful retreat' (as per the subtitle to 'Lines, Written at Bridgewater') suggests that the lost community of Thelwall's youth finds a substitute in the dispersed reformist community that he encounters in the provinces.

65. See, for instance, Thompson, *Silenced Partner*, pp. 46–9; Fairer, *Organising Poetry*, pp. 255–7; Roe, '"Atmospheric Air Itself": Medical Science, Politics and Poetry in Thelwall, Coleridge and Wordsworth', in *1789: The Year of the Lyrical Ballads*, ed. Richard Cronin (Houndmills: Macmillan, 1998), pp. 194–7; and Richard Gravil, 'The Somerset Sound; or, the Darling Child of Speech', *Coleridge Bulletin* ns 26 (Winter 2005), 2–4.

66. Thelwall, letter to Susan Thelwall, 18 July 1797, repr. in Davies, *Presences that Disturb*, pp. 296–7. Nicholas Roe gives vivid accounts of Thelwall's visit and its aftermath in 'Coleridge and John Thelwall: The Road to Nether Stowey', in *The Coleridge Connection: Essays for Thomas McFarland*, ed. Richard Gravil and Molly Lefebure (Houndmills: Macmillan, 1990), pp. 60–80; and 'John Thelwall in the West Country: The Road to Nether Stowey Revisited', in *John Thelwall: Critical Reassessments*, ed. Yasmin Solomonescu, Romantic Circles, Sept. 2011, http://www.rc.umd.edu/praxis/thelwall/HTML/praxis.2011.roe.html (accessed 12 June 2012).

67. Coleridge, *Collected Letters*, vol. I, p. 344.

68. Thelwall, *Retirement*, p. xxxiv.

69. Thelwall, *Retirement*, p. 127.

70. Thelwall, *Retirement*, pp. 128, 129–30.

71. Thelwall, *Retirement*, p. 131.

72. Coleridge, *Collected Letters*, vol. I, p. 295. 'Stella' was Thelwall's poetic name for his wife Susan.

73. Roe, 'Atmospheric', p. 15.

74. Thelwall, *Retirement*, pp. 131–2.

75. Thelwall, *Retirement*, p. 132.

76. Thelwall, *Retirement*, p. xxxiv.

77. Peter Crompton is mentioned in the *Dictionary of National Biography* entry for his son. See Joshua S. Getzler, 'Crompton, Sir Charles John (1797–1865)', in *Oxford Dictionary of National Biography*, ed. H. C. G. Matthew and Brian Harrison (Oxford: Oxford University Press, 2004), online edn, ed. Lawrence Goldman, Oct. 2009, http://www.oxforddnb.com/view/article/6756 (accessed 1 Jan. 2012).

78. Thelwall mentions his acquaintance with Darwin in 'A Pedestrian Excursion through Parts of England and Wales during the Summer of 1797', *Monthly Magazine* 8–12 (1799–1801), repr. in *Selected Political Writings of John Thelwall*, ed. Robert Lamb and Corinna Wagner, 4 vols (London: Pickering and Chatto, 2009), vol. III, p. 37; and 'Mr. Thelwall's Lecture on the Enunciative Organs, and the Formation of Literal Elements', *Monthly Magazine* 60 (1825), 114.

79. Thelwall, letter to Thomas Hardy, 12 Dec. 1805, Hesburgh Library, University of Notre Dame, MSE/MD 3811-8.

80. Thelwall, 'Auto-Biography. (To Dr Crompton – Eaton – Liverpool) 1 Nov. 1822', in *Poems, Chiefly Suggested by the Scenery of Nature; to Which are Added Odes &c. Amatory and Congratulatory, Translations, and Attempts at Humour* ('Derby manuscript'), 3 vols, Derby Local Studies Library, Derby, England, 5868–70, vol. III, pp. 897. Felicity James points out in 'Coleridge and the Unitarian Ladies', *Coleridge Bulletin* ns 28 (Winter 2006), 50, that when Crompton lost the 1796 Nottingham election, 'windows were broken, soldiers had to be deployed to clear the mob, and a Tree of Liberty was planted in the Market Place'. Thelwall discusses Crompton's candidacy in *Rights of Nature*, repr. in *PEJ*, pp. 399, 403, and declares an intention to visit Crompton in Derby in a letter to Thomas Hardy of 24 Aug. 1796, Hesburgh Library, University of Notre Dame, MSE/MD 3811-1.

81. Thelwall, letter to Peter Crompton, 3 March 1798, repr. in Davies, *Presences that Disturb*, p. 300.

82. J. A. Hamilton, 'Gurney, Sir John (1768–1845)', rev. Catherine Pease-Watkin, in *Oxford Dictionary of National Biography*, ed. H. C. G. Matthew and Brian Harrison, Oxford: Oxford University Press, 2004, online edn, ed. Lawrence Goldman, http://www.oxforddnb.com/view/article/11767 (accessed 28 Oct. 2012).

83. On Crompton's radical connections in Liverpool, where he moved a few years later, see Ian Sellers, 'William Roscoe, the Roscoe Circle and Radical Politics in Liverpool, 1787–1807', *Transactions of the Historic Society of Lancashire and Cheshire* 120 (1969), 45–62.

84. Crompton, letter to John Thelwall, 11 Sept. 1800, Morgan Library, New York, MA 77 (19).

85. This may be owing to the *Retirement* collection's publication in two stages. Thelwall later explained that the collection was first printed 'in compliance with the solicitations of some friends, who were desirous of an opportunity of serving me; and the obscure neighbourhood in which I then resided had not furnished me with those advantages of paper and typography, which the taste of the times required. The general publication was, therefore, deferred till occasion should call for, and leizure [sic] should permit, a new and more elegant impression'. See *A Letter to Francis Jeffray* [sic]*, Esq., on Certain Calumnies and Misrepresentations in the Edinburgh Review* (Edinburgh, 1804), p. vii. Elsewhere Thelwall observes that '[a]fter the first 500 copies were worked off, a considerable alteration was made in the latter part of the Memoir; and the more perfect copies were, therefore, [...] distinguished' with the inscription 'Second Edition'. See *Mr. Thelwall's Reply to the Calumnies, Misrepresentations, and Literary Forgeries, Contained in the Anonymous Observations on His Letter to the Editor of the Edinburgh Review* (Glasgow, 1804), p. 29. On the format of first edition, see Thelwall's letter to George Dyer of 12 Aug. 1801, repr. in Davies, *Presences that Disturb*, p. 310.

86. Thelwall, 'To Dr. Peter Crompton', in *Poems, Chiefly Written in Retirement* (Hereford, 1801), n. pag., Cambridge University Library, Rare Books, Y.19.43 (no. 1).

87. Coleridge, *Collected Letters*, vol. II, p. 724.

88. Coleridge, 'Reflections on Having Left a Place of Retirement', ll. 51–3, 57–9, repr. in *Samuel Taylor Coleridge: The Major Works,* ed. H. J. Jackson (Oxford: Oxford University Press, 2000), p. 31.

89. Thelwall, 'To Dr. Peter Crompton', n. pag.

90. Thelwall, *Retirement*, p. 127. On this double loss, cf. Scrivener, *Seditious Allegories*, pp. 247–8.

91. Coleridge, *Collected Letters*, vol. II, p. 723.

92. Thelwall, *Retirement*, p. xlii.

93. Thompson, 'An Autumnal Blast, a Killing Frost: Coleridge's Poetic Conversation with John Thelwall', *Studies in Romanticism* 36 (1997), 451.

94. Thelwall, *Retirement*, p. 139.

95. Thelwall, letter to John Vellum, 10 March 1794, repr. in Davies, *Presences that Disturb*, p. 290.

96. Thelwall, *Retirement*, p. 144.

97. Thelwall, *Retirement*, pp. xxxviii, 147. Notice of Maria's death appeared in *Monthly Magazine* 9 (Feb. 1800), 98.

98. See Wordsworth's letter to Benjamin Robert Haydon of 20 Jan. 1817 in *The Letters of William and Dorothy Wordsworth: The Middle Years*, ed. Ernest de Selincourt, rev. Mary Moorman and Alan G. Hill, 2nd edn, 2 vols (Oxford: Clarendon Press, 1970), vol. II, p. 361.

99. Thelwall, *Animal Vitality*, repr. in *SPW,* vol. I, p. 18.

100. Thelwall, *Retirement*, p. 146.

101. Catherine E. Storey, 'Apoplexy: Changing Concepts in the Eighteenth Century', in *Brain, Mind and Medicine: Essays in Eighteenth-Century Neuroscience*, ed. Harry Whitaker, C. U. M. Smith and Stanley Finger (New York: Springer, 2007), pp. 233–43.

102. Thelwall, *Retirement*, pp. 146–7.

103. Thelwall, *Confinement*, p. 9; marginalia on Coleridge, 79.

104. Thelwall, *Retirement*, p. 148.

105. Coleridge, *Lectures 1795: On Politics and Religion*, ed. Lewis Patton and Peter Mann, Bollingen Series 75 (London: Routledge and Kegan Paul, 1971), p. 297; Thelwall, *Retirement*, p. 149.

106. Thelwall, 'The Phenomena of the Wye, during the Winter of 1797–8', *Monthly Magazine* 5 (1798), 343–6; 6 (1798), 20–1, repr. in *Selected Political Writings of John Thelwall*, ed. Robert Lamb and Corinna Wagner, 4 vols (London: Pickering and Chatto, 2009), vol. III, pp. 4–6.

107. Thelwall, *Retirement*, pp. 149–50.

108. Thelwall, *Retirement*, pp. 150–1.

109. Thelwall, *Retirement*, p. 151.

110. 'Description of a Machine' and 'Electric Shock', in *Biographical and Imperial Magazine* (June 1790), 339–40.

111. Thelwall, *Retirement*, p. 154.

112. Thelwall, *Retirement*, p. 156.

113. Samuel Homfray, letter to the Duke of Portland, 1 Oct. 1800, repr. in Penelope J. Corfield and Chris Evans, 'John Thelwall in Wales: New

Documentary Evidence', *Bulletin of the Institute for Historical Research* 59 (1986), 237–8, with underlining reproduced from the manuscript.

114. Thompson, 'Disenchantment or Default?', p. 47.

115. Roe, 'Coleridge and John Thelwall', p. 74.

116. Thelwall's letter to Crompton extends greetings to his family's 'kind bene-factor Miss C', who may have been Crompton's sister or daughter. Thelwall, letter to Peter Crompton, 3 March 1798, repr. in Davies, *Presences that Disturb*, pp. 300–5. For the other letters from this period see pp. 298–307.

117. Thelwall, *Retirement*, pp. 158–9.

118. *OED Online*, s.v. 'effusion, *n.*'.

119. James L. Stone, James T. Goodrich and George R. Cybulski, 'John Hunter's Contributions to Neuroscience', in *Brain, Mind and Medicine: Essays in Eighteenth-Century Neuroscience*, ed. Harry Witaker, C. U. M. Smith and Stanley Finger (New York: Springer, 2007), p. 79.

120. Thelwall, *Retirement*, p. 145.

121. *Collins Spurrell Welsh Dictionary*, 2nd edn, s.v. 'pen' and 'heol'.

122. Judith Thompson notes that Maria is not listed in Llyswen church records and may have been denied a consecrated burial. 'Citizen Juan Thelwall: In the Footsteps of a Free-Range Radical', *Studies in Romanticism* 48 (Spring 2009), 70.

123. Thelwall, *Retirement*, p. 162.

124. Thelwall, *Retirement*, p. 160. Cf. Milton, *Lycidas*, ll. 10–11, in *John Milton*, p. 39: 'Who would not sing for Lycidas? he knew / Himself to sing, and build the lofty rhyme'.

125. Thelwall, *Letter to Cline*, repr. in *SPW*, vol. IV, p. 10.

4   Between Hope and Necessity

1. Thelwall, *Poetical Recreations*, p. 114.

2. Thelwall, *Poetical Recreations*, p. 114. Thelwall's automaton metaphor was perhaps inspired by Erasmus Darwin's invention of a speaking machine con-sisting of 'a wooden mouth with lips of soft leather, and with a valve over the back part of it for nostrils, both [of] which could be quickly opened or closed by the pressure of the fingers'; *The Temple of Nature; or, the Origin of Society* (London, 1803; repr. Menston: Scolar, 1973), p. 120.

3. Thelwall, *Rights of Nature*, repr. in *PEJ*, p. 430

4. Thelwall, *Sober Reflections*, repr. in *PEJ*, p. 386.

5. Thelwall, *Rights of Nature*, repr. in *PEJ*, p. 430, which substitutes 'extraordinarily' for 'extraordinary'.

6. Thelwall, *Peripatetic*, pp. 224–5.

7. Coleridge, *Collected Letters*, vol. I, p. 137.

8. Thelwall, *The Daughter of Adoption; A Tale of Modern Times*, ed. Michael Scrivener, Yasmin Solomonescu and Judith Thompson (Peterborough, ON: Broadview, 2013), p. 270.

9. Godwin, *Educational and Literary Writings*, ed. Pamela Clemit, The Pickering Masters (London: Pickering and Chatto, 1993), pp. 298–9.

10. Clara Reeve, *The Progress of Romance, through Times, Countries, and Manners; with Remarks on the Good and Bad Effects of It, on Them Respectively; in a*

Course of Evening Conversations, 2 vols (Colchester, 1785), vol. I, p. 111, Eighteenth Century Collections Online, http://find.galegroup.com.proxy. library.nd.edu/ecco (accessed 28 Oct. 2012).

11. Klancher, 'Republican Romance', 159.

12. Klancher, 'Republican Romance', 155. Godwin concluded that writing historical romance was 'a task too great for the powers of man' because it would require 'a sagacity scarcely less than divine' to trace the effects of necessity on human character and conduct; *Educational and Literary Writings*, p. 301.

13. Williams, *Culture and Materialism: Selected Essays*, Radical Thinkers (London: Verso, 1980; repr. 2005), pp. 108–9.

14. See, for instance, Thelwall's characterization of Isabella of England and Emperor Frederick II of Germany as 'senseless automatons, moved by the strings and wires of political expediency, [... and] led, without will or inclination, to the altar', in *Peripatetic*, p. 188.

15. For footage and analysis of the 2009 production, see 'John Thelwall in Performance: *The Fairy of the Lake*', ed. Judith Thompson, Romantic Circles, Aug. 2012, http://www.rc.umd.edu/reference/thelwall_fairy/index.html (accessed 28 Oct. 2012).

16. Thelwall, *Retirement*, pp. 14, 78.

17. Scrivener, *Seditious Allegories*, pp. 250–1; Thompson, 'A "Double-Visag'd Fate": John Thelwall and the Hapless Hope of Albion', in *John Thelwall: Radical Romantic and Acquitted Felon*, ed. Steve Poole, The Enlightenment World 11 (London: Pickering and Chatto, 2009), pp. 128–9. By contrast, Alan Lupack's assessment of *The Fairy* as a critique of the hero's 'destructive vengeance' does not fit with Arthur's primarily self-destructive tendencies. Lupack (ed.), *Arthurian Drama: An Anthology* (New York: Garland, 1991), pp. xvi–xvii.

18. Thelwall, *Retirement*, p. 13.

19. Thelwall, *Retirement*, pp. 58, 42. Michael Scrivener notes Thelwall's debt to Dryden's *King Arthur* (1691) in *Seditious Allegories*, p. 249.

20. Thelwall, *Retirement*, p. 88.

21. Thelwall, *Retirement*, p. xxxv; 'Phenomena of the Wye', repr. in *SPW*, vol. III, p. 7.

22. Davies, 'Capital Crimes', 56.

23. See, for instance, Thelwall, *Rights of Nature*, repr. in *PEJ*, p. 419.

24. Thelwall, *Retirement*, pp. 3, 13.

25. Thelwall, *Retirement*, p. 16; Thompson, 'Double-Visag'd', p. 129. On Walsh and Thelwall, see Nicholas Roe, 'Who Was Spy Nozy?' *Wordsworth Circle* 15, no. 2 (1984), 46–50; and A. J. Eagleston, 'Wordsworth, Coleridge, and the Spy', in *Coleridge: Studies by Several Hands on the Hundredth Anniversary of His Death*, ed. Edmund Blunden and Earl Leslie Griggs (London: Constable, 1934), pp. 73–87. Patty O'Boyle suggests instead that Incubus might be modelled on Coleridge in 'Coleridge, Wordsworth and Thelwall's *Fairy of the Lake*', *Coleridge Bulletin* ns 28 (2006), 66–7.

26. Thelwall, *Retirement*, p. 6. Vortigern was the early fifth-century Brythonic (or Welsh-Briton) king who precipitated the loss of Britain to the Saxons by an act of political betrayal, and thereafter sought refuge in the Wye Valley. On the parallels between Thelwall and Vortigern, see Davies, *Presences that Disturb*, p. 59.

27. Thelwall, *Political Lectures*, pp. 27–8.
28. Thelwall, *Retirement*, p. 49.
29. Thelwall, *Confinement*, p. 9; *Retirement*, p. 147.
30. Thelwall, *Retirement*, pp. 50–1.
31. Thelwall, *Retirement*, p. 47; *Confinement*, p. 2.
32. Coleridge, *Collected Letters*, vol. III, p. 490.
33. Coleridge, *Collected Letters*, vol. II, p. 1019; Thelwall, 'Imagination', *Panoramic Miscellany* (1826), 761.
34. Mrs. Thelwall, *Life*, p. 196. The use of opium and wine to excite a sluggish nervous system was recommended by, among others, the Scottish physician John Brown in *Elementa Medicinae* (1780), published in English in 1788 and republished in a more accurate translation by Thomas Beddoes in 1795, as noted by Vickers, *Coleridge and the Doctors*, pp. 52–3.
35. See, notably, Thelwall, *Rights of Nature*, repr. in *PEJ*, pp. 389–500.
36. Thelwall, *Retirement*, pp. 74, 80.
37. Thelwall, *Retirement*, p. 36.
38. Thelwall, *Retirement*, p. 48; Thompson, 'Double-Visag'd', pp. 136–7.
39. Thelwall, *Retirement*, pp. 64, 55.
40. Thelwall, *Retirement*, p. 57.
41. Thelwall, *Retirement*, p. 59.
42. According to *Retirement*, pp. xxxvii–xxxix, Thelwall's neighbours at Llyswen included a local clergyman who launched 'pointed and inflammatory allusions [about him] from the pulpit', a farmer who assaulted him with a pick-axe and superstitious gossips who saw omens of evil in his solitary rambles and distaste for Welsh ale and tobacco. Thelwall's political notoriety also made him unwelcome in the local libraries, and his mail was subject to frequent interception.
43. Thelwall, *Retirement*, p. 78.
44. Thelwall, *Tribune*, repr. in *PEJ*, p. 309.
45. This moral is reinforced by the play's conclusion: as the castle is engulfed in flames, Rowenna realizes that in her blind pursuit of 'Empire, and Love, and Glory', she has disastrously misconstrued the Fatal Sisters' prophecy that 'Arthur's hand shall light the fire / In which [... her] sorrows all expire'. Her deception by a 'double-visag'd Fate' suggests that the fatalistic despair of Arthur and his modern British counterparts is equally unfounded. *Retirement*, pp. 47, 30, 13.
46. Thelwall, *Vestibule*, p. 115; *Poetical Recreations*, p. 115.
47. Thelwall, *Poetical Recreations*, p. 116.
48. Thelwall, 'Auto-Biography', Derby manuscript, vol. III, pp. 891v–905v, underlining Thelwall's. The lines contradict Henry Crabb Robinson's claim in *Diary*, vol. I, p. 473, that Thelwall had nearly finished *The Hope* by 1815. A complete version has never surfaced.
49. Thelwall, *Retirement*, p. 177. Some of the fragments published in the *Retirement* collection re-appear in Thelwall's elocutionary anthologies, notably the various editions of *Selections, and Original Articles, Read and Recited in Illustration of Mr. Thelwall's Lectures on the Science and Practice of Elocution* (1802). Additional fragments of *The Hope* appeared over the next several decades in various publications including *The Vestibule of Eloquence*, the *Champion* and the *Monthly Magazine*.

50. Thelwall, *Poetical Recreations*, p. 236; Hume, *The History of England*, 6 vols (Indianapolis, IN: Liberty Fund, 1983), vol. I, p. 36, The Online Library of Liberty, http://oll.libertyfund.org/title/1868 (accessed 7 Nov. 2012).
51. As noted by Steve Poole in '"Not Precedents to Be Followed but Examples to Be Weighed": John Thelwall and the Jacobin Sense of the Past', in *John Thelwall: Radical Romantic and Acquitted Felon*, ed. Steve Poole, The Enlightenment World 11 (London: Pickering and Chatto, 2009), p. 163.
52. Thelwall, *Poetical Recreations*, p. 237.
53. For a comparable analysis of the aims of Major John Cartwright, Joseph Gerrald and other radicals of the time, see Epstein, *Radical Expression*, p. 21.
54. Thelwall, *Poetical Recreations*, p. 117.
55. Thelwall, *Retirement*, p. 182.
56. Thelwall, *Poetical Recreations*, p. 118.
57. Roe, *Politics of Nature*, p. 92.
58. Thelwall, *Poetical Recreations*, p. 120.
59. Thelwall, *Poetical Recreations*, p. 123.
60. Thelwall, *Retirement*, p. 177; Mrs. Thelwall, *Life*, p. 68.
61. Thelwall, *Vestibule*, p. 124.
62. Thelwall, *Retirement*, p. 192.
63. Thelwall, *Retirement*, pp. 194–5.
64. Thelwall, *Retirement*, p. 198.
65. Thelwall, *Retirement*, p. 201.
66. Thelwall, *Retirement*, p. 197.
67. Uglow, *Lunar Men*, p. 12; Fara, *Entertainment for Angels*, p. 14. Thelwall may alternatively be thinking of Francis Hauksbee's machine consisting of a great wheel that twirled a ball of glass, which produced electricity when rubbed. Uglow notes in *Lunar Men*, p. 10, that 'after some time the inside of the glass globe shone with a strange purple, blue-green glow, and lines of light crackled like lightening within it'.
68. Jackson, *Science and Sensation*, p. 56. Thelwall offers a positive variant of the 'hermetic hand' scene in 'The Trident of Albion', his poem on the death of Horatio Nelson, in which patriot feeling is described spreading 'Unanimous, / From rank to rank, thro all her kindling sons. / With deep-breath'd vows of emulation'; *Vestibule*, p. 26.
69. Thelwall, *Vestibule*, p. 118.
70. Thelwall, *Vestibule*, p. 124.
71. Thelwall, *Vestibule*, p. 129.
72. Thelwall, *Rights of Nature*, repr. in *PEJ*, p. 401.
73. Burke, *Reflections*, p. 130.
74. Mee, *Romanticism, Enthusiasm, and Regulation*, pp. 94, 25. I respond more fully to Mee's and Mary Fairclough's views on Thelwall's faith in the rational self-regulation of the crowd in Chapter 5.
75. Thelwall, *Vestibule*, pp. 131, 134.
76. Thelwall, *Vestibule*, p. 140. Cf. the title of Thelwall's short pamphlet *Strike, but Hear! A Dedication to His Majesty's Ministers, the Crown Lawyers, and the Majority of Both Houses of Parliament* (London, 1796), which alludes to the Athenian politician and general Themistocles's words to his persecutor, 'Strike, but hear!'

77. Thelwall, *Vestibule*, p. 144. Thelwall would later suggest that the Wittena-gemot was an ancestor of the British Parliament and assert against Hume that 'all which is really valuable in our Constitution is of Saxon origin', including juries, a constitutional militia and the rights to 'a legislative voice' and a vote. 'Etymological Reasoning', *Champion* 4 April 1819, p. 211.
78. Thelwall, *Vestibule*, p. 147.
79. Thelwall, *Poetical Recreations*, p. 236.
80. Thompson, 'Double-Visag'd', pp. 137–8.
81. Curran, *Poetic Form*, p. 161.
82. Coleridge, *Collected Letters*, vol. II, p. 723.
83. Thelwall, *Poetical Recreations*, p. 237.
84. Thelwall, *Peripatetic*, p. 303.
85. The page count refers to the four-volume London edition published in 1801 by Richard Phillips; the same year's two-volume Dublin edition was published by Nicholas Kelly. Textual variants are discussed in Michael Scrivener, Yasmin Solomonescu and Judith Thompson (eds), *The Daughter of Adoption; A Tale of Modern Times* (Peterborough, ON: Broadview, 2013), pp. 41–2.
86. *The Daughter* specifies that Montfort's interests lie in 'the French part of the island of St. Domingo', p. 80, and thereafter uses the name of the island to designate the French colony that occupied its western part. I follow the modern scholarly practice of referring to the French colony as St. Domingue (now Haiti), thereby distinguishing it from the Spanish colony of Santo Domingo, which occupied the eastern part of the island.
87. Thelwall, *Daughter*, p. 139.
88. Thelwall, *Daughter*, p. 270.
89. Thelwall, *Daughter*, p. 249.
90. As Robert Southey explained to a friend in November 1801: 'The novel you mention is by John Thelwall, and in the assumed name of Beaufort you may trace the Lecturer in Beaufort Buildings'; *New Letters of Robert Southey*, ed. Kenneth Curry, 2 vols (New York: Columbia University Press, 1965), vol. I, p. 256.
91. Thelwall, *Retirement*, p. xli.
92. Thelwall claims in *Retirement*, p. xlvi, that he wrote more than two-thirds of the novel in just a few weeks. Prompts to the identification of Seraphina and Maria include the description of Seraphina as a '[w]ild woodbine of the hedge' – the flower that symbolises Maria in the 1797 poem 'The Woodbine' – and the account of Parkinson's adoption of Seraphina as a surrogate for his own dead daughter. Thelwall, *Daughter*, pp. 428, 151–8; *Retirement*, pp. 139–40.
93. Thelwall, *Daughter*, p. 48.
94. E. P. Thompson, 'Hunting', 121–2.
95. Scrivener, Solomonescu and Thompson (eds), *Daughter*, p. 9.
96. Kelly, *English Jacobin Novel*, p. 16.
97. Kelly, *English Jacobin Novel*, p. 12.
98. Klancher, 'Republican Romance', 161.
99. Thelwall, *Daughter*, p. 259.
100. Thelwall, *Retirement*, p. xlvi; *Daughter*, p. 251. The recurrent use of 'brain' instead of 'mind' in *The Daughter*, e.g., pp. 134, 254, 319, 326, 406, 435, is

another symptom of the influence of late eighteenth-century medical science on Thelwall's work. Alan Richardson credits him with helping bring the term into wider literary usage, in *Science of the Mind*, p. 147.

101. Thelwall, *Daughter*, pp. 64, 66–7.
102. Thelwall, *Daughter*, pp. 65, 67.
103. Srinivas Aravamudan (ed.), *Fiction* (London: Pickering and Chatto, 1999), p. xviii, vol. VI of *Slavery, Abolition and Emancipation: Writings in the British Romantic Period*, ed. Peter J. Kitson and Deborah Lee, 8 vols.
104. Thelwall, *Incle and Yarico and* The Incas: *Two Plays by John Thelwall*, ed. Michael Scrivener and Frank Felsenstein (Madison: Fairleigh Dickinson University Press, 2006).
105. The date given for the rebellion in the London and Dublin editions – 22 Aug. 1795 (p. 159) – is almost certainly the result of a typographical error. Various dates and ages specified in the novel confirm that the fictional rebellion, like the real one, takes place in 1791. We are told, for instance, that Henry is born just after his father's departure for the West Indies. This must be around 1770 since, when the novel opens in 1776, Montfort has been gone six years (p. 47). Moreover, Henry is 21 when the slave rebellion breaks out (p. 222). The 1791 dating of the fictional rebellion is also corroborated by Seraphina's age and date of birth, as well as by the fact that it is said to take place 30 years after a smaller slave revolt in Jamaica, Tacky's Rebellion, which occurred in 1760–61 (p. 171).
106. Baron de Wimpffen, *A Voyage to Saint Domingo, in the Years 1788, 1789, and 1790*, trans. J. Wright (London, 1797); Bryan Edwards, *The History, Civil and Commercial, of the British West Indies*, vol. III (London, 1798). The classic modern account of the rebellion is C. L. R. James's *The Black Jacobins: Toussaint L'Ouverture and the San Domingo Revolution* (New York: Dial, 1938; repr. London: Allison and Busby, 1980).
107. Although the *Amis* prided themselves on representing the national interest, they were sometimes accused of being English agents sent to weaken the French hold on the Antilles. See Robin Blackburn, *The Overthrow of Colonial Slavery, 1776–1848* (London: Verso, 1988), pp. 169–77.
108. Coleridge later recalled, 'We were once sitting in a beautiful recess in the Quantocks, when I said to him – "Citizen John! this is a fine place to talk treason in!" – "Nay! Citizen Samuel", replied he, "it is a place to make a man forget that there is any necessity for treason!"'. Coleridge, *Table Talk*, ed. Carl Woodring, 2 vols, Bollingen Series 75 (London: Routledge and Kegan Paul, 1990), vol. I, pp. 180–1; vol. II, p. 115. For Wordsworth's recollection of the episode, see his letter of 16 Nov. 1838 to Henrietta Cecil Thelwall, repr. in *The Letters of William and Dorothy Wordsworth: The Later Years*, ed. Ernest De Selincourt, rev. Alan G. Hill, 2nd edn, 4 vols (Oxford: Clarendon Press, 1982), vol. III, p. 640.
109. Thelwall, *Daughter*, p. 142. Unaccountably, part of the treason exchange is truncated in the Dublin edition.
110. The name 'Parkinson' also evokes Thelwall's friend James Parkinson (1755–1824), a leading member of the London Corresponding Society and the physician who first described the nerve disease that bears his name, as well as a Jamaican Maroon leader in the Trelawney uprising of 1795–96, as noted in Scrivener, Solomonescu and Thompson (eds), *Daughter*, p. 24.

111. Thelwall, *Daughter*, pp. 160–1.

112. Thelwall, *Daughter*, p. 164.

113. Thelwall, *Daughter*, p. 162.

114. Godwin, *Political Justice*, p. 50. Godwin argued that if one could save only a single person from a house fire, justice demanded that it be a socially useful person like Fenelon – the Archbishop of Cambray and author of an influential critique of Louis XIV – rather than his chambermaid, even if that chambermaid were one's own wife or mother.

115. Kitson, '"Bales of Living Anguish": Representations of Race and the Slave in Romantic Writing', *ELH* 67 (2000), 529–32. On the novel's representation of race see also Kitson, 'John Thelwall in Saint Domingue: Race, Slavery, and Revolution in *The Daughter of Adoption: A Tale of Modern Times* (1801)', *Romanticism* 16, no. 2 (2010), 126–9; Arnold A. Markley, *Conversion and Reform in the British Novel in the 1790s: A Revolution of Opinions* (New York: Palgrave Macmillan, 2009), pp. 106–14; and Scrivener, Solomonescu and Thompson (eds), *Daughter*, pp. 20–6.

116. Thelwall, *Daughter*, p. 165.

117. Thelwall, *Daughter*, p. 170.

118. Thelwall, *Daughter*, p. 217; Wollstonecraft, *A Vindication of the Rights of Woman*, ed. Miriam Brody (London: Penguin, 1992), p. 266.

119. Thelwall, *Daughter*, pp. 252, 230.

120. Thelwall, *Daughter*, p. 253.

121. Thelwall, *Daughter*, pp. 253, 409.

122. Thelwall, *Daughter*, pp. 270, 263.

123. Thelwall, *Retirement*, p. xxxviii.

124. Thelwall, *Daughter*, p. 301.

125. This flaw in Godwin's philosophy was more prevalent in the first edition of *Political Justice*, which he revised for that reason, among others, several times.

126. Thelwall, *Daughter*, pp. 385–7. By contrast, Beverly Sprague Allen finds *The Daughter* to be in consensus with Godwinism, including in its concessions to received opinion, in 'William Godwin's Influence upon John Thelwall', *PMLA* 37 (1922), 679–81. Seraphina and Henry's marriage at the end of the novel also celebrates the abolition of primogeniture, the legitimacy of children born outside of wedlock and the parity of 'natural' and adoptive relationships.

127. Thelwall, *Daughter*, p. 406.

128. Markley, *Conversion and Reform*, p. 113.

129. Thelwall, *Daughter*, p. 415.

130. Thelwall, *Daughter*, p. 197.

131. Thelwall, *Daughter*, p. 421.

132. L. T. Topsfield, *Troubadours and Love* (Cambridge: Cambridge University Press, 1975), pp. 42–69. Coleridge addresses Thelwall in a letter of February 1797 as 'amorous Jeffery Ruddell', a designation that Thelwall probably used self-referentially in a prior letter. *Collected Letters*, vol. I, p. 308.

133. Thelwall, *Daughter*, p. 226.

134. Smith, *Moral Sentiments*, p. 12.

135. Thelwall, *Daughter*, p. 223.

136. Thelwall, *Peripatetic*, pp. 224–5.

137. This is Paul Hamilton's reading of Godwin in 'Coleridge and Godwin in the 1790s', in *The Coleridge Connection: Essays for Thomas McFarland*, ed. Richard Gravil and Molly Lefebure (New York: St. Martin's, 1990), p. 55.
138. Thelwall, *A Letter to Francis Jeffray*, p. 57n. Thelwall makes fun here of a review in the *Edinburgh* of William Shepherd's biography of the Italian humanist Poggio Bracciolini, specifically the reviewer's suggestion that the 'restoration of letters' in the fifteenth century was 'a *step* in the natural history of man' that would have '*developed itself*' even without the efforts of Bracciolini and his circle.

5   The Language of Nature

1. Thelwall, *Selections for the Illustration of a Course of Instructions on the Rhythmus and Utterance of the English Language* (London, 1812), p. xvi. Thelwall also refers to this work as *Illustrations of English Rhythmus*.
2. Wordsworth, *The Poetical Works of William Wordsworth*, ed. Ernest De Selincourt and Helen Darbishire, 5 vols (Oxford: Clarendon, 1940–49), vol. I, p. 363; Coleridge, *Lectures 1795*, p. 297.
3. Hazlitt, *The Complete Works of William Hazlitt*, ed. P. P. Howe, 21 vols (London: Dent, 1930–34), vol. XII, p. 264. Cf. Godwin, *Political Writings, II*, pp. 131–2.
4. Thelwall, *Tribune*, repr. in *PEJ*, p. 309.
5. Thelwall, *Prospectus*, p. 6.
6. Thomas Amyot, letter to Henry Crabb Robinson, 8 June 1796, repr. in *Youth and Revolution in the 1790s: Letters of William Pattison, Thomas Amyot and Henry Crabb Robinson*, ed. Penelope J. Corfield and Chris Evans (Stroud: Sutton, 1996), p. 138.
7. D'Israeli, *Vaurien*, p. 30.
8. See George Walker's *The Vagabond* (1799) and Robert Bisset's *Douglas; or, The Highlander* (1800) respectively. Thelwall also appears as an aged elocutionist who demonstrates his skills to ludicrous effect in George Borrow's *Lavengro: The Scholar–The Gypsy–The Priest*, 3 vols (London, 1851), vol. II, pp. 124–34, as noted in A. Boyle, 'Portraiture in *Lavengro* VI: The Teacher of Oratory–John Thelwall', *Notes and Queries*, 197 (1952), 38–9.
9. Britton, *Autobiography*, p. 145.
10. Thelwall, *Rights of Nature*, repr. in *PEJ*, p. 409.
11. Thelwall, letter to Joseph Strutt, 20 Dec. 1801, repr. in Davies, *Presences that Disturb*, pp. 312–13.
12. Thelwall, *Rhythmus*, cover page. In *Rights of Nature*, repr. in *PEJ*, p. 415n, Thelwall had praised Denis O'Bryen, author of the 'spirited and well-written' pamphlet *Utrum Horum? The Government, or the Country* (1796), for not having 'daubed his title-page either with *Mr.* or *Esq.*'.
13. Saintsbury, *A History of English Prosody from the Twelfth Century to the Present Day*, vol. III (London: Macmillan, 1910), p. 157. Andrew McCann argues that by training students for careers in parliament, the law and the church Thelwall was helping to 'assimilate' them into the institutions of bourgeois public life and consolidating its values; 'Romantic Self-Fashioning: John Thelwall and the Science of Elocution', *Studies in Romanticism* 40 (2001),

215–32. Steve Poole likewise contends that in the early nineteenth century Thelwall did not so much redirect his earlier energies as dissipate them in uncontroversial professional channels; 'Gillray, Cruikshank and Thelwall: Visual Satire, Physiognomy and the Jacobin Body', in *John Thelwall: Critical Reassessments*, ed. Yasmin Solomonescu, Romantic Circles, Sept. 2011, http://romantic.arhu.umd.edu/praxis/thelwall/HTML/praxis.2011.poole. html (accessed 12 June 2012), para. 18.

14. Thelwall, *Prospectus*, p. 18; *Sober Reflections*, repr. in *PEJ*, p. 376.

15. [Thelwall], 'Elocution', *Cyclopaedia; or, a New Universal Dictionary of Arts, Sciences, and Literature*, ed. Abraham Rees, vol. XIII (London, 1819), n. pag.

16. Judith Thompson, 'Re-Sounding Romanticism: John Thelwall and the Science and Practice of Elocution', in *Spheres of Action: Speech and Performance in Romantic Culture*, ed. Angela Esterhammer and Alexander Dick (Toronto: University of Toronto Press, 2009), pp. 21–45, borrowing the terms 'logopaedic' from Denyse Rockey, 'The Logopaedic Thought of John Thelwall, 1764–1834: First British Speech Therapist', *British Journal of Disorders of Communication* 12 (1977), 83–95.

17. Richardson, *Science of the Mind*, pp. 1–31, 118–24.

18. Thelwall, *Vestibule*, p. 2.

19. Thelwall, *Vestibule*, pp. 5–6, the definitions originally in italics.

20. [Thelwall], 'Emotion' and 'Enthusiasm', *Cyclopaedia*, vol. XIII, n. pag.

21. Thelwall, *Letter to Cline*, repr. in *SPW*, vol. IV, p. 8.

22. Thelwall, *Letter to Cline*, repr. in *SPW*, vol. IV, pp. 10–11.

23. Thelwall, *Letter to Cline*, repr. in *SPW*, vol. IV, pp. 12–13.

24. On the outside of the letter, however, Birkbeck added a note informing Anderson that he was 'not by any means decided' to pursue 'the plan mentioned by Mr. T.' and would probably remain in Scotland. Thelwall, letter to Robert Anderson, 9 Feb. 1804, National Library of Scotland, Edinburgh, 22.4.14. In 1823 Birkbeck founded the London Mechanics' Institution at which Thelwall would lecture. See Matthew Lee, 'Birkbeck, George (1776–1841)', in *Oxford Dictionary of National Biography*, online edn, ed. Lawrence Goldman (Oxford: Oxford University Press), http://www.oxforddnb.com/view/article/2454 (accessed 20 June 2012).

25. See, for instance, the announcement in *Monthly Magazine* 21 (1806), 247. Fittingly, the building at 57 Lincoln's Inn Fields that housed Thelwall's Institution is now occupied by a legal firm committed to human rights and social justice.

26. Thelwall, *Vestibule*, pp. 1–32 (i.e., 'Plan and Terms of the Institution', independently paginated).

27. Frederick W. Haberman, 'John Thelwall: His Life, His School, and His Theory of Elocution', in *Historical Studies of Rhetoric and Rhetoricians*, ed. Raymond F. Howes (Ithaca, NY: Cornell University Press, 1961), p. 191; Judith Thompson, 'From Forum to Repository: A Case Study in Romantic Cultural Geography', *European Romantic Review* 15, no. 2 (2004), 187; 'Mr. Thelwall', *Gentleman's Magazine* ns 2 (1834), 549–50.

28. For example, *Selections and Original Articles, Read and Recited in Illustration of Mr. Thelwall's Lectures on the Science and Practice of Elocution* (Wakefield, 1802), and *Selections, &c., for Mr. Thelwall's Lectures on the Science and Practice of Elocution* (York, 1802).

29. Thelwall, *Letters to Cline*, repr. in *SPW*, vol. IV, p. 62.

30. See the entries for 'Element', 'Elocution', 'Emotion', 'Emphasis', 'Energy', 'Enthusiasm', 'Enunciation', 'Euphony' and 'Expression' in *Cyclopaedia*, vol. XIII, n. pag. Thelwall claims authorship of the entries in *Monthly Magazine* 30 (1810), 302; and *Rhythmus*, p. xiv.

31. Thelwall, letter to the editor, *Monthly Magazine* 19 (1805), 348.

32. For an overview of these lectures see Thelwall, *Rhythmus*, pp. xxvii–lxxii.

33. Henrietta Cecil Thelwall, letter to the Rev. William Shepherd, March 1835, repr. in Davies, *Presences that Disturb*, p. 326.

34. A. S. Thelwall, *Exercises in Elocution, in Verse and Prose: To which is Prefixed, A Lecture on the Importance of Elocution in Connexion with Ministerial Usefulness, Delivered at King's College, London, on Entering upon the Duties of Lecturer on Public Reading, Jan. 30, 1850* (London, 1850); and S. Thelwall, *The Syllabic Primer and Reading Book, Based on the Principle That the Sound of Letters Is Determined by Their Position in a Syllable or Word* (London, 1859).

35. Robin Thelwall, 'The Phonetic Theory of John Thelwall (1764–1834)', in *Towards a History of Phonetics: Essays Contributed in Honour of David Abercrombie*, ed. R. E. Asher and Eugénie J. A. Henderson (Edinburgh: Edinburgh University Press, 1981), p. 188; Rockey, 'John Thelwall and the Origins of British Speech Therapy', *Medical History* 23 (1979), 156.

36. *OED Online*, s.v. 'rhythmus, *n.*'.

37. Shaftesbury, *Characteristicks of Men, Manners, Opinions, Times*, 4th edn, vol. I (London, 1727), p. 218, Eighteenth Century Collections Online, http://find.galegroup.com.proxy.library.nd.edu/ecco (accessed 29 Oct. 2012).

38. Thelwall, *Rhythmus*, p. ii.

39. Thelwall, *Letter to Cline*, repr. in *SPW*, vol. IV, p. 7.

40. Thelwall, *Rhythmus*, pp. xxviii–xxxv. Thelwall's understanding of the role of the chest and other 'secondary organs' is indebted to the blind natural philosopher John Gough, whom he met while lecturing in Kendal in 1803 and corresponded with thereafter. *Letter to Cline*, repr. in *SPW*, vol. IV, pp. 17–22.

41. [Thelwall], 'Elocution', *Cyclopaedia*, vol. XIII, n. pag.

42. The 'quantity' of a syllable depended on the length of time necessary for its pronunciation, which could be relatively 'long' or 'short'. 'Accent' referred to the inflection or slide of a syllable along the musical scale, which could be 'acute', 'grave' or 'circumflex'. 'Breath' designated the loudness of a syllable's pronunciation. Thelwall, 'Mr. Thelwall's Lecture on the Articulation and Qualities of Syllables, and the Educational Causes of Impediments of Speech', *Panoramic Miscellany* 1 (1826), 349.

43. Paul Fussell, Jr., *Theory of Prosody in Eighteenth-Century England* (1954; Hamden, CT: Archon, 1966), pp. 141–42.

44. Thelwall, *Rhythmus*, pp. iii–vii.

45. Steele, *Prosodia Rationalis: Or, an Essay towards Establishing the Melody and Measure of Speech, to Be Expressed and Perpetuated by Peculiar Symbols*, 2nd edn (London, 1779).

46. Thelwall, 'On the Application of the Principles of Musical Proportion in the Treatment of Impediments of Speech', *Monthly Magazine* 30 (1810), 105.

47. Thelwall, *Rhythmus*, p. xlvi, quoting Dryden's translation of the *Aeneid* (1697) and his *Absalom and Achitophel* (1681). I have omitted the musical notations that appear in the first line around 'who' and after 'fate', and in the second line before 'Auspicious' and 'at'.

48. Thelwall, *Rhythmus*, p. iii.
49. Thelwall, *Rhythmus*, p. xlvi.
50. Patricia Howell Michaelson notes that the linguistic specificity of eighteenth-century elocutionists' textual analyses anticipated that of twentieth-century New Critics, but was distinctly '*un*modern' in its insistence that close reading produced correct readings. *Speaking Volumes: Women, Reading, and Speech in the Age of Austen* (Stanford: Stanford University Press, 2002), p. 108.
51. Thelwall, *Rhythmus*, pp. xxi, xxiv.
52. Thelwall, 'Mr. Thelwall's Lecture on the Inherent and Incidental Properties of Syllables that Constitute the Bases of Prosodial Metre, and of the Rhythmus and Harmony of Speech', *Panoramic Miscellany* 1 (1826), 640.
53. The recitation of *Comus* is recorded in Robinson, *Diary*, vol. I, p. 492. On Thelwall's 'metronomic' elocution see Haberman, 'John Thelwall', p. 196; on his '*lèse-prosodie*' see Saintsbury, *English Prosody*, p. 158; on his insensitivity to the effects of metre and rhythm compared notably with Wordsworth, see Brennan O'Donnell, *The Passion of Meter: A Study of Wordsworth's Metrical Art* (Kent, OH: Kent State University Press, 1995), pp. 31–2; and Simon Jarvis, *Wordsworth's Philosophic Song*, Cambridge Studies in Romanticism 67 (Cambridge: Cambridge University Press, 2007), pp. 10–11.
54. Wordsworth, *The Letters of William and Dorothy Wordsworth: The Early Years, 1787–1805*, ed. Ernest De Selincourt, rev. Chester L. Shaver, 2nd edn (Oxford: Clarendon Press, 1967), p. 432. The square bracket insertions are the editor's.
55. [Francis Jeffrey], rev. of *Thalaba the Destroyer: A Metrical Romance*, by Robert Southey, *Edinburgh Review* 1 (1802), 73–4.
56. Wordsworth, *Early Years*, pp. 432–4. Wordsworth noted in his reply to Thelwall, 'The chief object of your Letter is to inquire whether the Preface to the L. B. be the manifesto alluded to. I never heard of any other, and have myself no doubt that [it] is'. He advised Thelwall to read the preface as it appeared in the third edition of the *Lyrical Ballads*, that is, the edition of 1802; *Early Years*, pp. 432, 435.
57. Thelwall, *Rhythmus*, p. xvi.
58. Tooke, *Diversions*, vol. I, pp. 36–7. 'H' replies that Locke would therefore have discussed the composition of terms rather than ideas, and of general and abstract terms rather than complex and simple ideas. *Diversions*, vol. I, p. 231. Thelwall and Tooke may also have had in mind Cordelia's remark to her father, 'Unhappy that I am, I cannot heave / My heart into my mouth', in *King Lear*, 1.1.90–1.
59. Thelwall, *Letter to Cline*, repr. in *SPW*, vol. IV, p. 76.
60. Mrs. Thelwall, *Life*, p. 40; Thelwall, *Letter to Cline*, repr. in *SPW*, vol. IV, pp. 27, 77. Thelwall devised the set of artificial teeth with the York dentist Mr Horner, the addressee of his comic poems 'Epistle from an Orator to his Dentist' and 'Impossibilities'. See *Letter to Cline*, repr. in *SPW*, vol. IV, p. 13; and *Poems, Chiefly Suggested by the Scenery of Nature; to Which are Added Odes &c. Amatory and Congratulatory, Translations, and Attempts at Humour* ('Derby manuscript'), 3 vols, Derby Local Studies Library, Derby, England, 5868–5870, vol. II, pp. 549–57.
61. Thelwall, *Letter to Cline*, repr. in *SPW*, vol. IV, p. 33.
62. Thelwall, *Letter to Cline*, repr. in *SPW*, vol. IV, p. 28. On Thelwall's pioneering empirical approach to speech therapy, see Rockey, 'Origins of British

Speech Therapy'; Rockey, 'Logopaedic Thought'; and Judith Felson Duchan, 'The Conceptual Underpinnings of John Thelwall's Elocutionary Practices', in *John Thelwall: Radical Romantic and Acquitted Felon*, ed. Steve Poole, The Enlightenment World 11 (London: Pickering and Chatto, 2009), pp. 139–45. Emily B. Stanback discusses Thelwall's progressive approach to mental illness in 'Disability and Dissent: Thelwall's Elocutionary Project', in *John Thelwall: Critical Reassessments*, ed. Yasmin Solomonescu, Romantic Circles, Sept. 2011, http://romantic.arhu.umd.edu/praxis/thelwall/HTML/praxis.2011. stanback.html (accessed 12 June 2012).

63. Haberman, 'John Thelwall', p. 197. Because of the centrality to his system of the links among perception, volition and bodily action, Thelwall would not admit to his Institution pupils with deafness or 'amentia'. He used the latter term to describe cases in which 'from the neglects or accidents of early education, the senses have not been properly developed, or the connective faculty of the mind has not been called into action'. *Letter to Cline*, repr. in *SPW*, vol. IV, p. 62.

64. Thelwall, *Letter to Cline*, repr. in *SPW*, vol. IV, p. 32.

65. Thelwall, *Poetical Recreations*, p. 114.

66. Darwin, *Temple of Nature*, p. 120.

67. Thelwall, *Letter to Cline*, repr. in *SPW*, vol. IV, p. 22.

68. Wilbur Samuel Howell, *Eighteenth-Century British Logic and Rhetoric* (Princeton: Princeton University Press, 1971), pp. 152–9.

69. See, for instance, Michael Shortland, 'Moving Speeches: Language and Elocution in Eighteenth-Century Britain', *History of European Ideas* 8 (1987), 684; and Murray Cohen, *Sensible Words: Linguistic Practice in England, 1640–1785* (Baltimore, MD: Johns Hopkins University Press, 1977), p. 114.

70. Sheridan, *A Course of Lectures on Elocution: Together with Two Dissertations on Language, and Some Other Tracts Relative to Those Subjects* (London, 1762; repr. Menston: Scolar, 1968), pp. xiii, 80. Similarly, William Enfield called for 'a natural, forcible, and varied EMPHASIS' in his popular anthology *The Speaker: Or, Miscellaneous Pieces, Selected from the Best English Writers, and Disposed under Proper Heads, with a View to Facilitate the Improvement of Youth in Reading and Speaking* (London, 1774), p. xvi.

71. Lucy Newlyn, *Reading, Writing, and Romanticism: The Anxiety of Reception* (Oxford: Oxford University Press, 2000), pp. 355–60.

72. On the 'natural' elocutionists, including Sheridan, William Cockin and John Rice, see Shortland, 'Moving Speeches', 645–6; on Blair see Howell, *British Logic and Rhetoric*, pp. 664–5. By contrast, 'artificial' elocutionists, including John Walker and James Burgh, stressed the artistic, imitative character of oral delivery and set out precise rules for the management of the voice.

73. Thelwall, *Rhythmus*, p. lxvii.

74. Thelwall, *Rhythmus*, p. xvi; Newlyn, *Reading, Writing, and Romanticism*, p. 360.

75. Hazlitt, *Complete Works*, vol. XVII, p. 118. Lucy Newlyn argues that in criticizing the poets' 'chaunting' Hazlitt was accusing them of 'an incipient political apostasy'; *Reading, Writing, and Romanticism*, p. 370. David Perkins suggests, moreover, that Wordsworth adhered more closely than Coleridge to the Augustan practices of contracting words to avoid trisyllabic feet and promoting syllables in stress positions to maintain a regular rhythm; 'How the Romantics Recited Poetry', *Studies in English Literature, 1500–1900* 31 (1991), 657.

76. Thelwall, marginalia on Coleridge, 88. Several of Thelwall's marginal comments restate the elocutionary principles that he explained more fully in his treatises and articles.

77. Thelwall, *Rights of Nature*, repr. in *PEJ*, pp. 399–400.

78. Thelwall, 'Mr. Thelwall's Lecture on the Articulation and Qualities of Syllables', 349, 350. For Thelwall's dispute with Burke about natural rights and 'Gothic' custom, see *Rights of Nature*, repr. in *PEJ*, pp. 439–61.

79. Thelwall, *Letter to Cline*, repr. in *SPW*, vol. IV, p. 16.

80. Thelwall, *Rights of Nature*, repr. in *PEJ*, p. 400. Susan Manly discusses the parallels between 1790s' debates about 'correct' language and Thelwall's arguments for the popular right of free speech in *Rights of Nature*, and she looks briefly at his attempts as an elocutionist to spread eloquence among the people in *Language, Custom and Nation in the 1790s: Locke, Tooke, Wordsworth, Edgeworth* (Aldershot: Ashgate, 2007), pp. 89–99.

81. McCann, 'Self-Fashioning', 225.

82. [Thelwall], 'Emotion', *Cyclopaedia*, vol. XIII, n.pag.

83. [Thelwall], 'Emotion', *Cyclopaedia*, vol. XIII, n. pag; Thelwall, *Vestibule*, p. 20.

84. Thelwall, *Vestibule*, p. 21.

85. Fliegelman, *Declaring Independence: Jefferson, Natural Language, and the Culture of Performance* (Stanford: Stanford University Press, 1993), p. 2; Michaelson, *Speaking Volumes*, pp. 44–8.

86. Thelwall, *Vestibule*, pp. 19–20. Like Sheridan, Thelwall had a longstanding interest in Johann Kaspar Lavater's taxonomy of facial expressions as indices of character in *Essays on Physiognomy* (1775). He may also have been familiar with Gilbert Austin's development of an elaborate system of notation for the body's natural language in *Chironomia: Or a Treatise on Rhetorical Delivery* (1806) and with Charles Bell's *Essays on the Anatomy of Expression in Painting* (1806).

87. Baillie quoted in Alan Richardson, 'Joanna Baillie's "Plays on the Passions"', in *Joanna Baillie, Romantic Dramatist*, ed. Thomas C. Crochunis (London: Routledge, 2004), p. 134.

88. Thelwall, *Vestibule*, pp. 20–2.

89. Cockin, *The Art of Delivering Written Language; or, an Essay on Reading* (London, 1775), pp. 1–17; [Thelwall], 'Elocution', *Cyclopaedia*, vol. XIII, n. pag.

90. Mee, *Romanticism, Enthusiasm, and Regulation*, pp. 119–20.

91. Thelwall, *Letter to Cline*, repr. in *SPW*, vol. IV, p. 10; Jon Mee, for instance, argues that while Thelwall's frequent calls for moderation in his lectures and speeches of the 1790s might betray latent anxieties about the enthusiasm of the crowd, he 'for the most part trusted his audience to regulate themselves'; '"The Press and Danger of the Crowd": Godwin, Thelwall, and the Counter-Public Sphere', in *Godwinian Moments: From the Enlightenment to Romanticism*, ed. Robert M. Maniquis and Victoria Myers (Toronto: University of Toronto Press, 2011), p. 93. Mary Fairclough claims more emphatically that unlike Godwin, Wollstonecraft and Burke, Thelwall refused to pathologize the physical processes underlying the communication of sympathy, regarding them as unfailingly 'wholesome'; *Romantic Crowd*, pp. 62, 107–21.

92. [Thelwall], 'Emotion', *Cyclopaedia*, vol. XIII, n. pag.

93. [Thelwall], 'Enthusiasm', *Cyclopaedia*, vol. XIII, n. pag.

94. [Thelwall], 'Enthusiasm', *Cyclopaedia*, vol. XIII, n. pag.

95. [Thelwall], 'Enthusiasm', *Cyclopaedia*, vol. XIII, n. pag.

96. The comparative advantages of written language were 'permanency – transmission – precision'. Thelwall, *Letter to Jeffray*, p. 85n.

97. The *Scenery of Nature* collection makes up volumes 1 and 2 of the Derby manuscript.

98. Thompson, *Silenced Partner*, pp. 200–2.

99. Thelwall, Derby manuscript, vol. I, n. pag. The 'obvious reason' for beginning with the Anacreontics is unclear.

100. Thelwall, 'Scenery of Nature', *Poetical Recreations*, p. 77.

101. Thelwall, *Peripatetic*, pp. 286–8; Thompson, *Silenced Partner*, pp. 200–18.

102. Thelwall, Derby manuscript, vol. I, pp. 1v–11v; vol. III, pp. 845v–850v. See also 'Sylvanus; or, the Pupil of the Groves', in *Champion* 16 Sept. 1820, republished two years later in *Poetical Recreations*, pp. 77–84. The dating is discussed in Thompson, *Silenced Partner*, pp. 203, 216.

103. Thelwall, Derby manuscript, vol. I, pp. 7v–9v.

104. Thelwall, Derby manuscript, vol. III, pp. 845v–848v; and vol. I, p. 7v.

105. Cooper quoted in Richardson, *Science of the Mind*, p. 124.

106. Curran, *Poetic Form*, pp. 63, 70.

107. Thelwall, 'Anacreontic IV', in Derby manuscript, vol. II, pp. 509–11, repr. in *Poetical Recreations*, pp. 25–6. Thelwall married Henrietta Cecil Boyle less than a year after his first wife Susan's death in 1816.

108. Thompson, 'Citizen Juan Thelwall', 89–95.

109. Thelwall, Derby manuscript, vol. II, p. 497, emphasis Thelwall's. Teos was an ancient Ionian city on the western coast of Asia Minor (*OED Online*, s.v. 'Teian, *adj.*').

110. Thelwall, Derby manuscript, vol. II, p. 457v, repr. as 'The Stranger. – To Miss Grahame', in *Poetical Recreations*, pp. 215–16. In *English Bards and Scotch Reviewers* (1809) Byron immortalized James Graham, author of *The Sabbath* (1804), as 'the Sabbath Bard, / Sepulchral Grahame', who 'pours his notes sublime / In mangled prose, nor e'en aspires to rhyme' – prompting Thelwall's defence of meditative blank verse and his own 'Sabbath Meditation' in the *Champion*. See *Poetical Recreations*, pp. 16–18. Thelwall sends regards to a 'Mr Grahame' in his letter to Robert Anderson of 12 March 1804, National Library of Scotland, Edinburgh, 22.4.14. Thelwall's daughters were Manon Roland, born March 1799, and Sara Maria, born February 1801.

111. Thelwall, Derby manuscript, vol. II, p. 463, repr. in *Poetical Recreations*, pp. 219–21. The addressee of 'To Miss Bannatine' may have been a relation of George Bannatine, the cousin of Hugh Blair, or of Blair's wife Katherine Bannatine (d. 1795). Richard B. Sher, 'Blair, Hugh (1718–1800)', in *Oxford Dictionary of National Biography*, ed. H. C. G. Matthew and Brian Harrison (Oxford: Oxford University Press, 2004), online edn, ed. Lawrence Goldman, Oct. 2009, http://www.oxforddnb.com/view/article/2563 (accessed 29 Oct. 2012).

112. Hugh Blair, *Lectures on Rhetoric and Belles Lettres* (1783), ed. Linda Ferreira-Buckley and S. Michael Hallon (Carbondale: Southern Illinois University Press, 2005), pp. 35–6. It is unclear which side of the debate about the authenticity of Macpherson's Ossianic poems Thelwall endorsed.

113. Thelwall, *Vestibule*, pp. 157, 160.

114. Thelwall, *Vestibule*, p. 158.

115. Thelwall, *Vestibule*, p. 158.

116. Richard Gravil, 'Mr. Thelwall's Ear; or, Hearing *The Excursion*', in *Grasmere, 2011: Selected Papers from the Wordsworth Summer Conference*, comp. Richard Gravil (Tirril: Humanities-Ebooks, 2011), pp. 188–9; Richardson, *Science of the Mind*, p. 70.

117. For Thelwall's 'harmonic classification' of the elements ('element' being his term for 'any simple enunciated sound') and his criticism of contemporary systems, see [Thelwall], 'Element', *Cyclopaedia*, vol. XII, n. pag; and 'Mr. Thelwall's Lecture on the Harmonic Qualities', repr. in *Selected Political Writings of John Thelwall*, ed. Robert Lamb and Corinna Wagner, 4 vols (London: Pickering and Chatto, 2009), vol. IV, pp. 209–12.

118. [Thelwall], 'Expression', *Cyclopaedia*, vol. XIII, n. pag.

119. Thelwall, *Poetical Recreations*, p. 149, where he defines the sonnet as 'an Ode of a single stanza'. That definition may explain why he could rename the 'Sonnet to Stella' 'Ode from the Land of Mountains'.

120. [Jeffrey], rev. of *Poems, Chiefly Written in Retirement*, 197–202; Thelwall, *Letter to Francis Jeffray*, pp. 70–1.

121. Henry Cockburn, *Life of Lord Jeffrey: With a Selection from His Correspondence*, vol. I (Edinburgh, 1852), p. 150. Cockburn notes that Thelwall and Jeffrey met amicably several years later.

122. Thelwall, *Letter to Jeffray*, p.75n.

123. Thelwall, *Letter to Jeffray*, pp. 88–9.

124. Thelwall, *Political Lectures*, pp. 8–9.

125. Mrs. Thelwall, *Life*, p. 367.

126. Thus it was not only the 'radical idealism' of Thelwall's message that his audience found objectionable, as Lucy Newlyn remarks in *Reading, Writing, and Romanticism*, p. 355, but specifically its materialism.

127. [Jeffrey], rev. of *Poems, Chiefly Written in Retirement*, by John Thelwall, *Edinburgh Review* 1 (April 1803), 199.

128. [Jeffrey], *Observations on Mr. Thelwall's Letter to the Editor of the Edinburgh Review* (Edinburgh, 1804), pp. 10, 14.

129. Thelwall would later compose a new ending for Collins's ode 'The Passions' that replaced its nostalgia for ancient song with a celebration of Eros as prime mover of the other passions: a 'living instrument; – all voice – / All harmony'. See Derby manuscript, vol. I, pp. 305–11, repr. in *Rhythmus*, pp. 9–14. Jeffrey derisively singles out the 'hermetic hand' passage of *The Hope of Albion* to show 'what incalculable improvements our modern poetry may expect from the philosophical skill of its votaries'; rev. of *Poems, Chiefly Written in Retirement*, 201.

130. [Jeffrey], *Observations*, pp. 4–5.

131. In the decades following Jeffrey's attack on Thelwall, the *Edinburgh Review* and other periodicals would level accusations of atheism and political subversion against a new generation of brain scientists, including William Lawrence in England and F. J. Gall and J. G. Spurzheim on the continent, as noted in Richardson, *Science of the Mind*, pp. 23–9.

132. Thelwall, *Mr. Thelwall's Reply*, p. 27.

133. Thelwall, *Letter to Cline*, repr. in *SPW*, vol. IV, p. 46.

134. Thelwall, *Results of Experience in the Treatment of Cases of Defective Utterance* (London, 1814), repr. in *Selected Political Writings of John Thelwall*,

ed. Robert Lamb and Corinna Wagner, 4 vols (London: Pickering and Chatto, 2009), vol. IV, p. 161.

135. See Thelwall, marginalia on Coleridge, 92, where he refers to 'Knitch' [*sic*], 'Who published a work on the Kantean philosophy while he was in England Which I have in my library, & attempted to establish a Kantean school or society here, of which I was a member, & in which I held several disputations with him on the principles of that professor'. Nitsch was the author of *A General and Introductory View of Professor Kant's Principles concerning Man, the World and the Deity* (1796). See also Manfred Kuehn, 'Hamilton's Reading of Kant: A Chapter in the Early Scottish Development of Kant's Thought', in *Kant and His Influence*, ed. George Macdonald Ross and Tony McWalter (London: Continuum, 2005), p. 318.

136. Thelwall, *Letter to Cline*, repr. in *SPW*, vol. IV, p. 36.

6   The Materialist Imagination

1. Thelwall, marginalia on Coleridge, 79.
2. Coleridge, *Collected Letters*, vol. II, p. 723.
3. Coleridge, *Biographia Literaria*, repr. in *Major Works*, p. 208.
4. [Jeffrey], *Observations*, p. 14.
5. J. T. [John Thelwall], 'Observations upon the Theory Adopted by Mr. Burke in His Examination of the Effects Produced upon the Mind by Words', *Monthly Magazine* 16 (Oct.–Nov. 1803), 212–17, 317–20. I follow the second instalment of the essay in substituting 'Adopted' for 'Adapted' in the title. While the strongest evidence for the identification of 'J. T.' as Thelwall lies in his views on language and cognition, that identification is supported by the fact that Thelwall had been a regular contributor to the *Monthly* since the mid-1790s, signing himself 'J. T.' on several occasions. His authorship is also consistent with the essay's praise for Burke's 'usual acuteness' and 'ingenuity': Thelwall had just included Burke's apostrophe to Marie Antoinette as a 'beautiful specimen' of 'oratorical enthusiasm' in *Selections, &c., for Mr. Thelwall's Lectures on the Science and Practice of Elocution* (York, 1802), n. pag. Morevoer, like Thelwall, the essayist is wary of the 'sort of implicit obedience which is paid to reputation', and he identifies as an autodidact who taught himself to appreciate Virgil's *Aeneid* using an English translation. 'Observations', 213, 318. The timing of the essay's appearance, some 50 years after the publication of Burke's *Philosophical Enquiry* but contemporaneous with the early stages of Thelwall's elocutionary career, also supports the case for his authorship. He contributed numerous articles on elocution to the *Monthly Magazine* thereafter. He was also a friend of the magazine's publisher Richard Phillips, to whom he sold *The Daughter of Adoption* in 1801.
6. Thelwall, *Retirement*, pp. xxii–xxiii.
7. Burke, *A Philosophical Enquiry into the Origin of our Ideas of the Sublime and Beautiful*, ed. Adam Phillips (Oxford: Oxford University Press, 1990; repr. 1998), p. 150.
8. Burke, *Philosophical Enquiry*, p. 157.
9. See, for instance, Stephen K. Land, *From Signs to Propositions: The Concept of Form in Eighteenth-Century Semantic Theory* (London: Longman, 1974), pp. 46–7.

10. Burke, *Philosophical Enquiry*, pp. 159–60.
11. [Thelwall], 'Observations', 212, 214.
12. [Thelwall], 'Observations', 216–17, italicized in the original.
13. [Thelwall], 'Observations', 213, 214.
14. Godwin, *Political Justice*, pp. 177–83.
15. According to Hartley, we begin in childhood to associate words with ideas through the repeated impressions made on the retina by the things those words denote. Each impression produces a simple idea, while impressions that occur in regular or vivid conjunction with one another form complex ideas, as, for instance, of qualities, passions, processes and other abstractions; *Observations on Man*, pp. 271, 273–77. Although Godwin's *Political Justice* was a likely source for Thelwall's understanding of Hartley's doctrine of association, the 1803 essay suggests a more direct acquaintance with *Observations on Man*. Thelwall may also be drawing on Priestley's abridged 1775 edition of that work (which did away with Hartley's theory of vibrations) or on the Unitarian minister Thomas Belsham's *Elements of the Philosophy of the Mind, and of Moral Philosophy* (London, 1801), drawn chiefly from Hartley and Priestley. Thelwall defends Belsham's necessitarianism in *A Letter to Francis Jeffray*, pp. 112–13.
16. [Thelwall], 'Observations', 214.
17. [Thelwall], 'Observations', 214. Thelwall would later assert that sounds are not material things but 'only perceptions of the sentient mind, originating in impressions on the tympanum of the ear'. Therefore, '[i]f all organized beings were deaf, there would be no sound in the universe'; 'The Anatomy of Speech', *Monthly Magazine* 59 (March 1825), 121.
18. Burke, *Philosophical Enquiry*, p. 156. Thelwall quotes Christopher Pitt's translation of the passage in question, *Aeneid* VIII. 429–32: 'Three points of rain, three forks of hail conspire; / Three arm'd with wind; and three were barbed with fire. / The mass they tempered thick with livid rays, / Fear, wrath and terror, and the lightning's blaze'. 'Observations', 318.
19. [Thelwall], 'Observations', 319.
20. Butler (ed.), *Burke, Paine, Godwin*, p. 207; Smith, *Politics of Language*, p. 87.
21. Furniss, *Edmund Burke's Aesthetic Ideology: Language, Gender, and Political Economy in Revolution*, Cambridge Studies in Romanticism 4 (Cambridge: Cambridge University Press, 1993), p. 107. On Godwin's views, see Angela Esterhammer, 'Godwin's Suspicion of Speech Acts', *Studies in Romanticism* 39, no. 4 (Winter 2000), 553–78; and Lucyle Werkmeister, 'Coleridge and Godwin on the Communication of Truth', *Modern Philology* 55, no. 3 (Feb. 1958), 170–7.
22. [Thelwall], 'Observations', 319. We might also glance here at Thelwall's 1798 essay 'The Phenomena of the Wye', repr. in *SPW*, vol. III, p. 3, where he asserts that the 'mingled impressions of sublimity and beauty' are not strictly dependent on 'diversities of light' and 'varied masses of light and shadows', but can proceed with equal, if not greater, effect from 'the power of mere outline' – Milton's 'darkness visible'.
23. Thelwall, *Poetical Recreations*, p. 155n. Thelwall explains here that having intelligible 'premises' – that is, appealing as much to 'correct' philosophy as to imagination – is what makes the difference between Thomas Gray's ludicrous description of an eagle '"perched on the sceptered hand of Jove",

dropping the thunderbolts from his talons, and closing his eyes in slumber', and Milton's beautiful image of Jupiter who 'on Juno smiles, / When he impregns the clouds that shed sweet May flowers'. The former is all about 'non-existent' entities, while the latter alludes to the 'solar region of the air' and 'lower atmosphere'.

24. Coleridge, *Collected Letters*, vol. I, pp. 277, 204.

25. Coleridge, *Collected Letters*, vol. I, pp. 204–5. It is clear from Coleridge's next reply that Thelwall actually objected to an essay in *The Watchman* in which Coleridge denounced the immorality and atheism of 'Modern Patriots', especially those who endorsed Godwinism; *Collected Letters*, vol. I, pp. 212–14.

26. Warren E. Gibbs, 'An Unpublished Letter from John Thelwall to S. T. Coleridge', *Modern Language Review* 25 (1930), 87.

27. Duncan Wu notes that Thelwall's criticism may have inspired Coleridge's self-parody in the 'Nehemiah Higginbottom' sonnets, in 'Coleridge, Thelwall, and the Politics of Poetry', *Coleridge Bulletin* ns 4 (1994), 40–1.

28. Gibbs, 'Unpublished Letter', 88; Coleridge, *Collected Letters*, vol. I, p. 215.

29. Coleridge, *Collected Letters*, vol. I, p. 221.

30. Coleridge, *Collected Letters*, vol. I, p. 286.

31. Thelwall, Marginalia on William Lisle Bowles's *Sonnets and Other Poems*, 4th edn (London, 1796), p. 45, National Art Library, London, Dyce 8vo 1298.

32. Thelwall, marginalia on Bowles, p. 50.

33. Thelwall, 'The Shrine of Howard', in *Poems on Various Subjects*, vol. II, pp. 180–8.

34. Thelwall, marginalia on Bowles, p. 58.

35. Fairer, *Organising Poetry*, pp. 251, 248.

36. Fairer, *Organising Poetry*, pp. 240, 249.

37. Thelwall, marginalia on Bowles, p. 28.

38. For the ca. 1797 dating of the marginalia on Bowles, see Fairer, *Organising Poetry*, p. 245; Thelwall's annotations on Coleridge's letters are reproduced in Coleridge, *Collected Letters*, vol. I, pp. 279, 281–2.

39. Although critics have long stressed the anti-materialist tenour of Coleridge's thought, a few have noted the persistence of a materialist strain within it. Alan Richardson describes the 'ambiguous role' of materialism in Coleridge's embodied notions of psyche and the emotions in *Science of the Mind*, pp. 39–65, 41; Richard Sha examines Coleridge's physiological understanding of the imagination's functions in 'Romantic Physiology'; Paul Gilmore notes the influence of materialist theories of nervous communication on Coleridge's idealist aesthetics in *Aesthetic Materialism*, pp. 26–32; and Gavin Budge argues that Coleridge is a materialist 'in the sense that the focus of his attention is the materially embodied situation in which human thought takes place', in 'Indigestion and Imagination in Coleridge's Critical Thought', in *Romantic Empiricism: Poetics and the Philosophy of Common Sense, 1780–1830*, ed. Gavin Budge (Lewisburg, PA: Bucknell University Press, 2007), p. 155.

40. Thelwall, marginalia on Coleridge, 81.

41. Thelwall, marginalia on Coleridge, 93–4.

42. Responding to Heather Jackson's suggestion that Thelwall read the *Biographia* with relative equanimity, Judith Thompson emphasizes the combative nature of his marginalia as it engages Coleridge on philosophical, political and poetic fronts. See H. J. Jackson, *Romantic Readers: The Evidence of*

Marginalia (New Haven, CT: Yale University Press, 2005), pp. 282–96; and Thompson, *Silenced Partner*, pp. 96–9.

43. Thelwall, marginalia on Coleridge, 84–5.
44. Thelwall, marginalia on Coleridge, 78.
45. Erving, 'Politics of Matter', 219–32.
46. Thelwall, marginalia on Coleridge, 79.
47. [Thelwall], 'Metaphysics', *Panoramic Miscellany* 1 (1826), 374.
48. Thelwall, *Animal Vitality*, repr. in *SPW*, vol. I, p. 27.
49. Thelwall, marginalia on Coleridge, 79.
50. Thelwall, marginalia on Coleridge, 94. In 1826 Thelwall would take another swipe at Coleridge in a brief article in the *Panoramic Miscellany*, distinguishing inspiration arising from 'the depths of intellectual meditation' from 'inspiration derived from physical stimuli', and insisting that real genius has 'little obligation to the Tuscan Bacchus, or to the Turkish Poppy'; 'Imagination', *Panoramic Miscellany* 1 (1826), 761.
51. Coleridge, *Biographia Literaria*, repr. in *Major Works*, p. 221.
52. Coleridge, *Collected Letters*, vol. I, pp. 294–5.
53. Coleridge, *Biographia Literaria*, repr. in *Major Works*, p. 255
54. Coleridge, *Biographia Literaria*, repr. in *Major Works*, pp. 255, 218–20.
55. Coleridge, *Biographia Literaria*, repr. in *Major Works*, p. 313.
56. Coleridge, *The Notebooks of Samuel Taylor Coleridge*, ed. Kathleen Coburn, vol. I (New York: Pantheon, 1957), p. 156.
57. Thelwall, marginalia on Coleridge, 80. Thelwall remarks elsewhere that we can conceive of the existence of things beyond our knowledge (such as eternity or infinitude) because 'the denial of them involves a contradiction'. On this basis his notes that 'no man can be in reality an Atheist', whatever name or attributes he chooses to give 'eternal and infinite consciousness, whether impersonated or diffused'; *Poetical Recreations*, p. 20. Diffused consciousness recalls Thelwall's definition of the universe as a 'continuous system of animated being'; *Tribune*, repr.,in *PEJ*, p. 106. Thelwall grapples further with these ideas in the manuscript poem 'Visions of Philosophy, by the Platonist', in Derby manuscript, vol. I, pp. 351v–373v, a revision of a poem in *The Peripatetic* that he apparently left incomplete at his death.
58. For further discussion of Thelwall's literary criticism in these journals, including his reviews of Byron and Scott, see Scrivener, 'John Thelwall and the Press', pp. 120–36.
59. [Thelwall], 'The Poetry of Miss Landen [*sic*]', *Panoramic Miscellany* 1 (1826), 74–82.
60. It is unclear whether Thelwall was aware of allegations circulating in the gutter press around this time that Landon was romantically involved with Jerdan, as noted in Jerome McGann and Daniel Riess (eds), *Letitia Elizabeth Landon: Selected Writings* (Peterborough, ON: Broadview, 1997), pp. 12–13.
61. Thelwall, 'Landen', 74–5.
62. Coleridge, *Biographia Literaria*, repr. in *Major Works*, p. 320; Thelwall, marginalia on Coleridge, 84.
63. *OED Online*, s.v. 'limbeck, *n.*'; Thelwall, 'Landen', 75.
64. Keats, letter to George and Thomas Keats, [21, 27?] Dec. 1817, repr. in *John Keats: Selected Poems and Letters*, ed. Douglas Bush (Boston: Houghton Mifflin, 1959), p. 260.

65. Thelwall, 'Landen', 78.
66. Wordsworth, *Lyrical Ballads*, p. 752; Wordsworth, *Early Years*, p. 435.
67. Mee, *Romanticism, Enthusiasm, and Regulation*, pp. 217–22.
68. Thelwall, 'Landen', 77.
69. Thelwall, Derby manuscript, vol. III, pp. 731v–771v, 954–72v. One portion of *Musalogia* appears at the end of Volume 3, another on the blank recto pages at the beginning of the same volume. Thelwall apparently ran out of pages at the end of the volume and began writing on the recto pages that he had left blank for emendations. The extant fragments comprise in all some 420 lines of Canto I, including the 165-line Proem (and its copious footnotes about the various writers and works it lists), and the 670 lines of Canto II. The 'Argument' of Canto I makes it clear that some passages were either never written or omitted from the Derby volumes. I am grateful to Judith Thompson for her assistance in dating the contents of Volume 3 based on the autobiographical and historical events referred to therein.
70. Thelwall, Derby manuscript, vol. III, p. 742v.
71. Thelwall, Derby manuscript, vol. III, pp. 731–33v.
72. Thelwall, Derby manuscript, vol. III, pp. 971–2.
73. Thelwall, Derby manuscript, vol. III, pp. 732v, 751–52v.
74. Thelwall, Derby manuscript, vol. III, p. 742v. In the Argument of Canto I, Thelwall catalogues the various poetic schools of the day according to their characteristic faults, including affectation ('The Dashing & Flowery' school), rule-boundness ('the Fastidious & precise'), Gothicism or supernaturalism ('Ghosts & Bugaboos', 'Hobgoblinisms of the Stage & Press'), apocalypticism ('Plague Willson & Mrs. Bysche Shelley' [*sic*]), abstraction ('Stilts, Balloons, Metaphysics & Bedlamitisms'), licentiousness ('Boudoir Poets, or Superfines', 'Jollities & Bacchanaliads', 'Capt. Morris & the Whiggery'), vulgarity ('Cocknies & Vulgarians'), immorality ('Byron') and political conservatism ('a digressive chart of the road from Jacobinism to laureate-ship & Treasury-benches'). See Derby manuscript, vol. III, pp. 740–41v. The passages on 'Boudoir Poets, or Superfines', 'Jollities & Bacchanaliads', 'Capt. Morris & the Whiggery' and 'Cocknies & Vulgarians' are among those missing from the poem as it appears in the Derby volumes.
75. Thelwall, Derby manuscript, vol. III, p. 955, with underlining reproduced from the manuscript.
76. Thelwall, marginalia on Coleridge, 86–7.
77. Coleridge criticizes the 'matter-of-factness' of Wordsworth's poetry in *Biographia Literaria*, repr. in *Major Works*, p. 391.
78. Thelwall, Derby manuscript, vol. III, pp. 746v–747v. I use the angular brackets to indicate that 'lot' appears above 'state' as a possible substitution.
79. Thelwall, marginalia on Coleridge, 82.
80. Poetry and politics are also linked in the other extended apostrophe of Canto I, an 80-line address to 'gentle Southey' that laments his poetic 'demonology' and chaotic metrical experimentation, as well as his political apostasy, but defends him from the 'burning' criticisms of Byron by celebrating the '<u>moral</u> strain' of his youth; Derby manuscript, vol. III, pp. 747v–749v. Canto I was meant to conclude with an apostrophe to 'genuine Freedom & Philosophy' that showed 'their dependence on the Social Virtues', culminating in 'an exhortation to moral purity in all poetical Offerings to the

Shrine of Liberty'; Derby manuscript, vol. III, p. 742v. Canto II, however, announces that 'moral themes' and the 'fervid chaunt of Liberty' are not appropriate to *Musalogia*'s 'stunted wing' and 'shepherd's pipe'. The phrases refer to the poem's tetrametric 'doggril', as distinct from the pentameter of 'A Milton's deep-ton'd harmony', but may also allude to the renewed repression of Thelwall's political voice in 1821, when he was arrested and indicted for seditious libel for an editorial in the *Champion* about the Peterloo crisis; Derby manuscript, vol. III, p. 742v.

81. Thelwall, Derby manuscript, vol. III, pp. 751v, 753v. Thelwall now calls Landon 'Sappho', after the ancient Greek lyric poet whom Landon invokes in *The Improvisatrice*. Landon had apparently taken offence at Thelwall's strictures in the January 1826 issue of the *Panoramic Miscellany*, which led him in the March issue to publish a 'Sonnet. To L. E. L.' that advised, 'Ponder awhile, and thou the strain wilt find, / Tho seeming harsh, more kindly far to be / Than the loud plaudit of o'erweening praise'. See 'Ausonia', 'Sonnet. To L. E. L. On Hearing that She had Been Grieved by Some Remarks upon Her Poetry in the *Panoramic Miscellany*', *Panoramic Miscellany* 1 (1826), 375.

82. Thelwall, Derby manuscript, vol. III, pp. 756v–758v.

83. Thelwall, Derby manuscript, vol. III, p. 765v.

84. Thelwall, *Poetical Recreations*, p. 155n.

85. Thelwall, Derby manuscript, vol. III, p. 972.

86. Thelwall, 'The Star that Shone When Other Stars Were Dim', *Monthly Magazine* 59 Supplement (1825), 661–3; and Derby manuscript, vol. III, pp. 920v–926v, which differs in the irregular indentation of the poem's lines. Subsequent references are to the page numbers of published version.

87. Boyd Hilton, *A Mad, Bad, and Dangerous People? England 1783–1846* (Oxford: Oxford University Press, 2006), pp. 290–1. In 1808 Thelwall had composed an 'Ode Addressed to the Energies of Britain in behalf of the Spanish Patriots' in which Iberia figures as the last hope of a continent under siege by Napoleon; *Vestibule*, pp. 65–72. When Henry Crabb Robinson visited Thelwall after Napoleon's defeat at Waterloo in 1815, he found him 'in unaffected low spirits', anticipating 'a revival of ancient despotism in France'; *Diary*, vol. I, p. 491. For Thelwall's later 'Address to the Armed Patriots of Spain', see *Poetical Recreations*, pp. 128–31.

88. Thelwall, 'The Star', 661.

89. Thelwall, 'The Star', 661.

90. Thelwall, 'The Star', 662.

91. Thelwall, 'The Star', 661.

92. Thelwall, 'The Star', 663.

93. 'Francisco Espoz y Mina', in *Encyclopædia Britannica Online Academic Edition*, http://www.britannica.com/EBchecked/topic/192771/Francisco-Espoz-y-Mina (accessed 25 May 2012).

94. Thelwall, 'The Star', 663.

95. Thompson, *Silenced Partner*, pp. 248–9.

96. Thelwall, 'The Star', 662.

97. Wordsworth, 'I wandered lonely as a Cloud', ll. 14–16, in *William Wordsworth*, p. 146.

98. Richardson, *Neural Sublime*, p. 55.

99. Richardson, *Neural Sublime*, p. 37.

100. In this respect 'The Star' also bears comparison with Coleridge's 'This Lime-Tree Bower My Prison', especially ll. 39–41, in *Major Works*, p. 39, in which the poet imagines Charles Lamb 'gazing round / On the wide landscape, [...] till all doth seem / Less gross than bodily'. Coleridge quoted the passage in his letter to Thelwall of 14 Oct. 1797, repr. in *Collected Letters*, vol. I, p. 350.

101. Wordsworth, *The Prelude* (1805), Book X, ll. 725–7, in *The Prelude: The Four Texts (1798, 1799, 1805, 1850)*, ed. Jonathan Wordsworth (London: Penguin, 1995), p. 442.

102. Michael J. Tolly, 'Preromanticism', in *A Companion to Romanticism*, ed. Duncan Wu (Oxford: Blackwell, 2007), p. 17; Coleridge, 'To John Thelwall', in *Poetical Works*, vol. I, p. 265.

103. *On the Sublime*, quoted in [Thelwall], 'Observations', 319–20.

104. Coleridge, *Biographia Literaria*, repr. in *Major Works*, p. 325.

105. Thelwall, *Retirement*, pp. 129–30; the poem is the aptly titled 'Lines, Written at *Bridge*water' (emphasis added).

Appendices

1. Maria Hawes, daughter of Thelwall's friend William Hawes (founder of the Humane Society) and wife of John Gurney (junior counsel for the defence at Thelwall's trial in 1794).

2. The Liverpool Unitarian minister and politician William Shepherd, whom Thelwall's widow would later ask for advice regarding her *Life of John Thelwall*. See Henrietta Cecil Thelwall, letter to William Shepherd, March 1835, repr. in Davies, *Presences that Disturb*, pp. 322–6.

3. Possibly *The Hope of Albion*, as noted in Chapter 3.

4. Cf. Coleridge's letter of 24 July 1800 to Thomas Poole: 'At Liverpool we took up our quarters with Dr Crompton, who lives at Eton, a noble seat four miles & a half from the town—he received us with joyous hospitality, & Mrs Crompton, who is all I can conceive of an angel, with most affectionate gladness. Here we stayed 8 or 9 days'; *Collected Letters*, vol. I, p. 607.

5. The Liverpool historian and abolitionist William Roscoe.

6. Unidentified.

7. The chemist, physician and political radical Thomas Beddoes, a friend of Coleridge and Robert Southey, founded in 1799 in Bristol the Pneumatic Institute, which used gases in the treatment of illness. See Michael Neve, 'Beddoes, Thomas (1760–1808)', in *Oxford Dictionary of National Biography*, online edn, ed. Lawrence Goldman, Oxford: Oxford University Press, http://www.oxforddnb.com/view/article/1919 (accessed 28 Nov. 2012).

8. Elizabeth Evans, daughter of the Derby inventor and cotton manufacturer Jedediah Strutt, and a friend of the Coleridges.

9. William Strutt, the father of Jedediah Strutt and grandfather of Elizabeth Evans and William and Joseph Strutt, the latter a friend and patron of Thelwall's.

10. This may be a reference to the missionary and journalist William Ward, editor of the *Derby Mercury* from 1789 to 1791 and founder, with Joseph Strutt, Samuel Fox and Erasmus Darwin, of the Derby Society for Political Information in 1792. Ward sailed to India as a missionary in May 1799

but did not actually 'give up the Ghost' until 1823. See Goodwin, *Friends of Liberty*, p. 230; and E. I. Carlyle, 'Ward, William (1769–1823)', rev. Brian Stanley, in *Oxford Dictionary of National Biography*, ed. H. C. G. Matthew and Brian Harrison (Oxford: Oxford University Press, 2004), online edn, ed. Lawrence Goldman, http://www.oxforddnb.com/view/article/28710 (accessed 28 Nov. 2012). On Crompton's being 'almost knock'd on the head', see Thelwall, 'Auto-Biography', in Derby manuscript, vol. III, pp. 897: 'A stone, thrown at his head, / Miss'd him, 'tis said, / And had well nigh brain'd "dear Doctor"'.

11. Untraced.

12. A reference to Thelwall's grief at the death of his daughter Maria in December 1799.

13. Cf. Coleridge, 'Reflections on Having Left a Place of Retirement', ll. 51–3, repr. in *Major Works*, p. 30: 'And he that works me good with unmoved face, / Does it but half: he chills me while he aids, / My benefactor, not my brother man!'. The allusion is discussed in Chapter 3 of this book.

14. In 1822–23 the British Parliament debated the legitimacy of the Continental allies' support for a French invasion of Spain intended to restore the absolutist Bourbon king Ferdinand VII, who had been deposed by the liberal revolution of 1820. 'Mina' is the Spanish revolutionary Francisco Espoz y Mina, who in 1823 led the Liberal army in Catalonia against the French and thereafter sought refuge in London. See Hilton, *Dangerous People*, pp. 290–1; and 'Francisco Espoz y Mina'.

15. The square brackets around this prefatory note appear in the original.

16. Thelwall's symbol for the 'thesis' (as opposed to the 'arsis') of prosody, by which he sometimes signed his periodical contributions.

Bibliography

Primary works

Abernethy, John, *An Enquiry into the Probability and Rationality of Mr. Hunter's Theory of Life; Being the Subject of the First Two Anatomical Lectures Delivered before the Royal College of Surgeons, of London*, London, 1814, Eighteenth Century Collections Online, http://find.galegroup.com.proxy.library.nd.edu/ecco (accessed 16 Oct. 2012).

Ambulator: Or, a Pocket Companion in a Tour Round London, within the Circuit of Twenty-Five Miles, Describing Whatever is Most Remarkable for Antiquity, Grandeur, Elegance, or Rural Beauty, 4th edn, London, 1792.

Aristotle, *Nicomachean Ethics*, trans. Terence Irwin, Indianapolis, IN: Hackett, 1985.

'Ausonia', 'Sonnet. To L. E. L. On Hearing that She had Been Grieved by Some Remarks upon her Poetry in the *Panoramic Miscellany*', *Panoramic Miscellany* 1 (1826), 375.

Bisset, Robert, *Douglas; or, The Highlander*, ed. Richard Cronin, London: Pickering and Chatto, 2005.

Blair, Hugh, *Lectures on Rhetoric and Belles Lettres*, ed. Linda Ferreira-Buckley and S. Michael Hallon, Carbondale: Southern Illinois University Press, 2005.

Borrow, George Henry, *Lavengro: The Scholar–The Gypsy–The Priest*, 3 vols, London, 1851.

Britton, John, *The Auto-Biography of John Britton*, 3 vols, London, 1849.

Brombert, Victor, 'The Bastille and the Poetry of Prison Literature', *American Society Legion of Honor Magazine* 39 (1968), 73–85.

'Bull, Jack', 'On Mister Surgeon Thelwall', *Tomahawk* 27 Oct. 1795; repr. in *British War Poetry in the Age of Romanticism 1793–1815*, comp. Betty T. Bennett, digital edn, ed. Orianne Smith, Romantic Circles, Sept. 2004, http://www.rc.umd.edu/editions/warpoetry/1795/1795_17.html (accessed 23 Oct. 2012).

Burke, Edmund, *A Letter from the Right Honourable Edmund Burke to a Noble Lord, on the Attacks Made upon Him and His Pension, in the House of Lords, by the Duke of Bedford and the Earl of Lauderdale, Early in the Present Sessions of Parliament*, 2nd edn, London, 1796, Eighteenth Century Collections Online, http://find.galegroup.com.proxy.library.nd.edu/ecco (accessed 27 Oct. 2012).

Burke, Edmund, *Letters on a Regicide Peace*, in *The Revolutionary War, 1794–1797, and Ireland*, ed. R. B. McDowell, The Writings and Speeches of Edmund Burke, Oxford: Clarendon Press, 1996, pp. 44–119, 187–386.

Burke, Edmund, *A Philosophical Enquiry into the Origin of our Ideas of the Sublime and Beautiful*, ed. Adam Phillips, Oxford: Oxford University Press, 1990; repr. 1998.

Burke, Edmund, *Reflections on the Revolution in France*, in *The French Revolution, 1790–1794, and Ireland*, ed. L. G. Mitchell, The Writings and Speeches of Edmund Burke, Oxford: Clarendon Press, 1989, pp. 53–293.

Cockburn, Henry, *Life of Lord Jeffrey: With a Selection from His Correspondence*, vol. I, Edinburgh, 1852.

Cockin, William, *The Art of Delivering Written Language; or, an Essay on Reading*, London, 1775.

Coleridge, Samuel Taylor, *The Collected Letters of Samuel Taylor Coleridge*, ed. Earl Leslie Griggs, 6 vols, Oxford: Clarendon, 1956–71.

Coleridge, Samuel Taylor, *Lectures 1795: On Politics and Religion*, ed. Lewis Patton and Peter Mann, Bollingen Series 75, London: Routledge and Kegan Paul, 1971.

Coleridge, Samuel Taylor, *Poetical Works*, ed. J. C. C. Mays, 3 vols, Bollingen Series 75, London: Routledge and Kegan Paul, 2001.

Coleridge, Samuel Taylor, *Samuel Taylor Coleridge: The Major Works*, ed. H. J. Jackson, 1985; Oxford: Oxford University Press, 2000.

Coleridge, Samuel Taylor, *Table Talk*, ed. Carl Woodring, 2 vols, Bollingen Series 75, London: Routledge and Kegan Paul, 1990.

Cooper, Bransby Blake, *The Life of Sir Astley Cooper*, 2 vols, London, 1843.

Crompton, Peter, Letter to John Thelwall, 11 Sept. 1800, Morgan Library, New York, MA 77 (19).

Darwin, Erasmus, *The Botanic Garden: A Poem, in Two Parts*, London, 1791, Eighteenth Century Collections Online, http://find.galegroup.com.proxy. library.nd.edu/ecco (accessed 16 Oct. 2012).

Darwin, Erasmus, *The Temple of Nature; or, the Origin of Society*, London, 1803; repr. Menston: Scolar, 1973.

'Description of a Machine Invented by M. Roulaud, Professor of Natural Philosophy at the University of Paris, for Restoring Respiration to Persons Drowned, or Otherwise Suffocated', *Biographical and Imperial Magazine* (June 1790), 339–40.

D'Israeli, Isaac, *Vaurien: Or, Sketches of the Times*, ed. Nicola Trott, London: Pickering and Chatto, 2005.

'The Electric Shock, a Test of Remaining Life', *Biographical and Imperial Magazine* (June 1790), 340.

Enfield, William, *The Speaker: Or, Miscellaneous Pieces, Selected from the Best English Writers, and Disposed under Proper Heads, with a View to Facilitate the Improvement of Youth in Reading and Speaking*, London, 1774.

Godwin, William, *Caleb Williams*, ed. Pamela Clemit, The Pickering Masters, London: Pickering and Chatto, 1992.

Godwin, William, *Educational and Literary Writings*, ed. Pamela Clemit, The Pickering Masters, London: Pickering and Chatto, 1993.

Godwin, William, *An Enquiry Concerning Political Justice*, ed. Mark Philp, The Pickering Masters, London: Pickering and Chatto, 1993.

Godwin, William, *An Enquiry Concerning Political Justice: Variants*, ed. Mark Philp, The Pickering Masters, London: Pickering and Chatto, 1993.

Godwin, William, *Political Writings II*, ed. Mark Philp, The Pickering Masters, London: Pickering and Chatto, 1993.

Goethe, Johann Wolfgang von, *Elective Affinities: A Novel*, trans. of *Die Wahlverwandtschaften*, 1809, ed. David Constantine, Oxford: Oxford University Press, 1994; repr. 1999.

Hartley, David, *Observations on Man, His Frame, His Duty, and His Expectations*, vol. I, London, 1749; repr. [1791], Eighteenth Century Collections Online, http://find.galegroup.com.proxy.library.nd.edu/ecco (accessed 24 Oct. 2012).

Hazlitt, William, *The Complete Works of William Hazlitt*, ed. P. P. Howe, 21 vols, London: Dent, 1930–4.

Holcroft, Thomas, *Alwyn, or the Gentleman Comedian*, London, 1780, Eighteenth Century Collections Online, http://find.galegroup.com.proxy.library.nd.edu/ecco (accessed 2 Nov. 2012).

Howell, T. B., and Thomas Jones Howell, *A Complete Collection of State Trials and Proceedings for High Treason and Other Crimes and Misdemeanors*, vol. XXV, London, 1818.

Hume, David, *The History of England*, 6 vols, Indianapolis: Liberty Fund, 1983, The Online Library of Liberty, http://oll.libertyfund.org/title/1868 (accessed 7 Nov. 2012).

Hunter, John, *A Treatise on the Blood, Inflammation, and Gun-Shot Wounds*, London, 1794, Eighteenth Century Collections Online, http://find.galegroup.com.proxy.library.nd.edu/ecco (accessed 15 Feb. 2014).

[Jeffrey, Francis], *Observations on Mr. Thelwall's Letter to the Editor of the Edinburgh Review*, Edinburgh, 1804.

[Jeffrey, Francis], rev. of *Poems, Chiefly Written in Retirement*, by John Thelwall, *Edinburgh Review* 1 (April 1803), 197–202.

[Jeffrey, Francis], rev. of *Thalaba the Destroyer: A Metrical Romance*, by Robert Southey, *Edinburgh Review* 1 (Oct. 1802), 63–83.

Johnson, Samuel, *A Dictionary of the English Language*, 2 vols, London, 1786, Eighteenth Century Collections Online, http://find.galegroup.com.proxy.library.nd.edu/ecco (accessed 22 Oct. 2012).

Kames, Lord (Henry Home), *Elements of Criticism*, ed. Peter Jones, vol. I, Indianapolis: Liberty Fund, 2005, The Online Library of Liberty, http://oll.libertyfund.org/title/1430 (accessed 28 June 2012).

Keats, John, *John Keats: Selected Poems and Letters*, ed. Douglas Bush, Boston: Houghton Mifflin, 1959.

Milton, John, *John Milton: The Major Works*, ed. Stephen Orgel and Jonathan Goldberg, Oxford: Oxford University Press, 1991.

'Mr. Thelwall', *Gentleman's Magazine* ns 2 (1834), 550.

The Parliamentary History of England, from the Earliest Period to the Year 1803, ed. William Cobbett, T. C. Hansard and J. Wright, vol. XXXI, London, 1818.

'Phocion', 'To the Right Hon. William Pitt', *Morning Chronicle* 13 Nov. 1794, p. 2.

Preface, *Monthly Magazine* 1 (1796), iii–iv.

Priestley, Joseph, *Disquisitions Relating to Matter and Spirit*, 2nd edn, Birmingham, 1782, Eighteenth Century Collections Online, http://find.galegroup.com.proxy.library.nd.edu/ecco (accessed 12 June 2012).

Priestley, Joseph, *The History and Present State of Electricity*, London, 1767.

Reeve, Clara, *The Progress of Romance, through Times, Countries, and Manners; with Remarks on the Good and Bad Effects of It, on Them Respectively; in a Course of Evening Conversations*, 2 vols, [Colchester], 1785, Eighteenth Century Collections Online, http://find.galegroup.com.proxy.library.nd.edu/ecco (accessed 28 Oct. 2012).

Robinson, Henry Crabb, *Diary, Reminiscences, and Correspondence of Henry Crabb Robinson*, ed. Thomas Sadler, 2nd edn, 3 vols, London: Macmillan, 1869.

Shaftesbury, Anthony Ashley Cooper, Third Earl of, *Characteristicks of Men, Manners, Opinions, Times*, 4th edn, vol. I, London, 1727, Eighteenth Century Collections Online, http://find.galegroup.com.proxy.library.nd.edu/ecco (accessed 29 Oct. 2012).

Shelley, Percy, *Percy Bysshe Shelley: The Major Works*, ed. Zachary Leader and Michael O'Neill, Oxford: Oxford University Press, 2003; repr. 2009.

Sheridan, Thomas, *A Course of Lectures on Elocution: Together with Two Dissertations on Language, and Some Other Tracts Relative to Those Subjects*, London, 1762; repr. Menston: Scolar, 1968.

Smith, Adam, *The Theory of Moral Sentiments*, ed. D. D. Raphael and A. L. Macfie, Oxford: Clarendon Press, 1976.

Smith, Charlotte, *The Poems of Charlotte Smith*, ed. Stuart Curran, New York: Oxford University Press, 1993.

Southey, Robert, *New Letters of Robert Southey*, ed. Kenneth Curry, 2 vols, New York: Columbia University Press, 1965.

Steele, Joshua, *Prosodia Rationalis: Or, an Essay towards Establishing the Melody and Measure of Speech, to Be Expressed and Perpetuated by Peculiar Symbols*, 2nd edn, London, 1779.

Sterne, Lawrence, *A Sentimental Journey and Other Writings*, ed. Ian Jack and Tim Parnell, Oxford: Oxford University Press, 2003; repr. 2008.

Thelwall, A. S., *Exercises in Elocution, in Verse and Prose: To which is Prefixed, A Lecture on the Importance of Elocution in Connexion with Ministerial Usefulness, Delivered at King's College, London, on Entering upon the Duties of Lecturer on Public Reading, Jan. 30, 1850*, London, 1850.

Thelwall, John, *An Address to the Inhabitants of Yarmouth, on the Violent Outrage Lately Committed in Their Town, by a Selected Band of Desperate Ruffians*, Yarmouth, 1796.

Thelwall, John, 'The Anatomy of Speech', *Monthly Magazine* 59 (1825), 120–2, 196–9, 305–8, 397–9, 489–92.

Thelwall, John, *An Appeal to Popular Opinion, against Kidnapping and Murder; Including a Narrative of the Late Atrocious Proceedings, at Yarmouth; with the Statements, Hand-Bills, &c. Pro and Con*, London, 1796.

Thelwall, John, 'On the Application of the Principles of Musical Proportion in the Treatment of Impediments of Speech', *Monthly Magazine* 30 (1810), 104–8.

Thelwall, John, *The Daughter of Adoption; A Tale of Modern Times*, ed. Michael Scrivener, Yasmin Solomonescu and Judith Thompson, Peterborough, ON: Broadview, 2013.

Thelwall, John, 'To Dr. Peter Crompton', in *Poems, Chiefly Written in Retirement*, Hereford, 1801, Cambridge University Library, Rare Books, Y.19.43 (no. 1).

Thelwall, John, 'Elocution', *Cyclopaedia; or, a New Universal Dictionary of Arts, Sciences, and Literature*, ed. Abraham Rees, vol. XIII, London, 1819, n. pag.

Thelwall, John, 'Emotion', *Cyclopaedia; or, a New Universal Dictionary of Arts, Sciences, and Literature*, ed. Abraham Rees, vol. XIII, London, 1819, n. pag.

Thelwall, John, 'Emphasis', *Cyclopaedia; or, a New Universal Dictionary of Arts, Sciences, and Literature*, ed. Abraham Rees, vol. XIII, London, 1819, n. pag.

Thelwall, John, 'Enthusiasm', *Cyclopaedia; or, a New Universal Dictionary of Arts, Sciences, and Literature*, ed. Abraham Rees, vol. XIII, London, 1819, n. pag.

Thelwall, John, *An Essay, Towards a Definition of Animal Vitality*, London, 1793; repr. in *Selected Political Writings of John Thelwall*, ed. Robert Lamb and Corinna Wagner, 4 vols, London: Pickering and Chatto, 2009, vol. I, pp. 11–30.

Thelwall, John, 'Etymological Reasoning', *Champion* 4 April 1819, p. 211.

[Thelwall, John], 'Imagination', *Panoramic Miscellany* 1 (1826), 761.

Thelwall, John, *Incle and Yarico and The Incas: Two Plays by John Thelwall*, ed. Frank Felsenstein and Michael Scrivener, Madison, NJ: Fairleigh Dickinson University Press, 2006.

Thelwall, John, 'On the Influence of the Scenery of Nature on the Intellectual and Moral Character, as well as on the Taste and Imagination', *Champion* 9 Sept. (1820), repr. in *The Poetical Recreations of* The Champion, *and His Literary Correspondents; with a Selection of Essays, Literary and Critical, Which Have Appeared in* The Champion *Newspaper*, London, 1822, pp. 73–7.

Thelwall, John, 'King Chaunticlere; or, the Fate of Tyranny', *Politics for the People: Or a Salmagundy for Swine* 1 (1794), 102–7; repr. in *Selected Political Writings of John Thelwall*, ed. Robert Lamb and Corinna Wagner, 4 vols, London: Pickering and Chatto, 2009, vol. I, pp. 33–6.

Thelwall, John, 'Letter to the Editor', *Monthly Magazine* 19 (1805), 348–52.

Thelwall, John, *A Letter to Francis Jeffray* [sic], *Esq., on Certain Calumnies and Misrepresentations in the Edinburgh Review; the Conduct of Certain Individuals on the Night of Mr. Thelwall's Probationary Lecture, at Bernard's Rooms, Edinburgh; and the Ignorance of the New Critical Junto of the Simplest Elements of English Composition and English Grammar*, Edinburgh, 1804.

Thelwall, John, *A Letter to Henry Cline, Esq., on Imperfect Developments of the Faculties, Mental and Moral, as well as Constitutional and Organic; and on the Treatment of Impediments of Speech*, London, 1810; repr. in *Selected Political Writings of John Thelwall*, ed. Robert Lamb and Corinna Wagner, 4 vols, London: Pickering and Chatto, 2009, vol. IV, pp. 3–111.

Thelwall, John, Letter to Robert Anderson, 9 Feb. 1804, National Library of Scotland, Edinburgh, 22.4.14.

Thelwall, John, Letter to Robert Anderson, 12 March 1804, National Library of Scotland, Edinburgh, 22.4.14.

Thelwall, John, Letter to Thomas Hardy, 24 Aug. 1796, Hesburgh Library, University of Notre Dame, MSE/MD 3811-1.

Thelwall, John, Letter to Thomas Hardy, 19 May 1797, Hesburgh Library, University of Notre Dame, MSE/MD 3811-3.

Thelwall, John, Letter to Thomas Hardy, 12 Dec. 1805, Hesburgh Library, University of Notre Dame, MSE/MD 3811-8.

Thelwall, John, Marginalia on Coleridge's *Biographia Literaria*; repr. in Burton R. Pollin and Redmond Burke, 'John Thelwall's Marginalia in a Copy of Coleridge's *Biographia Literaria*', *Bulletin of the New York Public Library* 74 (1970), 73–94.

Thelwall, John, Marginalia on William Lisle Bowles's *Sonnets and Other Poems*, 4th edn, London, 1796, National Art Library, London, Dyce 8vo 1298.

[Thelwall, John], 'Metaphysics', *Panoramic Miscellany* 1 (1826), 374.

Thelwall, John, 'Mr. Thelwall's Lecture on the Articulation and Qualities of Syllables, and the Educational Causes of Impediments of Speech', *Panoramic Miscellany* 1 (1826), 347–54.

Thelwall, John, 'Mr. Thelwall's Lecture on the Enunciative Organs, and the Formation of Literal Elements', *Monthly Magazine* 60 (1825), 5–8, 113–17, 202–4, 305–8.

Thelwall, John, 'Mr. Thelwall's Lecture. On the Harmonic Qualities of the Literal Elements, and Their Classification, According to Their Musical and Other Inherent Properties', *Panoramic Miscellany* 1 (1826), 41–6, 193–8; repr. in *Selected Political Writings of John Thelwall*, ed. Robert Lamb and Corinna Wagner, 4 vols, London: Pickering and Chatto, 2009, vol. IV, pp. 201–13.

Thelwall, John, 'Mr. Thelwall's Lecture on the Inherent and Incidental Properties of Syllables that Constitute the Bases of Prosodial Metre, and of the Rhythmus and Harmony of Speech', *Panoramic Miscellany* 1 (1826), 635–42.

Thelwall, John, Mr. *Thelwall's Reply to the Calumnies, Misrepresentations, and Literary Forgeries, Contained in the Anonymous Observations on His Letter to the Editor of the Edinburgh Review: With a Further Exposition of the Ungrammatical Ignorance of the Writers and Vindicators of that Defamatory Journal*, Glasgow, 1804.

Thelwall, John, *The Natural and Constitutional Right of Britons to Annual Parliaments, Universal Suffrage, and the Freedom of Popular Association*, London, 1795; repr. in *The Politics of English Jacobinism: Writings of John Thelwall*, ed. Gregory Claeys, University Park: Pennsylvania State University Press, 1995, pp. 4–63.

Thelwall, John, 'Ode to Science. Recited at the Anniversary Meeting of the Philomathian Society, June 20, 1791', London, 1791; repr. in *Selected Political Writings of John Thelwall*, ed. Robert Lamb and Corinna Wagner, 4 vols, London: Pickering and Chatto, 2009, vol. I, pp. 3–8.

Thelwall, John, *A Particular Account of the Late Outrages at Lynn and Wisbeach; Being a Postscript to the Appeal to Popular Opinion, against Kidnapping and Murder*, London, 1796.

Thelwall, John, 'A Pedestrian Excursion through Parts of England and Wales during the Summer of 1797', *Monthly Magazine* 8–12 (1799–1801), repr. in *Selected Political Writings of John Thelwall*, ed. Robert Lamb and Corinna Wagner, 4 vols, London: Pickering and Chatto, 2009, vol. III, pp. 17–55.

Thelwall, John, *The Peripatetic*, ed. Judith Thompson, Detroit, MI: Wayne State University Press, 2001.

Thelwall, John. *The Peripatetic; or, Sketches of the Heart, of Nature and Society; in a Series of Politico-Sentimental Journals, in Verse and Prose of the Eccentric Excursions of Sylvanus Theophrastus, Supposed to be Written by Himself*, [Southwark], 1793, Eighteenth Century Collections Online, http://find.galegroup.com. proxy.library.nd.edu/ecco (accessed 21 Nov. 2012).

Thelwall, John, 'The Phenomena of the Wye, during the Winter of 1797–8', *Monthly Magazine* 5 (1798), 343–46; 6 (1798), 20–1; repr. in *Selected Political Writings of John Thelwall*, ed. Robert Lamb and Corinna Wagner, 4 vols, London: Pickering and Chatto, 2009, vol. III, pp. 3–13.

Thelwall, John, *Poems, Chiefly Suggested by the Scenery of Nature; to Which are Added Odes &c. Amatory and Congratulatory, Translations, and Attempts at Humour*, 3 vols, manuscript, Derby Local Studies Library, England, 5868–5870.

Thelwall, John, *Poems, Chiefly Written in Retirement*, Hereford, 1801; repr. Oxford: Woodstock, 1989.

Thelwall, John, *Poems on Various Subjects*, 2 vols, London, 1787; repr. in *Literature Online*, Cambridge: Chadwyck-Healey, 1992, http://lion.chadwyck.com.proxy. library.nd.edu/ (accessed Aug. 13, 2013).

Thelwall, John, *Poems Written in Close Confinement in the Tower and Newgate, under a Charge of High Treason*, London, 1795; repr. Otley: Woodstock, 2000.

Thelwall, John, 'Poems Written in the Tower', *Champion* 12 May–14 July and 4 Aug.–8 Sept. 1821.

Thelwall, John, *The Poetical Recreations of* The Champion, *and His Literary Correspondents; with a Selection of Essays, Literary and Critical, Which Have Appeared in* The Champion *Newspaper*, London, 1822.

[Thelwall, John], 'The Poetry of Miss Landen [*sic*]', *Panoramic Miscellany* 1 (1826), 74–82.

Thelwall, John, *Political Lectures. Volume the First—Part the First: Containing the Lecture on Spies and Informers, and the First Lecture on Prosecutions for Political Opinion*, London, 1795.

Thelwall, John, *Prospectus of a Course of Lectures, to Be Delivered every Monday, Wednesday, and Friday, during the Ensuing Lent. In Strict Conformity with the Restrictions of Mr. Pitt's Convention Act*, London, 1796.

Thelwall, John, *Results of Experience in the Treatment of Cases of Defective Utterance, from Deficiencies in the Roof of the Mouth, and Other Imperfections and Mal-Conformations of the Organs of Speech; with Observations on Cases on Amentia, and Tardy and Imperfect Developments of the Faculties*, London, 1814.

Thelwall, John, *Rights of Nature, against the Usurpations of Establishments*, London, 1796; repr. in *The Politics of English Jacobinism: Writings of John Thelwall*, ed. Gregory Claeys, University Park: Pennsylvania State University Press, 1995, pp. 389–500.

[Thelwall, John], 'The Sceptic. (No. IV.)', *Biographical and Imperial Magazine* (Feb. 1790), 103–6.

Thelwall, John, *Selected Political Writings of John Thelwall*, ed. Robert Lamb and Corinna Wagner, 4 vols, London: Pickering and Chatto, 2009.

Thelwall, John, *Selections and Original Articles, Read and Recited in Illustration of Mr. Thelwall's Lectures on the Science and Practice of Elocution*, Wakefield, 1802.

Thelwall, John, *Selections, &c., for Mr. Thelwall's Lectures on the Science and Practice of Elocution*, York, 1802.

Thelwall, John, *Selections for the Illustration of a Course of Instructions on the Rhythmus and Utterance of the English Language; with an Introductory Essay on the Application of Rhythmical Science to the Treatment of Impediments, and the Improvement of Our National Oratory; and an Elementary Analysis of the Science and Practice of Elocution, Composition, &c.*, London, 1812.

Thelwall, John, 'A Sheep-Shearing Song'; repr. in Mrs. Thelwall [Henrietta Cecil Thelwall], *The Life of John Thelwall*, London, 1837, pp. 447–9.

Thelwall, John, *Sober Reflections on the Seditious and Inflammatory Letter of the Right Hon. Edmund Burke, to a Noble Lord*, London, 1796; repr. in *The Politics of English Jacobinism: Writings of John Thelwall*, ed. Gregory Claeys, University Park: Pennsylvania State University Press, 1995, pp. 329–87.

Thelwall, John, *The Speech of John Thelwall, at the General Meeting of the Friends of Parliamentary Reform, Called by the London Corresponding Society, and Held in the Neighbourhood of Copenhagen-House; on Monday, October 26, 1795*, 3rd edn, London, 1795.

Thelwall, John, *The Speech of John Thelwall, at the Second Meeting of the London Corresponding Society, and Other Friends of Reform, Held at Copenhagen-House, on Thursday, November 12, 1795*, London, 1795.

Thelwall, John, 'The Star that Shone When Other Stars Were Dim', *Monthly Magazine* 59 Supplement (1825), 661–3.

Thelwall, John, *Strike, but Hear! A Dedication to His Majesty's Ministers, the Crown Lawyers, and the Majority of Both Houses of Parliament*, London, 1796.

Thelwall, John, *The Tribune*, 3 vols, London, 1795–96; repr. in *The Politics of English Jacobinism: Writings of John Thelwall*, ed. Gregory Claeys, University Park: Pennsylvania State University Press, 1995, pp. 65–327.

Thelwall, John, *The Tribune, a Periodical Publication, Consisting Chiefly of the Political Lectures of J. Thelwall*, 3 vols, London, 1795–96, Cambridge University Library, Rare Books, Acton.c.25.418.

Thelwall, John, *The Vestibule of Eloquence: Original Articles, Oratorical and Poetical, Intended as Exercises in Recitation, at the Institution, Bedford Place, Russell Square*, London, 1810.

Thelwall, Mrs. [Henrietta Cecil Thelwall], *The Life of John Thelwall*, London, 1837.

Thelwall, S., *The Syllabic Primer and Reading Book, Based on the Principle That the Sound of Letters Is Determined by Their Position in a Syllable or Word*, London, 1859.

'T., J.' [John Thelwall], 'Observations upon the Theory Adopted by Mr. Burke in his Examination of the Effects Produced upon the Mind by Words', *Monthly Magazine* 16 (1803), 212–17, 317–20.

Tooke, John Horne, *Epea Pteroenta: or, The Diversions of Purley, Part I*, 2nd edn, London, 1798, Eighteenth Century Collections Online, http://find.galegroup.com.proxy.library.nd.edu/ecco (accessed 27 Oct. 2012).

Tooke, John Horne, *The Prison Diary (16 May–22 November 1794) of John Horne Tooke*, ed. A. V. Beedell and A. D. Harvey, Leeds: Leeds Philosophical and Literary Society, 1995.

Walker, George. *The Vagabond*, 3rd edn, 2 vols, London, 1799.

Wollstonecraft, Mary, *A Vindication of the Rights of Woman*, ed. Miriam Brody, London: Penguin, 1992.

Wordsworth, William, *The Letters of William and Dorothy Wordsworth: The Early Years, 1787–1805*, ed. Ernest De Selincourt, rev. Chester L. Shaver, 2nd edn, Oxford: Clarendon Press, 1967.

Wordsworth, William, *The Letters of William and Dorothy Wordsworth: The Later Years*, ed. Ernest De Selincourt, rev. Alan G. Hill, 2nd edn, 4 vols, Oxford: Clarendon Press, 1982.

Wordsworth, William, *The Letters of William and Dorothy Wordsworth: The Middle Years*, ed. Ernest de Selincourt, rev. Mary Moorman and Alan G. Hill, 2nd edn, 2 vols, Oxford: Clarendon Press, 1970.

Wordsworth, William, *Lyrical Ballads, and Other Poems, 1797–1800*, ed. James Butler and Karen Green, The Cornell Wordsworth, Ithaca, NY: Cornell University Press, 1992.

Wordsworth, William, *The Poetical Works of William Wordsworth*, ed. Ernest De Selincourt and Helen Darbishire, 5 vols, Oxford: Clarendon, 1940–9.

Wordsworth, William, *The Prelude: The Four Texts (1798, 1799, 1805, 1850)*, ed. Jonathan Wordsworth, London: Penguin, 1995.

Wordsworth, William, *William Wordsworth: Selected Poetry*, ed. Stephen Gill and Duncan Wu, Oxford: Oxford University Press, 1998.

Secondary works

Abrams, M. H., *The Mirror and the Lamp: Romantic Theory and the Critical Tradition*, Oxford: Oxford University Press, 1953; repr. New York: Norton, 1958.

Abrams, M. H., 'Structure and Style in the Greater Romantic Lyric', in *From Sensibility to Romanticism: Essays Presented to Frederick A. Pottle*, ed. Frederick W. Hilles and Harold Bloom, New York: Oxford University Press, 1965, pp. 527–60.

Allard, James Robert, *Romanticism, Medicine, and the Poet's Body*, The Nineteenth Century, Aldershot: Ashgate, 2007.

Allen, Beverly Sprague, 'William Godwin's Influence upon John Thelwall', *PMLA* 37 (1922), 662–82.

Aravamudan, Srinivas (ed.), *Fiction*, London: Pickering and Chatto, 1999, vol. VI of *Slavery, Abolition and Emancipation: Writings in the British Romantic Period*, ed. Peter J. Kitson and Deborah Lee, 8 vols.

Barrell, John, 'Imaginary Treason, Imaginary Law: The State Trials of 1794', in *The Birth of Pandora and the Division of Knowledge*, Houndmills: Macmillan, 1992, pp. 119–43.

Barrell, John, *Imagining the King's Death: Figurative Treason, Fantasies of Regicide, 1793–1796*, Oxford: Oxford University Press, 2000.

Barrell, John, *The Spirit of Despotism: Invasions of Privacy in the 1790s*, Oxford: Oxford University Press, 2006.

Barrell, John, and Jon Mee (eds), *Trials for Treason and Sedition, 1792–1794*, 8 vols, London: Pickering and Chatto, 2006.

Bate, Walter Jackson, *From Classic to Romantic: Premises of Taste in Eighteenth-Century England*, New York: Harper Torchbooks, 1961.

Bender, John, *Imagining the Penitentiary: Fiction and the Architecture of Mind in Eighteenth-Century England*, Chicago: University of Chicago Press, 1987.

Bertucci, Paola, 'Therapeutic Attractions: Early Applications of Electricity to the Art of Healing', in *Brain, Mind and Medicine: Essays in Eighteenth-Century Neuroscience*, ed. Harry Whitaker, C. U. M. Smith and Stanley Finger, New York: Springer, 2007, pp. 271–83.

Bevan, Michael, 'Parkinson, James (1755–1824)', in *Oxford Dictionary of National Biography*, ed. H. C. G. Matthew and Brian Harrison, Oxford: Oxford University Press, 2004, online edn, ed. Lawrence Goldman, Oct. 2009, http://www. oxforddnb.com/view/article/21371 (accessed 16 Oct. 2012).

Blackburn, Robin, *The Overthrow of Colonial Slavery 1776–1848*, London: Verso, 1988.

Blackburn, Simon, *The Oxford Dictionary of Philosophy*, Oxford: Oxford University Press, 1994.

Boulton, James T., *The Language of Politics in the Age of Wilkes and Burke*, London: Routledge and Kegan Paul, 1963; repr. Westport, CT: Greenwood, 1975.

Boyle, A., 'Portraiture in *Lavengro* VI: The Teacher of Oratory – John Thelwall', *Notes and Queries* 197 (1952), 38–9.

Brunton, Deborah, 'Walker, John (1759–1830)', in *Oxford Dictionary of National Biography*, ed. H. C. G. Matthew and Brian Harrison, Oxford: Oxford University Press, 2004, online edn, ed. Lawrence Goldman, Oct. 2009, http://www. oxforddnb.com/view/article/28500 (accessed 22 June 2011).

Budge, Gavin, 'Indigestion and Imagination in Coleridge's Critical Thought', in *Romantic Empiricism: Poetics and the Philosophy of Common Sense, 1780–1830*, ed. Gavin Budge, Lewisburg, PA: Bucknell University Press, 2007, pp. 141–81.

Bugg, John, 'Close Confinement: John Thelwall and the Romantic Prison', *European Romantic Review* 20, no. 1 (2009), 37–56.

Burch, Druin, *Digging up the Dead: The Life and Times of Astley Cooper, an Extraordinary Surgeon*, London: Vintage, 2008.

Butler, Marilyn (ed.), *Burke, Paine, Godwin, and the Revolution Controversy,* Cambridge: Cambridge University Press, 1984.

Carlyle, E. I., 'Ward, William (1769–1823)', rev. Brian Stanley, in *Oxford Dictionary of National Biography,* ed. H. C. G. Matthew and Brian Harrison, Oxford: Oxford University Press, 2004, online edn, ed. Lawrence Goldman, http://www.oxforddnb.com/view/article/28710 (accessed 28 Nov. 2012).

Cestre, Charles, *John Thelwall: A Pioneer of Democracy and Social Reform in England during the French Revolution,* London: Swan Sonnenschein, 1906.

Chandler, James, *An Archaeology of Sympathy: The Sentimental Mode in Literature and Cinema,* Chicago: University of Chicago Press, 2013.

Claeys, Gregory, 'The Origins of the Rights of Labour: Republicanism, Commerce, and the Construction of Modern Social Theory in Britain, 1796–1805', *Journal of Modern History* 66 (1994), 249–90.

Claeys, Gregory (ed.), *The Politics of English Jacobinism: Writings of John Thelwall,* University Park: Pennsylvania State University Press, 1995.

Clemit, Pamela (ed.), *The Letters of William Godwin,* vol. I: *1778–1797,* Oxford: Oxford University Press, 2011.

Cohen, Murray, *Sensible Words: Linguistic Practice in England, 1640–1785,* Baltimore, MD: Johns Hopkins University Press, 1977.

Colley, Linda, 'Radical Patriotism in Eighteenth-Century England', in *Patriotism: The Making and Unmaking of British National Identity,* ed. Raphael Samuel, London: Routledge, 1989, vol. I, pp. 169–87.

Collings, David, 'The Harsh Delights of Political Duty: Thelwall, Coleridge, Wordsworth, 1795–99', in *Romantic Wars: Studies in Culture and Conflict, 1793–1822,* ed. Philip Shaw, Aldershot: Ashgate, 2000, pp. 57–79.

Coole, Diana, and Samantha Frost (eds), *New Materialisms: Ontology, Agency, and Politics,* Durham: Duke University Press, 2010.

Cordasco, Francesco, 'Junius (fl. 1768–1773)', in *Oxford Dictionary of National Biography,* ed. H. C. G. Matthew and Brian Harrison, Oxford: Oxford University Press, 2004, online edn, ed. Lawrence Goldman, Jan. 2008 http://www.oxforddnb.com/view/article/45912 (accessed 27 Oct. 2012).

Corfield, Penelope J., and Chris Evans, 'John Thelwall in Wales: New Documentary Evidence', *Bulletin of the Institute for Historical Research* 59 (1986), 231–9.

Corfield, Penelope J., and Chris Evans (eds), *Youth and Revolution in the 1790s: Letters of William Pattison, Thomas Amyot and Henry Crabb Robinson,* Stroud: Sutton, 1996.

Craig, Cairns, *Associationism and the Literary Imagination: From the Phantasmal Chaos,* Edinburgh: Edinburgh University Press, 2007.

Cronin, Richard, *The Politics of Romantic Poetry: In Search of the Pure Commonwealth,* London: Macmillan, 2000.

Cunningham, Andrew, and Nicholas Jardine (eds), *Romanticism and the Sciences,* Cambridge: Cambridge University Press, 1990.

Cunningham, Hugh, 'The Language of Patriotism', in *Patriotism: The Making and Unmaking of British National Identity,* ed. Raphael Samuel, London: Routledge, 1989, vol. I, pp. 57–89.

Curran, Stuart, *Poetic Form and British Romanticism,* Oxford: Oxford University Press, 1986.

Davies, Damian Walford, 'Capital Crimes: John Thelwall, "Gallucide" and Psychobiography', *Romanticism* 18, no. 1 (2012), 55–69.

Davies, Damian Walford, *Presences that Disturb: Models of Romantic Identity in the Literature and Culture of the 1790s*, Cardiff: University of Wales Press, 2002.

Davis, Michael T., 'Tooke, John Horne (1736–1812)', in *Oxford Dictionary of National Biography*, ed. H. C. G. Matthew and Brian Harrison, Oxford: Oxford University Press, 2004, online edn, ed. Lawrence Goldman, Oct. 2009, http://www.oxforddnb.com/view/article/27545 (accessed 23 Oct. 2012).

Davis, Michael T., et al. (eds), *London Corresponding Society, 1792–1799*, 6 vols, London: Pickering and Chatto, 2002.

Davis, Wayne A., *Meaning, Expression, and Thought*, Cambridge: Cambridge University Press, 2003.

Deane, Phyllis, *The First Industrial Revolution*, 2nd edn, Cambridge: Cambridge University Press, 1998.

Desjardins, Molly, 'John Thelwall and Association', in *John Thelwall: Critical Reassessments*, ed. Yasmin Solomonescu, Romantic Circles, Sept. 2011, http://romantic.arhu.umd.edu/praxis/thelwall/HTML/praxis.2011.desjardins.html (accessed 12 June 2012).

Duchan, Judith Felson, 'The Conceptual Underpinnings of John Thelwall's Elocutionary Practices', in *John Thelwall: Radical Romantic and Acquitted Felon*, ed. Steve Poole, The Enlightenment World 11, London: Pickering and Chatto, 2009, pp. 139–45.

Eagleston, A. J., 'Wordsworth, Coleridge, and the Spy', in *Coleridge: Studies by Several Hands on the Hundredth Anniversary of His Death*, ed. Edmund Blunden and Earl Leslie Griggs, London: Constable, 1934, pp. 73–87.

Epstein, James A., *Radical Expression: Political Language, Ritual, and Symbol in England, 1790–1850*, New York: Oxford University Press, 1994.

Erving, George S., 'The Politics of Matter: Newtonian Science and Priestleyan Metaphysics in Coleridge's "Preternatural Agency"', *European Romantic Review* 19, no. 3 (2008), 219–32.

Esterhammer, Angela, 'Godwin's Suspicion of Speech Acts', *Studies in Romanticism* 39, no. 4 (Winter 2000), 553–78.

Fairclough, Mary, *The Romantic Crowd: Sympathy, Controversy and Print Culture*, Cambridge Studies in Romanticism 97, Cambridge: Cambridge University Press, 2013.

Fairer, David, *Organising Poetry: The Coleridge Circle, 1790–1798*, Oxford: Oxford University Press, 2009.

Fallon, Stephen M., *Milton among the Philosophers: Poetry and Materialism in Seventeenth-Century England*, Ithaca, NY: Cornell University Press, 1991.

Fara, Patricia, *An Entertainment for Angels: Electricity in the Enlightenment*, Revolutions in Science, New York: Columbia University Press, 2002.

Fliegelman, Jay, *Declaring Independence: Jefferson, Natural Language, and the Culture of Performance*, Stanford: Stanford University Press, 1993.

Foucault, Michel, *The Birth of the Clinic: An Archaeology of Medical Perception*, trans. A. M. Sheridan Smith, London: Tavistock, 1973; repr. New York: Vintage, 1994.

'Francisco Espoz y Mina', in *Encyclopædia Britannica Online Academic Edition* http://www.britannica.com/EBchecked/topic/192771/Francisco-Espoz-y-Mina (accessed 25 May 2012).

Fulford, Tim, Debbie Lee and Peter J. Kitson, *Literature, Science and Exploration in the Romantic Era: Bodies of Knowledge*, Cambridge Studies in Romanticism 60, Cambridge: Cambridge University Press, 2004.

Furniss, Tom, *Edmund Burke's Aesthetic Ideology: Language, Gender, and Political Economy in Revolution*, Cambridge Studies in Romanticism 4, Cambridge: Cambridge University Press, 1993.

Fussell, Paul, Jr., *Theory of Prosody in Eighteenth-Century England*, Hamden, CT: Archon, 1954; repr. 1966.

Gallop, Geoffrey, 'Ideology and the English Jacobins: The Case of John Thelwall', *Enlightenment and Dissent* 5 (1986), 3–20.

Getzler, Joshua S., 'Crompton, Sir Charles John (1797–1865)', in *Oxford Dictionary of National Biography*, ed. H. C. G. Matthew and Brian Harrison, Oxford: Oxford University Press, 2004, online edn, ed. Lawrence Goldman, Oct. 2009, http://www.oxforddnb.com/view/article/6756 (accessed 1 Jan. 2012).

Gibbs, Warren E., 'An Unpublished Letter from John Thelwall to S. T. Coleridge', *Modern Language Review* 25 (1930), 85–90.

Gigante, Denise, *Life: Organic Form and Romanticism*, New Haven, CT: Yale University Press, 2009.

Gilmore, Paul, *Aesthetic Materialism: Electricity and American Romanticism*, Stanford: Stanford University Press, 2009.

Goodwin, Albert, *The Friends of Liberty: The English Democratic Movement in the Age of the French Revolution*, Cambridge, MA: Harvard University Press, 1979.

Gravil, Richard, 'Mr. Thelwall's Ear; or, Hearing *The Excursion*', in *Grasmere, 2011: Selected Papers from the Wordsworth Summer Conference*, comp. Richard Gravil, Tirril: Humanities-Ebooks, 2011, pp. 171–203.

Gravil, Richard, 'The Somerset Sound; or, the Darling Child of Speech', *Coleridge Bulletin* ns 26 (Winter 2005), 1–21.

Haberman, Frederick W., 'John Thelwall: His Life, His School, and His Theory of Elocution', in *Historical Studies of Rhetoric and Rhetoricians*, ed. Raymond F. Howes, Ithaca, NY: Cornell University Press, 1961, pp. 189–97.

Hamilton, J. A., 'Gurney, Sir John (1768–1845)', rev. Catherine Pease-Watkin, in *Oxford Dictionary of National Biography*, ed. H. C. G. Matthew and Brian Harrison, Oxford: Oxford University Press, 2004, online edn, ed. Lawrence Goldman, http://www.oxforddnb.com/view/article/11767 (accessed 28 Oct. 2012).

Hamilton, Paul, 'Coleridge and Godwin in the 1790s', in *The Coleridge Connection: Essays for Thomas McFarland*, ed. Richard Gravil and Molly Lefebure, New York: St. Martin's, 1990, pp. 41–59.

Hampsher-Monk, Iain, 'John Thelwall and the Eighteenth-Century Radical Response to Political Economy', *Historical Journal* 34 (1991), 1–20.

Hartman, Geoffrey, 'Wordsworth and Metapsychology', in *Wordsworth's Poetic Theory: Knowledge, Language, Experience*, ed. Alexander Regier and Stefan H. Uhlig, Houndmills: Palgrave Macmillan, 2010, pp. 195–211.

Hill, Christopher, 'The Norman Yoke', in *Democracy and the Labour Movement: Essays in Honour of Dona Torr*, ed. John Saville, London: Lawrence and Wishart, 1954, pp. 11–66.

Hilton, Boyd, *A Mad, Bad, and Dangerous People? England 1783–1846*, Oxford: Oxford University Press, 2006.

Holmes, Richard, *The Age of Wonder: How the Romantic Generation Discovered the Beauty and Terror of Science*, London: Harper, 2008.

Howell, Wilbur Samuel, *Eighteenth-Century British Logic and Rhetoric*, Princeton: Princeton University Press, 1971.

Jackson, H. J., *Romantic Readers: The Evidence of Marginalia*, New Haven, CT: Yale University Press, 2005.

Jackson, Noel, *Science and Sensation in Romantic Poetry*, Cambridge Studies in Romanticism 73, Cambridge: Cambridge University Press, 2008.

Jacyna, L. S, 'Immanence or Transcendence: Theories of Life and Organization in Britain, 1790–1835', *Isis* 74, no. 3 (1983), 311–29.

James, C. L. R., *The Black Jacobins: Toussaint L'Ouverture and the San Domingo Revolution*, New York: Dial, 1938; repr. London: Allison and Busby, 1980.

James, Felicity, 'Coleridge and the Unitarian Ladies', *Coleridge Bulletin* ns 28 (Winter 2006), 46–53.

Janowitz, Anne, *Lyric and Labour in the Romantic Tradition*, Cambridge Studies in Romanticism 30, Cambridge: Cambridge University Press, 1998.

Jarvis, Robin, *Romantic Writing and Pedestrian Travel*, Houndmills: Macmillan, 1997.

Jarvis, Simon, *Wordsworth's Philosophic Song*, Cambridge Studies in Romanticism 67, Cambridge: Cambridge University Press, 2007.

Johnston, Kenneth R., *Wordsworth and* The Recluse, New Haven, CT: Yale University Press, 1984.

Jones, Chris, *Radical Sensibility: Literature and Ideas in the 1790s*, London: Routledge, 1993.

Kallich, Martin, *The Association of Ideas and Critical Theory in Eighteenth-Century England*, The Hague: Mouton, 1970.

Kelly, Gary, *The English Jacobin Novel, 1780–1805*, Oxford: Clarendon Press, 1976.

Kelly, Gary, 'The Limits of Genre and the Institution of Literature: Romanticism between Fact and Fiction', in *Romantic Revolutions: Criticism and Theory*, ed. Kenneth R. Johnston et al, Bloomington: Indiana University Press, 1990, pp. 158–75.

Kitson, Peter J., '"Bales of Living Anguish": Representations of Race and the Slave in Romantic Writing', *ELH* 67 (2000), 515–37.

Kitson, Peter J., 'John Thelwall in Saint Domingue: Race, Slavery, and Revolution in *The Daughter of Adoption: A Tale of Modern Times* (1801)', *Romanticism* 16, no. 2 (2010), 120–38.

Klancher, Jon P., 'Godwin and the Republican Romance: Genre, Politics, and Contingency in Cultural History', *Modern Language Quarterly* 56, no. 2 (June 1995), 145–65.

Knellwolf, Christa, and Jane Goodall (eds), *Frankenstein's Science: Experimentation and Discovery in Romantic Culture, 1780–1830*, Aldershot: Ashgate, 2008.

Kramnick, Isaac, 'On Anarchism and the Real World: William Godwin and Radical England', *American Political Science Review* 66 (1972), 114–28.

Kramnick, Isaac, 'Eighteenth-Century Science and Radical Social Theory: The Case of Joseph Priestley's Scientific Liberalism', *Journal of British Studies* 25, no. 1 (Jan. 1986), 1–30.

Kuehn, Manfred, 'Hamilton's Reading of Kant: A Chapter in the Early Scottish Development of Kant's Thought', in *Kant and His Influence*, ed. George Macdonald Ross and Tony McWalter, London: Continuum, 2005, pp. 315–47.

Lamb, Jonathan, 'Language and Hartleian Associationism in *A Sentimental Journey*', *Eighteenth-Century Studies* 13, no. 3 (Spring 1980), 285–312.

Lamb, Robert, 'Labour, Contingency, Utility: Thelwall's Theory of Property', in *John Thelwall: Radical Romantic and Acquitted Felon*, ed. Steve Poole, The Enlightenment World 11, London: Pickering and Chatto, 2009, pp. 51–60.

Land, Stephen K., *From Signs to Propositions: The Concept of Form in Eighteenth-Century Semantic Theory*, Longman Linguistics Library 16, London: Longman, 1974.

Lawrence, Christopher, 'The Nervous System and Society in the Scottish Enlightenment', in *Natural Order: Historical Studies of Scientific Culture*, ed. Barry Barnes and Steven Shapin, Sage Focus Editions 6, Beverly Hills, CA: Sage, 1979, pp. 19–40.

Lee, Matthew, 'Birkbeck, George (1776–1841)', in *Oxford Dictionary of National Biography*, online edn, ed. Lawrence Goldman, Oxford: Oxford University Press, http://www.oxforddnb.com/view/article/2454 (accessed 20 June 2012).

Levinson, Marjorie, 'A Motion and a Spirit: Romancing Spinoza', *Studies in Romanticism* 46 (Winter 2007), 367–408.

Levinson, Marjorie, *Wordsworth's Great Period Poems: Four Essays*, Cambridge: Cambridge University Press, 1986.

Lupack, Alan (ed.), *Arthurian Drama: An Anthology*, New York: Garland, 1991.

Lyon, Judson Stanley, The Excursion: *A Study*, Yale Studies in English 114, New Haven, CT: Yale University Press, 1950.

Macherey, Pierre, 'In a Materialist Way', in *Philosophy in France Today*, ed. Alan Montefiore, Cambridge: Cambridge University Press, 1983, pp. 136–54.

Magnuson, Paul, *Reading Public Romanticism*, Princeton: Princeton University Press, 1998.

Manly, Susan, *Language, Custom and Nation in the 1790s: Locke, Tooke, Wordsworth, Edgeworth*, Aldershot: Ashgate, 2007.

Markley, Arnold A., *Conversion and Reform in the British Novel in the 1790s: A Revolution of Opinions*, New York: Palgrave Macmillan, 2009.

McCann, Andrew, *Cultural Politics in the 1790s: Literature, Radicalism and the Public Sphere*, Houndmills: Macmillan, 1999.

McCann, Andrew, 'Romantic Self-Fashioning: John Thelwall and the Science of Elocution', *Studies in Romanticism* 40 (2001), 215–32.

McFarland, Thomas, *Coleridge and the Pantheist Tradition*, Oxford: Clarendon Press, 1969.

McGann, Jerome J., *The Romantic Ideology: A Critical Investigation*, Chicago: University of Chicago Press, 1983.

McGann, Jerome J., and Daniel Riess (eds), *Letitia Elizabeth Landon: Selected Writings*, Peterborough, ON: Broadview, 1997.

Mee, Jon, *Conversable Worlds: Literature, Contention, and Community 1762 to 1830*, Oxford: Oxford University Press, 2011.

Mee, Jon, 'The Dungeon and the Cell: The Prison Verse of Coleridge and Thelwall', in *John Thelwall: Radical Romantic and Acquitted Felon*, ed. Steve Poole, The Enlightenment World 11, London: Pickering and Chatto, 2009, pp. 107–16.

Mee, Jon, '"Examples of Safe Printing": Censorship and Popular Radical Literature in the 1790s', in *Literature and Censorship*, ed. Nigel Smith, Essays and Studies ns 46, Cambridge: Brewer, 1993, pp. 81–95.

Mee, Jon, '"The Press and Danger of the Crowd": Godwin, Thelwall, and the Counter-Public Sphere', in *Godwinian Moments: From the Enlightenment to Romanticism*, ed. Robert M. Maniquis and Victoria Myers, Toronto: University of Toronto Press, 2011, pp. 83–102.

Mee, Jon, *Romanticism, Enthusiasm, and Regulation: Poetics and the Policing of Culture in the Romantic Period*, Oxford: Oxford University Press, 2003; repr. 2005.

Michaelson, Patricia Howell, *Speaking Volumes: Women, Reading, and Speech in the Age of Austen*, Stanford: Stanford University Press, 2002.

Neve, Michael, 'Beddoes, Thomas (1760–1808)', in *Oxford Dictionary of National Biography*, online edn, ed. Lawrence Goldman, Oxford: Oxford University Press, http://www.oxforddnb.com/view/article/1919 (accessed 28. Nov. 2012).

Newlyn, Lucy, *Reading, Writing, and Romanticism: The Anxiety of Reception*, Oxford: Oxford University Press, 2000.

O'Boyle, Patty, 'Coleridge, Wordsworth and Thelwall's *Fairy of the Lake*', *Coleridge Bulletin* ns 28 (2006), 63–71.

O'Donnell, Brennan, *The Passion of Meter: A Study of Wordsworth's Metrical Art*, Kent, OH: Kent State University Press, 1995.

Packham, Catherine, *Eighteenth-Century Vitalism: Bodies, Culture, Politics*, Palgrave Studies in the Enlightenment, Romanticism and the Cultures of Print, Houndmills: Palgrave Macmillan, 2012.

Perkins, David, 'How the Romantics Recited Poetry', *Studies in English Literature 1500–1900* 31 (1991), 655–71.

Philp, Mark, 'The Fragmented Ideology of Reform', in *The French Revolution and British Popular Politics*, ed. Mark Philp, Cambridge: Cambridge University Press, 1991, pp. 50–77.

Philp, Mark, *Godwin's Political Justice*, Ithaca, NY: Cornell University Press, 1986.

Piper, H. W., *The Active Universe: Pantheism and the Concept of the Imagination in the English Romantic Poets*, London: Athlone, 1962.

Pollin, Burton R., and Redmond Burke, 'John Thelwall's Marginalia in a Copy of Coleridge's *Biographia Literaria*', *Bulletin of the New York Public Library* 74 (1970), 73–94.

Poole, Steve, 'Gillray, Cruikshank and Thelwall: Visual Satire, Physiognomy and the Jacobin Body', in *John Thelwall: Critical Reassessments*, ed. Yasmin Solomonescu, Romantic Circles, Sept. 2011, http://romantic.arhu.umd.edu/praxis/thelwall/HTML/praxis.2011.poole.html (accessed 12 June 2012).

Poole, Steve (ed.), *John Thelwall: Radical Romantic and Acquitted Felon*, The Enlightenment World 11, London: Pickering and Chatto, 2009.

Poole, Steve, '"Not Precedents to Be Followed but Examples to Be Weighed": John Thelwall and the Jacobin Sense of the Past', in *John Thelwall: Radical Romantic and Acquitted Felon*, ed. Steve Poole, The Enlightenment World 11, London: Pickering and Chatto, 2009, pp. 161–73.

Porter, Roy, *Flesh in the Age of Reason: How the Enlightenment Transformed the Way We See Our Bodies and Souls*, London: Allen Lane, 2003; repr. London: Penguin, 2004.

Porter, Roy, 'Medical Science and Human Science in the Enlightenment', in *Inventing Human Science: Eighteenth-Century Domains*, ed. Christopher Fox, Roy Porter and Robert Wokler, Berkeley: University of California Press, 1995, pp. 53–87.

Poynter, J. R., *Society and Pauperism: English Ideas on Poor Relief, 1795–1834*, London: Routledge and Kegan Paul, 1969.

Rajan, Tilottama, 'Wollstonecraft and Godwin: Reading the Secrets of the Political Novel', *Studies in Romanticism* 27 (1988), 221–51.

Reiman, Donald (ed.), *Ode to Science, John Gilpin's Ghost, Poems, The Trident of Albion*, by John Thelwall, New York: Garland, 1978.

Richards, Graham, *Mental Machinery: The Origins and Consequences of Psychological Ideas. Part I: 1600–1850*, London: Athlone, 1992.

Richardson, Alan, *British Romanticism and the Science of the Mind*, Cambridge Studies in Romanticism 47, Cambridge: Cambridge University Press, 2001.

Richardson, Alan, 'Joanna Baillie's "Plays on the Passions"', in *Joanna Baillie, Romantic Dramatist*, ed. Thomas C. Crochunis, London: Routledge, 2004, pp. 130–45.

Richardson, Alan, *The Neural Sublime: Cognitive Theories and Romantic Texts*, Baltimore, MD: Johns Hopkins University Press, 2010.

Richardson, Alan, 'Reimagining the Romantic Imagination', *European Romantic Review* 24, no. 4 (2013), 385–402.

Robbins, Caroline, *The Eighteenth-Century Commonwealthman*, Cambridge, MA: Harvard University Press, 1959.

Robinson, Jeffrey C., *The Walk: Notes on a Romantic Image*, Norman: University of Oklahoma Press, 1989.

Rockey, Denyse, 'John Thelwall and the Origins of British Speech Therapy', *Medical History* 23 (1979), 156–75.

Rockey, Denyse, 'The Logopaedic Thought of John Thelwall, 1764–1834: First British Speech Therapist', *British Journal of Disorders of Communication* 12 (1977), 83–95.

Roe, Nicholas, '"Atmospheric Air Itself": Medical Science, Politics and Poetry in Thelwall, Coleridge and Wordsworth', in *1789: The Year of the Lyrical Ballads*, ed. Richard Cronin, Houndmills: Macmillan, 1998, pp. 185–202.

Roe, Nicholas, 'Coleridge and John Thelwall: The Road to Nether Stowey', in *The Coleridge Connection: Essays for Thomas McFarland*, ed. Richard Gravil and Molly Lefebure, Houndmills: Macmillan, 1990, pp. 60–80.

Roe, Nicholas, *John Keats and the Culture of Dissent*, Oxford: Clarendon Press, 1997.

Roe, Nicholas, 'John Thelwall in the West Country: The Road to Nether Stowey Revisited', in *John Thelwall: Critical Reassessments*, ed. Yasmin Solomonescu, Romantic Circles, Sept. 2011, http://www.rc.umd.edu/praxis/thelwall/HTML/praxis.2011.roe.html (accessed 12 June 2012).

Roe, Nicholas, 'The Lives of John Thelwall: Another View of the "Jacobin Fox"', in *John Thelwall: Radical Romantic and Acquitted Felon*, ed. Steve Poole, The Enlightenment World 11, London: Pickering and Chatto, 2009, pp. 13–24.

Roe, Nicholas (ed.), *Samuel Taylor Coleridge and the Sciences of Life*, Oxford: Oxford University Press, 2001.

Roe, Nicholas, 'Thelwall, John (1764–1834)', in *Oxford Dictionary of National Biography*, ed. H. C. G. Matthew and Brian Harrison, Oxford: Oxford University Press, 2004, online edn, ed. Lawrence Goldman, Sept. 2012, http://www.oxforddnb.com/view/article/27167 (accessed 16 Nov. 2012).

Roe, Nicholas, 'Who Was Spy Nozy?', *Wordsworth Circle* 15, no. 2 (1984), 46–50.

Roe, Nicholas, *Wordsworth and Coleridge: The Radical Years*, Oxford: Clarendon Press, 1988.

Rogers, John, *The Matter of Revolution: Science, Poetry, and Politics in the Age of Milton*, Ithaca, NY: Cornell University Press, 1996.

Rothstein, Eric, '"Ideal Presence" and the "Non Finito" in Eighteenth-Century Aesthetics', *Eighteenth-Century Studies* 9, no. 3 (1976), 307–32.

Rousseau, George S., *Nervous Acts: Essays on Literature, Culture and Sensibility*, Houndmills: Palgrave Macmillan, 2004.

Rousseau, George S., 'The Perpetual Crises of Modernism and the Traditions of Enlightenment Vitalism: with a Note on Mikhail Bakhtin', in *The Crisis of*

Modernism: Bergson and the Vitalist Controversy, ed. Frederick Burwick and Paul Douglass, Cambridge: Cambridge University Press, 1992, pp. 15–75.

Rousseau, George S., 'Science and the Discovery of the Imagination in Enlightened England', *Eighteenth-Century Studies* 3, no. 1 (Autumn 1969), 108–35.

Royden, Michael, 'Rushton, Edward (1756–1814)', in *Oxford Dictionary of National Biography*, online edn, ed. Lawrence Goldman, Oxford: Oxford University Press, 2004, http://www.oxforddnb.com/view/article/24286 (accessed 24 Nov. 2012).

Ruston, Sharon, *Shelley and Vitality*, Houndmills: Palgrave Macmillan, 2005; repr. 2012.

Saintsbury, George, *A History of English Prosody from the Twelfth Century to the Present Day*, 3 vols, London: Macmillan, 1910.

Schofield, Robert E., *The Enlightened Joseph Priestley: A Study of His Life and Work from 1773 to 1804*, University Park: Pennsylvania State University Press, 2004.

Schofield, Robert E., *Mechanism and Materialism: British Natural Philosophy in an Age of Reason*, Princeton: Princeton University Press, 1970.

Scrivener, Michael, 'John Thelwall and Popular Jacobin Allegory, 1793–95', *ELH* 67 (2000), 951–71.

Scrivener, Michael, 'John Thelwall and the Press', in *Romanticism, Radicalism and the Press*, ed. Stephen C. Behrendt, Detroit, MI: Wayne State University Press, 1997, pp. 120–36.

Scrivener, Michael, 'The Rhetoric and Context of John Thelwall's "Memoir"', in *Spirits of Fire: English Romantic Writers and Contemporary Historical Methods*, ed. G. A. Rosso and Daniel P. Watkins, Rutherford, NJ: Fairleigh Dickinson University Press, 1990, pp. 112–30.

Scrivener, Michael, *Seditious Allegories: John Thelwall and Jacobin Writing*, University Park: Pennsylvania State University Press, 2001.

Scrivener, Michael, Yasmin Solomonescu and Judith Thompson (eds), *The Daughter of Adoption; A Tale of Modern Times*, by John Thelwall, Peterborough, ON: Broadview, 2013.

Sellers, Ian, 'William Roscoe, the Roscoe Circle and Radical Politics in Liverpool, 1787–1807', *Transactions of the Historic Society of Lancashire and Cheshire* 120 (1969), 45–62.

Seymour, Miranda, *Mary Shelley*, New York: Grove, 2000.

Sha, Richard, 'Imagination as Inter-Science', *European Romantic Review* 20, no. 5 (Dec. 2009), 661–9.

Sha, Richard, 'Romantic Physiology and the Work of Romantic Imagination: Hypothesis and Speculation in Science and Coleridge', *European Romantic Review* 24, no. 4 (2013), 403–19.

Sha, Richard, 'Towards a Physiology of the Romantic Imagination', *Configurations* 17 (2009), 197–226.

Sheldon, Richard, '"A Loud, a Fervid, and Resolute Remonstrance with our Rulers": John Thelwall, the People and Political Economy', in *John Thelwall: Radical Romantic and Acquitted Felon*, ed. Steve Poole, The Enlightenment World 11, London: Pickering and Chatto, 2009, pp. 61–70.

Sher, Richard B., 'Blair, Hugh (1718–1800)', in *Oxford Dictionary of National Biography*, ed. H. C. G. Matthew and Brian Harrison, Oxford: Oxford University

Press, 2004, online edn, ed. Lawrence Goldman, Oct. 2009, http://www. oxforddnb.com/view/article/2563 (accessed 29 Oct. 2012).

Shortland, Michael, 'Moving Speeches: Language and Elocution in Eighteenth-Century Britain', *History of European Ideas* 8 (1987), 639–53.

Simpson, David, 'Public Virtues, Private Vices: Reading between the Lines of Wordsworth's "Anecdote for Fathers"', in *Subject to History: Ideology, Class, Gender*, ed. David Simpson, Ithaca, NY: Cornell University Press, 1991, pp. 163–90.

Smeed, J. W., *The Theophrastan 'Character': The History of a Literary Genre*, Oxford: Clarendon Press, 1985.

Smith, Olivia, *The Politics of Language, 1791–1819*, Oxford: Clarendon Press, 1984.

Solomonescu, Yasmin (ed.), *John Thelwall: Critical Reassessments*, Romantic Circles, Sept. 2011, http://www.rc.umd.edu/praxis/thelwall/index.html (accessed 30 Jan. 2014).

Stanback, Emily B., 'Disability and Dissent: Thelwall's Elocutionary Project', in *John Thelwall: Critical Reassessments*, ed. Yasmin Solomonescu, Romantic Circles, Sept. 2011, http://romantic.arhu.umd.edu/praxis/thelwall/HTML/ praxis.2011.stanback.html (accessed 12 June 2012).

St. Clair, William, *The Godwins and the Shelleys: The Biography of a Family*, New York: Norton, 1989; repr. Baltimore, MD: Johns Hopkins University Press, 1991.

Stone, James L., James T. Goodrich and George R. Cybulski, 'John Hunter's Contributions to Neuroscience', in *Brain, Mind and Medicine: Essays in Eighteenth-Century Neuroscience*, ed. Harry Whitaker, C. U. M. Smith and Stanley Finger, New York: Springer, 2007, pp. 67–84.

Storey, Catherine E, 'Apoplexy: Changing Concepts in the Eighteenth Century', in *Brain, Mind and Medicine: Essays in Eighteenth-Century Neuroscience*, ed. Harry Whitaker, C. U. M. Smith and Stanley Finger, New York: Springer, 2007, pp. 233–43.

Thale, Mary (ed.), *Selections from the Papers of the London Corresponding Society, 1792–1799*, Cambridge: Cambridge University Press, 1983.

Thelwall, Robin, 'The Phonetic Theory of John Thelwall (1764–1834)', in *Towards a History of Phonetics: Essays Contributed in Honour of David Abercrombie*, ed. R. E. Asher and Eugénie J. A. Henderson, Edinburgh: Edinburgh University Press, 1981, pp. 186–203.

Thompson, E. P., 'Disenchantment or Default? A Lay Sermon', in *The Romantics: England in a Revolutionary Age*, New York: New Press, 1997, pp. 33–74.

Thompson, E. P., 'Hunting the Jacobin Fox', *Past and Present* 142 (1994), 94–140.

Thompson, E. P., *The Making of the English Working Class*, London: Victor Gollancz, 1963; repr. London: Penguin, 1991.

Thompson, Judith, 'An Autumnal Blast, a Killing Frost: Coleridge's Poetic Conversation with John Thelwall', *Studies in Romanticism* 36 (1997), 427–56.

Thompson, Judith, 'Citizen Juan Thelwall: In the Footsteps of a Free-Range Radical', *Studies in Romanticism* 48 (Spring 2009), 67–100.

Thompson, Judith, 'A "Double-Visag'd Fate": John Thelwall and the Hapless Hope of Albion', in *John Thelwall: Radical Romantic and Acquitted Felon*, ed.

Steve Poole, The Enlightenment World 11, London: Pickering and Chatto, 2009, pp. 125–38.

Thompson, Judith, 'From Forum to Repository: A Case Study in Romantic Cultural Geography', *European Romantic Review* 15, no. 2 (2004), 177–91.

Thompson, Judith (ed.), 'John Thelwall in Performance: *The Fairy of the Lake*', Romantic Circles, Aug. 2012, http://www.rc.umd.edu/reference/thelwall_fairy/index.html (accessed 28 Oct. 2012).

Thompson, Judith, 'John Thelwall and the Politics of Genre 1793/1993', *Wordsworth Circle* 25, no. 1 (1994), 21–5.

Thompson, Judith (ed.), 'John Thelwall in Time and Text', Romantic Circles, Aug. 2012, http://www.rc.umd.edu/reference/thelwall_chronology/index.html (accessed 27 Oct. 2012).

Thompson, Judith, *John Thelwall in the Wordsworth Circle: The Silenced Partner*, Nineteenth-Century Major Lives and Letters, New York: Palgrave Macmillan, 2012.

Thompson, Judith, 'Overlooking History: The Case of John Thelwall', in *Romanticism, History, Historicism: Essays on an Orthodoxy*, ed. Damian Walford Davies, Routledge Studies in Romanticism 11, New York: Routledge, 2009, pp. 103–25.

Thompson, Judith (ed.), *The Peripatetic*, by John Thelwall, Detroit, MI: Wayne State University Press, 2001.

Thompson, Judith, 'Re-Sounding Romanticism: John Thelwall and the Science and Practice of Elocution', in *Spheres of Action: Speech and Performance in Romantic Culture*, ed. Alexander Dick and Angela Esterhammer, Toronto: University of Toronto Press, 2009, pp. 21–45.

Tolly, Michael J., 'Preromanticism', in *A Companion to Romanticism*, ed. Duncan Wu, Oxford: Blackwell, 2007, pp. 12–22.

Topsfield, L. T., *Troubadours and Love*, Cambridge: Cambridge University Press, 1975.

Uglow, Jenny, *The Lunar Men: The Friends Who Made the Future, 1730–1810*, London: Faber and Faber, 2002.

Vickers, Neil, *Coleridge and the Doctors, 1795–1806*, Oxford: Clarendon Press, 2004.

Wallace, Anne D., *Walking, Literature, and English Culture: The Origins and Uses of Peripatetic in the Nineteenth Century*, Oxford: Oxford University Press, 1993.

Wallace, Miriam L., *Revolutionary Subjects in the English 'Jacobin' Novel, 1790–1805*, Bucknell Studies in Eighteenth-Century Literature and Culture, Lewisburg, PA: Bucknell University Press, 2009.

Werkmeister, Lucyle, 'Coleridge and Godwin on the Communication of Truth', *Modern Philology* 55, no. 3 (Feb. 1958), 170–7.

Wharam, Alan, *The Treason Trials, 1794*, Leicester: Leicester University Press, 1992.

White, R. S., *Natural Rights and the Birth of Romanticism in the 1790s*, Houndmills: Palgrave Macmillan, 2005.

Williams, Carolyn D., 'Hawes, William (1736–1808)', in *Oxford Dictionary of National Biography*, ed. H. C. G. Matthew and Brian Harrison, Oxford: Oxford University Press, 2004, online edn, ed. Lawrence Goldman, Oct. 2009, http://www.oxforddnb.com/view/article/12648 (accessed 11 June 2012).

Williams, Raymond, *Culture and Materialism: Selected Essays*, Radical Thinkers, London: Verso, 1980; repr. 2005.

Williams, Raymond, *Keywords: A Vocabulary of Culture and Society*, rev. ed., New York: Oxford University Press, 1983.

Wood, Marcus, 'William Cobbett, John Thelwall, Radicalism, Racism and Slavery: A Study in Burkean Parodics', *Romanticism on the Net* 15 (Aug. 1999), http://www.erudit.org/revue/ron/1999/v/n15/005873ar.html (accessed 23 May 2007).

Wu, Duncan, 'Coleridge, Thelwall, and the Politics of Poetry', *Coleridge Bulletin* ns 4 (1994), 23–44.

Wylie, Ian, *Young Coleridge and the Philosophers of Nature*, Oxford: Clarendon Press, 1989.

Yolton, John W., *Thinking Matter: Materialism in Eighteenth-Century Britain*, Minneapolis: University of Minnesota Press, 1983.

Index

Note: Page references in **bold** refer to illustrations; 'n.' after a page reference refers to a note on that page.

Printed and bound in Great Britain by
CPI Group (UK) Ltd, Croydon, CR0 4YY